Culture Wars

Culture Wars

Dispatches from the Front

Larry G. Johnson

Copyright © 2016 by Larry G. Johnson.
All rights reserved.

Published by Anvil House Publishers, LLC
Owasso, Oklahoma
www.anvilhousebooks.com

Printed in the United States of America.
Cover: Whitley Graphics

ISBN: 978-0-9839716-4-1

Library of Congress Control Number: 2016908405

In loving memory of my grandmother:

Sallie Pearl Hart

Contents

Preface ix

Acknowledgements xi

Beliefs Have Consequences

Part I – The Christian and the culture

In Defense of Labels 3
Tis the Season for Secular Silliness 7
How we choose to deal with our sin defines our destiny 11
Progressive Protestantism – Declining Faith 15
Criminalizing Christian beliefs and behavior 19
Joseph – Man in the shadows 25
Creative Evolution – Screwtape's science for Christians – Parts I-II 29
I'm so ashamed! I was a member of a hate group and didn't know it 39

Part II – Worldview

Why I believe 43
What is your purpose in life? – Parts I-II 47
Thrill killers, the ACLU, Benjamin Spock, and C. S. Lewis ... 53
Acts of God or Acts of Man? 57
Statistics: Facts often used to replace truth 61

Part III – Conflict of Worldviews

Liberalism explained 65
Conservatism explained 69
Mainstream Environmentalism – The Dark Side – Parts I-II 73
Progressivism's Fatal Flaw 81
Liberal Hypocrisy – The Hollywood Ten and the Friends of Abe 85
End of the Citizen-Soldier? 89

Part IV – Language

Liberal language and the trashing of truth 93
Who owns the language? 97
The *New* Ministry of Truth 2014 101
The most powerful weapon 105

Part IV – Islam

Liberal defense of Islam 109
Are Christianity and Islam morally equivalent? – Parts I-V 113
"Workplace violence" comes to Canada 129

Contents

Finding Truth In The Maze Of Freewill

Part I – Marriage & Family

Marriage – Parts I-V 135
Love and Commitment 149
Did father really know best? 153

Part II – Abortion

Postcard from Hell 157
Oh!? It's a matter of sanitation and not murder 161

Part III – Homosexuality

Equality – The homosexual agenda's Trojan horse in its
    battle for cultural acceptance 163
Mr. Jones's Childish Things – Parts I-II 167
Is God Out of Touch with Mainstream Views? 175
Does God lie? 179
Humanism's equality handcuffs freedom and violates
    the Constitution 183

Part IV – Education

Education in America – Parts I-III 187
Common Core Standards – The devil is in the details 197
Train up a child in the way he should go – Parts I-II 203
Shake and Bake History - Engineering the future while
    forgetting the past 211
Progressive view of American history: The good old days
    were all bad 215

Contents

Freedom Abused Is Freedom Lost

Part I – Government

Our Playdoh® Constitution	221
Death of the American Constitution	225
Government is not the problem, however…	229
The Christian's Role in Politics and Government	233
Would Jefferson label the modern Judiciary as the "Despotic Branch"?	237
Helicopter Government – Parts I-V	243
This was done by ordinary people – Parts I-IV	259

Part II – Socialism

The New Despotism – Parts I-II	275
March Madness: Nanny State 1 – Freedom 0	281
Work	285
Newspeak 2014: The Language of Socialism	289

Part III – America

Disunited States of America	293
American Exceptionalism – Parts I-III	297
Freedom	305
The Fragility of Free Speech in America	309
Notes	313
Selected Bibliography	339

Preface

The title of the book is indicative of the mindset of most Americans on whichever side of the cultural divide they find themselves. The articles posted in *culturewarrior.net* are dispatches from the front lines of this war for the soul of the American culture and Western civilization on a larger scale. The articles selected for this book were originally posted on *culturewarrior.net* which began in March 2013.

The culture wars are a battle among worldviews–Christianity, humanism, Islam, and various other Eastern religions. It is a war for supremacy in the America republic and on a larger scale in all of Western civilization. In America, the quest for dominance in the nation's central cultural vision is primarily between Christianity and humanism. However, Islam is gaining popular support under the guise of humanism's faulty definition of multiculturalism and tolerance. Because of humanism's historic opposition to Christianity, the rise of Islam in Western nations is being used by humanists as a temporal weapon in pursuing its war against Christianity.

Christianity has been the source of Western civilization's greatness, strength, and endurance for most of a millennia and a half. The American experience since the first Europeans set foot on its eastern shores has been centered on a Christian understanding of the world. America became the greatest nation in the world because its central cultural vision was informed and guided by those biblical principles upon which it was founded.

Since the nation's founding, this central cultural vision has been under assault by those holding the humanistic worldview and which gained dominance in America during the last half of the twentieth century. Having gained critical mass and leadership positions in the various spheres and institutions of American life, their humanistic policies, laws, and initiatives are being imposed on a nation whose citizens fundamentally still cling to the biblical worldview of the Founders.

As a result Christianity has been marginalized and driven from the public square. The conflict flows from humanism's *fundamental differences with Christianity's basic principles and beliefs that cannot be compromised* without destroying what Christians claim to be as individuals and as a nation. And it is in these basic differences of belief that we see the flashpoints in the culture wars which include abortion, same-sex marriage, and homosexuality. This is the heart of the culture wars—the struggle for supremacy in the American cultural vision between those holding humanistic and Christian worldviews and their respective truth claims.

The humanistic worldview regarding truth is one of cultural relativism which requires a suspension of judgment since all belief systems contain some elements of truth while no one belief system has all the truth. For humanists, all social constructions are culturally relative as they are shaped by class, gender, and ethnicity. Because there is no supernatural Creator or God, there can be no universal truths and therefore all viewpoints, lifestyles, and beliefs are equally valid. As a result, no man or group can claim to be infallible with regard to truth and virtue. Rather, truth is produced by the free give and take of competing claims and opinions of the moment. Therefore, truth can be manufactured to fit the mood and demands of the times in which we live.

For those holding the Christian worldview, the battle is about adhering to unchanging biblical principles and restoring the biblical understanding of truth in all spheres of national life. To do so Christians and like-minded non-Christians must speak the truth in the face of lies, defend biblical principles in the public square when others compromise, and pursue right actions in spite of consequences. A hostile culture, an adversarial government, and a culpable legal system will extract a price from those that dare to oppose humanism's agenda. Those who value the Judeo-Christian ethic but ignore or disengage from the culture wars place religious freedom and our nation in peril.

Topical moments in media and culture are often of great debate and concern but are largely forgotten within a short time. Such moments frequently command newspaper headlines and news cast sound bites that play repeatedly during the 24-hour news cycle. These singular, seemingly unrelated occurrences are often thought of as only of momentary concern. Yet, it is in examining the accumulation of such topical moments that we give a face and direction to the cultural drift. From this examination we may clearly define the reasons for "why we fight" in the raging culture wars.

This is the essential purpose of the articles presented in *culturewarrior.net*. From a thoughtful examination of the daily skirmishes in the culture wars we can understand the larger picture and expose the tactics, strategies, and goals of the opposition. Armed with such knowledge, Christians can and must give a forceful defense of the truth of the Judeo-Christian worldview and its historical preeminence as the central vision of American culture upon which the nation was founded.

Acknowledgements

The Apostle Paul wrote that for Christians speaking or writing, the ultimate source of truth must come from the Holy Spirit through His teaching, leading, and guidance and not from human wisdom.

> Now we have received not the spirit of the world, but the Spirit which is from God, that we might understand the gifts bestowed on us by God. And we impart this in words not taught by human wisdom but taught by the Spirit, interpreting spiritual truths to those who possess the Spirit. [1 Corinthians 1:12-13. RSV]

For what truth that I have spoken or written about in the articles posted on *culturewarrior.net* and in the other books I have written, I acknowledge my complete dependence on the Holy Spirit.

I must also thank those readers of *culturewarrior.net* and the other books that I have written. Their faithfulness in reading what I have written is shown by their kind words and encouragement to continue writing about Christianity and the culture.

But there is one other constant and invaluable source of help and encouragement that I must always acknowledge—Sherryl, my wife and best friend for 44 years.

Books by Larry G. Johnson

Tar Creek – A History of the Quapaw Indians, the World's Largest Lead and Zinc Discovery, and the Tar Creek Superfund Site. ©2008 [Finalist - Oklahoma Book Award Non-fiction Book of the Year 2010 by the Oklahoma Center for the Book, the state affiliate of the Center for the Book in the Library of Congress.]

Ye shall be as gods – Humanism and Christianity – The Battle for Supremacy in the American Cultural Vision. ©2011

Evangelical Winter – Restoring New Testament Christianity. ©2016

Culture Wars – Dispatches from the Front. ©2016

BELIEFS HAVE CONSEQUENCES

Part I – The Christian and the Culture

In Defense of Labels (11-15-13)

Max Lucado is a wonderful and inspiring writer. Few writers can match his ability to bring fresh insights, infuse substance, and bring clarity to both the commonplace and complex things of life. One of his recent website posts was titled "Simply 'Church'." He posed two questions, "…what would happen if all the churches agreed, on a given day, to change their names simply to 'church'?…if there are no denominations in heaven, why do we have denominations on earth?" His point was that we should not attend a church based on the sign outside, but we should join our hearts to the like-minded hearts of the people on the inside.[1]

This is a noble sentiment and reflects the Apostle Paul's admonition to the Romans, "Now the God of patience and consolation grant you to be like-minded one toward another according to Christ Jesus: That ye may with one mind and one mouth glorify God, even the Father of our Lord Jesus Christ." [Romans 15: 5-6. KJV] In other words, the church should be in unity in thought and message. Matthew Henry stated, "The foundation of Christian love and peace is laid in like-mindedness. This like-mindedness must be according to Christ Jesus…" In other words, Christ should be our pattern because the unity of Christians glorifies God. However, Henry warns that our prayers for like-mindedness "…must be first for *truth*, and then for *peace*…it is *first pure, then peaceable*."

Max Lucado's "Simply Church" may have worked in first century Israel for there were few churches and just one Christian church. But we live in twenty-first century America with many communities that have churches on almost every corner. There are many religions, thousands of denominations, and hundreds of thousands of churches. In America most are Christian churches, each professing to be a follower of Jesus Christ. So, using the Simply Church model, how does one know which church to join oneself with? How does one know whether the people inside are like-minded? Attend one Sunday? No, first impressions are often not reliable proofs of like-mindedness. Then attend a year? No, for one can spend much of life searching for instead of fellowshipping with like-minded Christians.

Thus, discovering like-minded believers without using labels can be a difficult and time-consuming task.

Labels are useful and compatible with divine order. God used labels during the Creation. He labeled trees in the Garden...the tree of life and the tree of knowledge of good and evil. He labeled the rivers going out of Eden. God brought the animals to Adam to see what he would call them, "...and whatsoever Adam called every living creature, that was the name thereof." And from Adam's side He made him a wife who "shall be called Woman." [Genesis 2:9-23. KJV]

In our search for like-mindedness with other Christians, we must return to Matthew Henry's admonition that our quest must first be for *truth* and then for *peace*.[2] In that quest for truth, labels are invaluable and become a type of shorthand for what we know to be true or not true (the written word as well as symbols, e.g., fish symbol, the cross, the dove).

Throughout the ages language has been the means of achieving order in culture. Knowledge of truth comes through the word which provides solidity in the "shifting world of appearances." Richard Weaver called words the storehouse of our memory. In our modern age humanists have effectively used semantics to neuter words of their meaning in historical and symbolic contexts, that is, words now mean what men want them to mean. By removing the fixities of language (which undermines an understanding of truth), language loses its ability to define and compel. As the meaning of words is divorced from truth, relativism gains supremacy, and a culture tends to disintegration without an understanding of eternal truths upon which to orient its self.[3]

Therefore, the problem with simply "Church" is that we live in a fallen world, and there are competing voices each professing truth. Removing the labels and being simply "Church" won't work when we must give priority to truth. Without truth, simply "Church" won't achieve like-mindedness in a world immersed in a relativistic sea of shifting appearances. In such a world labels become our anchors to truth.

I am thankful for my denomination, and I'm thankful that it is not labeled simply "Church." Without its label, many like-minded Christians would drive on by not knowing they have a fellow believer on the inside. Although I believe my denomination has the best understanding of God's truth, I have no animosity towards other Christians who genuinely seek God and believe their understanding of biblical truth is more accurate than mine. I wish them well for we are all followers of Jesus Christ on this earth and like-minded on the major tenets of our faith. And we'll all be members of simply Church when we get to heaven.

Labels also help us identify those with whom we should not be in fellowship. The Bible says that there are many churches with misleading labels who have false prophets and false teachers that have abandoned biblical truth and will not be a part of that gathering in heaven. Also, other religions have labels that may accurately depict what's on the inside, but what's on the inside is a false religion whose god is not the great I AM and does not lead to truth or a heavenly home.

When traveling I have occasionally driven along the streets of a city unfamiliar to me in search of a church to attend. First, I spot a cross on top of a steeple in the distance. I then look for the label on that local branch of Christianity. In a few seconds I have some understanding of the truth held by those inside and whether they are like-minded or not. I like labels here on earth, but I'm glad we won't need them in heaven for we'll be simply 'Church.'

Tis the Season for Secular Silliness (12-13-13)

A Holiday letter to my secular humanist friends

The first signs of the holiday shopping season peek from store shelves in September. October's chill warns that Halloween nears. We must select a costume that tops last year's. November heralds that most wonderful time of the year—Black Friday. But Oh My! What shall we do with December and that highly embarrassing "other" holiday? You know the one I mean. We once masked it by calling it Xmas. But the X could be misconstrued as a cross. And a cross can be associated with you know who, and that will never do. Now we call that "other" holiday by many names such as Winter Solstice celebration, Festival of Lights, and Winter Carnival. Those names are so inclusive, so democratic…so…so generic. (I almost said ecumenical, but that sounds too religious.) With these new names, the holiday season can mean whatever one wants it to mean rather than have a religious meaning crammed down our throats each December. Why must we be subjected to those old-fashioned myths and fables that have lingered for two thousand years? We have Santa Claus!

But there are still millions out there who haven't gotten the message. They are generally backward, unintelligent, and remain culturally insensitive unlike those of us who have progressed beyond those crude expressions of faith. Unfortunately, not everyone wants to join our shining, non-offensive, tolerant, all inclusive, sensitive secular society.

You hear those sentimental Christians whining every year at this time. They are always hiding behind the Constitution which they say guarantees their religious freedom. Well of course they have religious freedom as long as they don't flaunt it in public!

We must be ever vigilant and ready to crush any efforts to return to those bad old days. Just a couple of years ago, a group of carolers singing at various businesses in a Silver Springs, Maryland, shopping center entered a U.S. Post Office also located in the shopping center. Dressed in period costumes reminiscent of Dickens' "A Christmas Carol," they were only a few words into their first carol when the vigilant and brave Post Office manager rushed into the lobby to stop the indiscretion. "You can't do this on government property," the angry manager shouted. He ordered them to leave immediately because there was a Post Office policy prohibiting solicitation. They attempted to explain that they were going to all the businesses in the shopping center. But he would have none of it and insisted they leave in spite of boos from the patrons waiting in line.[1] Even though there was no such policy, this Post Office manager should serve as a role model for that small minority of managers who aren't so enlightened and have allowed caroling in their Post Offices. Fortunately, our government is filled with like-minded militant secularist bureaucrats rigorously defending society from such unauthorized merriment.

But we can never let down our guard. Just the other day the leadership of the U.S. House of Representatives announced that its members would be allowed to use previously banned holiday greetings in official mailings to their constituents. Representative Candice Miller said, "I feel it is entirely appropriate for members of Congress to include a simple holiday salutation, whether it is Merry Christmas, Happy Hanukkah, and so on."[2] Shameful! How could these legislators abuse their franking privileges by including messages of Merry Christmas to thousands of their constituents? Such episodes tend to be contagious and must not be allowed to go unchallenged.

Such blatant relapses can cause others to become weak-kneed when banning Christmas from any public display or expression. One example is the Bordentown, New Jersey, Regional School District administration that had banned religious Christmas music at winter public school concerts effective as of October 18th. Less than two weeks later the superintendent backed down after national attention was focused on the school's ban. The superintendent announced that religious Christmas music would be allowed for now "...after reviewing additional legal considerations and advice on this matter and the expressed sentiments of the community at large..." However, she promised that, "...the school board will continue to examine the issue to determine how the policy will be handled in the future."[3] Of course it is always wise to impose these unpopular restrictions on a low-key basis. The school administration should have imposed the restrictions banning religious Christmas music in, let's say, March. Once policies are established and in effect for a period of time, opposition to those policies can usually be attributed to a fringe element of religious fanatics bent on imposing their religion on others and which violates our constitutionally mandated separation of church and state. It doesn't matter that the words "separation of church and state" aren't in the Constitution; we know the Founders really meant freedom *from* religion instead of freedom *of* religion. You see, that Constitution thing can work both ways.

Wait a minute. I must go to the door. No, it can't be! There are carolers out there singing religious Christmas songs and indiscriminately shouting Merry Christmas right there on the *public* sidewalk for everyone to hear. Where's my cell phone? Hello! 911? Send the police. No, better yet send a SWAT team. We are having a major public insurrection right here in River City in direct violation of the Constitution. Hurry! There are children in the neighborhood being exposed to this brazen criminal activity!

I must go. I think I see one of my neighbors putting a nativity scene on his front lawn. Hmmm. Would that violation fall under the city's building code or advertising ordinance? Where's my cell phone?

How we choose to deal with our sin defines our destiny (11-7-14)

Bishop Edward J. Slattery, bishop of the Catholic Diocese of Tulsa, recently wrote of the confusion within the Catholic Church regarding its teaching on divorce, cohabitation, and people who experience same-sex attractions ("We are not defined by our sin"). He states that much of this confusion resulted from the Vatican's October publication of a working paper (Relatio post Disceptationem) of the Extraordinary General Assembly of the Synod of Bishops on the Family whose purpose was to raise awareness of significant pastoral issues concerning divorce, cohabitation, and homosexuality. The document was designed "...*to raise questions and indicate perspectives that will have to be matured.*"[4] [emphasis added]

One of Bishop Slattery's concerns is that much of the confusion results from contemporary commentators and even some in the church who use language that tends to diminish the human person through emphasis on their sinful activity. This is a legitimate concern, and as the bishop states, "...activity should never be confused with identity. The human person always remains greater than what he or she does or experiences."[5] The Bishop is correct in that the importance of man's identity is confirmed by the inestimable value God places on man. The tremendous value of man to God is undeniable when one considers that the cost of man's redemption from his sinful state was the sacrifice of God's own Son on the cross. Therefore, God does not condemn man nor can the church. But man was given freewill, and with freewill man made choices that are in conflict with God's commandments and plan for mankind and thereby condemned himself. When this happened, it was called sin and broke the relationship between God and man. It is at this point that man often attempts to *justify his activity because of his identity*, and the modern church is often a co-conspirator in excusing sinful activity.

From a broader perspective, it would appear that much of the confusion in the church world stems from the church's efforts (both Catholic and Protestant) to be inclusive of people who want to be accepted by the church but also want their sinful lifestyles to be accepted too. To do so they engage in theological contortions to answer questions and give perspective that will bring "maturity" (i.e., acceptance of the sinner *and* the sin within the church). It is in these efforts that the Bible is ignored even though it is the ultimate source of truth and is exceptionally clear in most cases as to God's answers and perspective with regard to both sin and the sinner.

An example of this confusion and blurring of lines with regard to sin, the pastoral teaching of the U.S. Conference of Catholic Bishops correctly states that, "God does not love someone any less simply because he or she is homosexual. God's love is always and everywhere offered to those who are open to receiving it."[6] However, this truthful teaching is often perverted to mean that love is all that is necessary by those wanting the church to embrace both the sinner and his sin. To do so dismisses the admonitions of Paul to the Romans regarding homosexuality which are clear-cut and still applicable in the twenty-first century (see Romans 1:18, 24-27). This is but one example of the great caustic of relativism seeping into the church and by which biblical truths are ignored and eroded.

To claim love is all that is necessary is to dismiss the centrality of the cross in the great meta-narrative of the Bible with regard to creation, the fall, and man's need for redemption. Christ died for the sins of the world to obtain forgiveness for man, and every man has a choice as to whether or not he will accept that forgiveness and follow Christ. To follow Christ is to follow His commandments. But, if love is all that is necessary, then the cross becomes irrelevant, sin is a misnomer, Satan is a myth, and God does not care about how we live our lives.

Bishop Slattery rightly says, "Chastity, after all, pertains not just to our behavior but also to the state of our hearts."[7] Acceptance of Christ is first a matter of the heart. We can't clean up our lives before we approach Christ. Every human approaches Christ as a sinner whether he is guilty of adultery, homosexual behavior, fornication, murder, theft, or one of a thousand other sins. I am a sinner saved by grace, the unmerited favor of Christ. I have repented of my sin and have been forgiven. Not only have I repented of past sins, I have turned from my sinful ways. Homosexuals, adulterers, fornicators, and any other label the sinner wears can repent, be saved, and fellowship with God for eternity. However, to do so, they *cannot stay in their sin*. When the sinner accepts Christ he must put away the sin and often this "putting away" can be a difficult and continuing struggle for the new Christian. But it is the struggle to lay down one's sin coupled with continued repentance which makes the difference, not a continuing indifference to one's sin.

In 1937, the Confessing Church in Germany was under severe persecution from Nazi rulers and that portion of the German church aligned with Hitler. Brilliant theologian, pastor, and opponent of the

Nazi regime, Dietrich Bonhoeffer wrote a dramatic paper in which he cautioned his fellow pastors in the Confessing Church.

> Anyone who turns from his sinful way at the word of proclamation and repents, receives forgiveness. Anyone who perseveres in his sin receives judgment. The church cannot loose the penitent from sin without arresting and binding the impenitent in sin...The promise of grace is not to be squandered; it needs to be protected from the godless. Grace cannot be proclaimed to anyone who does not recognize or distinguish or desire it...The world upon whom grace is thrust as a bargain will grow tired of it, and it will not only trample upon the Holy, but also will tear apart those who force it on them. For its own sake, for the sake of the sinner, and for the sake of the community, the Holy is to be protected from cheap surrender. The Gospel is protected by the preaching of repentance which calls sin sin and declares the sinner guilty...The preaching of grace can only be protected by the preaching of repentance.[8]

Americans are especially averse to pain and suffering, and much of the modern church has that mindset. This is why it is difficult for some in the church to require the often painful "putting away" of sin when it welcomes the sinner into the supposed "big tent" of Christianity under the banner of love. Many in the modern church insist that the problem is not "cheap grace" but "cheap laws." In other words, love and looking to Christ is all that matters. But grace without repentance is still cheap grace. Writing in his classic work *The Cost of Discipleship*, Bonhoeffer described this toxin within the church.

> Cheap grace is the deadly enemy of our Church...In such a Church the world finds a cheap covering for its sins; no contrition is required, still less any real desire to be delivered from sin...Cheap grace means the justification of sin without the justification of the sinner...Cheap grace is grace without discipleship, grace without the cross, grace without Jesus Christ, living and incarnate.[9]

When we approach the cross with a contrite heart, our destiny is defined by how we respond to Christ's invitation to be a part of His eternal kingdom. A person who willfully continues in his sin cannot be excused for they "…are [not] open to growing in virtue" and their heart remains unconverted. If the church does not make this distinction clear, it is guilty of misleading people as to their eternal destination.

Progressive Protestantism – Declining Faith (2-13-15)

The Reverend John M. Buchanan is the editor/publisher of *Christian Century*, the leading voice of mainline Protestantism and what some call Progressive Protestantism. Buchanan likens the current decline in many Protestant denominations to the equivalent of a rummage sale. "Things that are old and worn out get sold to make room for a new things. Every 500 years there's a major shift." He points to the Protestant Reformation of 500 years ago and claims that we're due for one of those major shifts. "I think we're in the middle of a rummage sale. We're trying to figure out what comes next. And I think something new is going to emerge out of this. We don't know what it is yet."[1]

For a brief overview of *Christian Century* and Progressive Protestantism, see recently published *culturewarrior.net* articles: Strange Fire – The American church's quest for cultural relevance – Part I[2] and Part II[3].

In spite of the decline of Protestant denominations in America and much of Western civilization, Buchanan believes that even though there are large number of those without religious affiliation, he states that people are still spiritual in that "…they believe in God, they pray, they read religious books, and they try to do the right thing with their lives."[4] But Buchanan's assumption that man's seemingly "spiritual" nature is a sign of hope completely misses the fundamental nature of man and his separation from God. It is because man is lost that those spiritual longings rise to the surface in every age and every culture. One hundred eighty years ago, Alexis de Tocqueville described these spiritual longings.

> …the imperfect joys of this world will never satisfy his heart. Man alone of all created beings shows a natural disgust for existence and an immense longing to exist; he despises life and fears annihilation. These different feelings constantly drive his soul toward the contemplation of another world and religion it is which directs him there. Religion is thus one particular form of hope as natural to the human heart as hope itself. Men cannot detach themselves from religious beliefs except by some wrong-headed thinking and by a sort of moral violence inflicted upon their true nature; they are

drawn back by an irresistible inclination. Unbelief is an accident; faith is the only permanent state of mankind.[5]

Every man is born with an inherent stain of sin that separates him from God. Buchanan's hope is merely recognition of man's spiritual condition and his yearning to be reunited with God. Simply stated, religion is man's search for God, and that search leads many to false religions and gods. Although claiming to represent the one true God, many Protestant denominations have failed to present Him *in truth and power* to those searchers. This is the reason for the declining number of denominational adherents in the Western world.

What are some of those old and tired things Buchanan believes that need to be thrown out? Although Buchanan says the church hasn't figured that out yet, it appears that some biblical truths that have directed and sustained the church for two thousand years are among the items to be tossed on the ash heap. On the issue of same-sex marriage, he states that *Christian Century* "...has gradually come to support a positive position, that it's a good thing. Let's get past this and make sure that everyone has the same opportunities to be married."[6] [emphasis added] Apparently, the Apostle Paul's condemnation of homosexuality in his letter to the Romans (1:18, 24-27) is one of those things to be consigned to the rummage sale. But, how does one *get past* a biblical commandment? For God and Paul, eternal truths are never subject to change, even in the midst of contemporary cultural imperatives that change frequently and rapidly.

Buchanan is also greatly concerned with achieving peace among the various religions and agrees with a Catholic theologian who stated that "...there will be no world peace until there is peace among religions, and that will not happen until there is *dialogue* between religions."[7] [emphasis added] Apparently, Buchanan believes that dialogue will lead to common ground through discovery of beliefs shared by various religions. As commendable as world peace may be, that is not the mission of the church. Christ came into the world to bear witness to the truth. [John 18:37] Likewise, dialogue to find common ground with false religions was not part of Christ's commission to His followers. Rather, He commanded them to "Go therefore and make disciples of all nations, baptizing them in the name of the Father and of the Son and of the Holy Spirit, teaching them to observe all that I have commanded you..." [Matthew 28:19-20a. RSV]

In his book *Storm*, Jim Cymbala has written an excellent diagnosis of the condition of the American church and the reasons for its decline. Cymbala states that many leaders of the church use "faith talk" or mental positivism (similar to that of Rev. Buchanan) to avoid the reality of a declining church. Many blame the decline on forces outside the church including failed political solutions and a decaying secular culture that is increasing hostile to the message of Christ and His followers.[8] Certainly these are contributing influences, but the Church has survived far worse in its two thousand year history. Cymbala cuts to the heart of the failure of the modern church.

> Yet, we simultaneously mimic the ways of the world in hopes of packaging our faith into "Christianity Lite"— a spiritual candy we can toss at nonbelievers rather than confronting the hostile reactions that can occur when we proclaim the real gospel of Jesus Christ. Pandering to the culture with prepackaged truth nuggets hasn't made us *more* effective; it has made us *ineffective*. Many devoted Christians see the warning signs and recognize our failed attempts to turn back the tide…They are frustrated with church services that are shallow and powerless…While our culture rapidly deteriorates, they aren't fooled by the hype in some religious quarters, nor the "Don't worry, God is sovereign!" attitude of others who have their heads in the sand…Most of all, they know it's impossible for any nation to change unless we Christians and our churches become the spiritual light and salt of which Jesus spoke.[9] [emphasis in original]

The church must discard its application of spiritual Band-Aids® to a hurting and lost world and recognize the dimensions of the battle. "For we are not contending against flesh and blood, but against the principalities, against the powers, against the world rulers of this present darkness, against the spiritual hosts of wickedness in heavenly places." [Ephesians 6:12. RSV]

The solutions for reversing the decline of the American church are not new and have served the church well for two thousand years. They brought spiritual renewal to America three times since the arrival of the first Americans on the eastern shore. Renewal begins with desperate, concerted prayer in which we humble ourselves, repent, and call upon God to heal our land and restore our Godly legacy. Preachers must preach the power-packed, unchanged, unadulterated Word of God centered on Jesus Christ, or as Cymbal puts it, "the real gospel of Jesus Christ." We must seek the manifest presence of the Holy Spirit within our church services. We must die to self as we become the salt and light so needed by a lost and dying world. Lastly, we must love our brothers and sisters in Christ as well as a lost world, be they Muslim, homosexual, atheist, and every other human who in their heart of hearts is seeking to know the one true God. "For God so loved the world that he gave His only Son, that whoever believes in him should not perish but have eternal life." [John 3:16. RSV]

Criminalizing Christian beliefs and behavior (4-10-15)

As Liberals see it, some people are just more equal than others.

Barronelle Stutzman is a florist and owner of Arlene's Flowers in the State of Washington who is in peril of losing her business, personal assets, and retirement. Because of her religious beliefs and her faithfulness to those beliefs, she was sued by the State of Washington and the ACLU in 2013. Her crime was telling Rob Ingersoll that she would not provide her services as a florist for his upcoming marriage to his same-sex partner because it was a violation of her belief that marriage was to be between a man and woman. In February 2015, a Washington judge ruled that Ms. Stutzman had broken the law by discriminating against Ingersoll. The court said that while recognizing her religious beliefs are protected by the Constitution, her discriminatory actions were not.[1]

On March 13, 2014 William Jack went to Denver's Azucar Bakery and requested two Bible-shaped cakes that were to be decorated and inscribed with Bible verses. Marjorie Silva refused to accept his order but agreed to bake the cakes and supply Jack with the necessary icing and decorations so that he could decorate the cake as he pleased. Jack's requested design offended Ms. Silva because one cake was to have the image of two groomsmen holding hands in front of a cross with a red "X" over them. The cake was to be inscribed with a Bible verse: "God hates sin. Psalm 45:7." On the second cake, Jack requested the image of the same two groomsmen with the red "X" but inscribed with the verses: "God loves sinners" and "While we were yet sinners Christ died for us. Romans 5:8." Following a complaint against Silva for discrimination, the Colorado Civil Rights Division ruled in March 2015 that Silva did not discriminate against Jack by refusing to make the cakes because the customer's requests included "derogatory language and imagery."[2]

Ms. Stutzman and Ms. Silva withheld their personal services because the provision of those services would have been in direct violation of their beliefs. Ms. Stutzman's beliefs were based on her religious convictions protected by the First Amendment. Ms. Silva's beliefs were based on her personal opinion as to what constituted "derogatory language and imagery." The Colorado Civil Rights commission ignored Silva's overt discrimination against Jack while the

Washington State judge convicted Stutzman of exercising her First Amendment freedom of religion.

By judicial and bureaucratic edicts across the nation, the First Amendment protection of religious freedom is being dismantled by *separating religious belief from actions in support of those beliefs* in order to achieve humanistic definitions of equality and political correctness. Without the ability to exercise one's religious beliefs, the First Amendment protections of religious freedom are rendered meaningless.

Religious Freedom Restoration Act

Because of legislative, judicial, and bureaucratic actions that compromised the First Amendment protection of religious freedom, the federal Religious Freedom Restoration Act of 1993 was unanimously passed by the House, and the Senate overwhelmingly approved the bill by a 97-3 vote. On November 16, 1993, President Clinton spoke to those gathered on the south lawn of the White House on the day of the signing of the bill. One particular statement from his speech is significantly applicable to today's debate on the government's efforts to curtail religious freedom.

> The free exercise of religion has been called the first freedom, that which originally sparked the development of the full range of the Bill of Rights. Our Founders cared a lot about religion…They knew that religion helps to give our people the character without which a democracy cannot survive. *They knew that there needed to be a space of freedom between Government and people of faith that otherwise Government might usurp.*[3] [emphasis added]

In 1997, the Supreme Court struck down the federal RFRA not because of the "compelling interest test" but because it ruled that Congress could not require the test be used by states in cases involving religious freedom.[4] This was followed by new federal legislation that reinstated protections of religious freedom from governmental interference.

Subsequently, a number of states passed RFRA legislation that closely followed the original federal law and its successors. On March 26, 2015, Governor Mike Pence signed into law a Religious Freedom and Restoration Act passed by the Indiana legislature. The heart of Indiana's protection of religious freedom act is found in Section 8.

Sec. 8. (a) Except as provided in subsection (b), a governmental entity may not substantially burden a person's exercise of religion, even if the burden results from a rule of general applicability.

(b) A governmental entity may substantially burden a person's exercise of religion only if the governmental entity demonstrates that application of the burden to the person: (1) is in furtherance of a compelling governmental interest; and (2) is the least restrictive means of furthering that compelling governmental interest.[5]

Irrespective of the approval the President and almost universal approval of Congress in 1993, as well as most Americans twenty-two years earlier, these eighty words have created a blistering firestorm of protests, threats, economic blackmail, and character assassination against states, legislators, and other RFRA supporters across America by the homosexual lobby and other supporters of the homosexual agenda. These supporters include the media and cultural elites, CEOs of major corporations, and liberal politicians and bureaucrats.

Is religious freedom decided by the First Amendment or the Chamber of Commerce?

Tim Cook, CEO of Apple, has called RFRA legislation in the various states as very dangerous and would allow people to discriminate against their neighbors. Cook lambasted the various RFRA supporters and linked them to segregation and discrimination in the south of the 1960s and 1970s.

America's business community recognized a long time ago that discrimination, in all forms, is *bad for business*...These bills rationalize injustice by pretending to defend something many of us hold dear. They go against the very principles our nation was founded on...This isn't a political issue. It isn't a religious issue. This is about how we treat each other as human beings.[6] [emphasis added]

In spite of Tim Cook's assertions to the contrary, *restrictions on the practice of one's religious beliefs is a religious issue and protection of religious freedom is a political issue.* Although Cook believes RFRA laws go against the very principles upon which the nation was founded, the real violation of those principles occurs when the full meaning and protections of the First Amendment are ignored and/or violated by a government that forces people to disobey their religious beliefs in order to achieve some arbitrary standard of equality.

Even pop star Miley Cyrus, not known as a paragon of moral virtue or for her intellectual gifts, vilified Indiana's RFRA supporters while giving an interview to *Time* magazine about the future of music and youth culture.

> They are dinosaurs, and they are dying off. We are the new generation, and with that will come so much...People are trying now to make the Indiana law look like something that it's not. They're trying to make it look like it's not discriminatory. It's confusing for my fans, so I'm happy to [speak up about it]. They won't listen to Tim Cook, maybe. But they'll listen to me, you know? And people are starting to listen, I think.[7]

To help alleviate the confusion of Ms. Cyrus and her fans, RFRA laws are not discriminatory because they apply to *everyone*.

Interdependence of the Constitution and moral virtue of the people

The primary reason for the loss of religious freedoms in America is *not* to be found in any supposed defects of the Constitution's plain wording or the Founders' clear meaning and intent. Rather, the reason for loss of religious freedom can be discovered in the words of two of America's most illustrious Founders.

> We have no government armed in power capable of contending in human passions unbridled by morality and religion...Our Constitution was made only for a *moral and religious people*. It is wholly inadequate to the government of any other.[8] [John Adams, signer of the Constitution and second president of the United States] [emphasis added]

> Only a *virtuous* people are capable of freedom. As nations become more corrupt and vicious, they have more need of masters.[9] [Benjamin Franklin, signer of

the Declaration of Independence and Constitution] [emphasis added]

The assault on religious freedom is occurring because there is a shortage of virtuous, moral, and religious leadership at the helms of the institutions of American life. Like Esau, Tim Cook and many other Chamber of Commerce types have despised their heritage and sold their birthright of religious freedom for a pot of stew. [Genesis 25:29-34] Ignoring the wishes of the people and the safeguards designed by the Founders, the liberal bullies and their cultural lackeys are now the masters—the new experts at determining what constitutes religious liberty but who are not to be bothered with the First Amendment's plain language.

Unlike the CEOs of mega-corporations and their humanistic colleagues, the Founders were far more concerned with religious liberty than their bank balances, the egalitarian notions of equality, the humanistic doctrines of French intellectuals, or the ridicule of cultural royalists. The Constitution continues to be unequivocal evidence of the Founders' strong concern for religious freedom because "… they knew that there needed to be a space of freedom between Government and people of faith that otherwise Government might usurp."

Joseph – Man in the shadows (12-19-14)

During my lifetime I have probably looked at dozens of nativity sets and observed many Christmas plays depicting the night of Christ's birth. The cast of characters includes baby Jesus, Mary, the shepherds, the three wise men (who actually appeared much later in time), assorted cows, chickens, sheep, and other animals typically found in a stable. Oh yes, we must not forget Joseph. In arranging our nativity scene, Jesus is always placed at the center with Mary hovering nearby or holding the child. Inconspicuous Joseph is standing there, seemingly as an afterthought, merely because of his status as the husband of Mary. In modern parlance, Joseph was the typical wallflower, a fifth wheel, the original invisible man. Never in the spotlight, Joseph was a man who always seemed to be in the shadows.

Prior to Jesus birth, Joseph is mentioned only once in Luke's first chapter, "To a virgin betrothed to a man whose name was Joseph, of house of David..." [Luke 1:27. RSV] In Chapter 2, Joseph is mentioned a second time when he traveled with his pregnant wife (but "who knew not a man" in the quaint phrasing of King James) from Nazareth to Bethlehem to be taxed in accordance with the decree of Caesar Augustus. [v. 4] Joseph's unimportance in the events surrounding Christ's birth appears to be confirmed by the sparse mention of his name in Luke's record of that first Christmas. He receives far less discussion than the lowly shepherds who had a remarkable encounter with an angel and a multitude of the heavenly host telling of Christ's birth. The shepherds then hurry from the fields where they tended their flocks to the stable to find "Mary and Joseph, and the babe lying in a manger." [v. 16] When the days of Mary's purification were completed according to the Mosaic law, Joseph and Mary traveled from Bethlehem to Jerusalem to present the babe to the Lord and to offer a sacrifice as commanded by the law of the Lord. When Joseph and Mary presented the child to Simeon and to receive a blessing as was the custom of the law, they marveled at Simeon's prophecy with regard to the Christ child. [v. 22-35]

We must look to Matthew's gospel to learn a little more of Joseph. Matthew tells us that after finding Mary was pregnant, "...her husband Joseph, being a just man and unwilling to put her to shame, resolved to divorce her quietly." [Matthew 1:19. RSV] But an angel appeared to Joseph in a dream and told him he should keep Mary as his wife because the baby was conceived by the Holy Spirit, that His name would be called Emanuel (God with us), and that He will save his people from their sins. "When Joseph awoke from sleep, he did as the angel of the Lord commanded him; he took his wife, but knew her not until she had borne a son; and he called His name Jesus." [v. 24-25]

Some period of time after their return to Nazareth, wise men from the east hoping to find Him who was born king of the Jews followed His star. They found the child residing with His parents and presented their treasures to the child king. [Matthew 2:1-12. RSV] Soon thereafter an angel of the Lord appeared unto Joseph in a dream, warning him to flee with his family to Egypt.

Joseph was obedient to the Lord and fled with Mary and Jesus because Herod sought to kill the baby. They stayed in Egypt until Herod's death. [v. 13-15]

We have only one more reference to Joseph twelve years after Jesus' birth. Mary and Joseph experienced every parent's nightmare—a missing child. After a day's journey on the way back to Nazareth following their annual pilgrimage to Jerusalem where they attended the feast of the Passover, Joseph and Mary discovered that Jesus was missing. They had presumed Jesus was with their kinsfolk and acquaintances traveling with them. Returning to Jerusalem, they sought Him for three days before they "...found him in the temple, sitting among the teachers, listening to them and asking them questions; and all who heard him were amazed at his understanding and his answers." [Luke 2:46-47. RSV]

It appears we have not discovered a lot of material in the scriptures to flesh-out the caricature of Joseph that most of us see as we look at our nativity sets. Yet, after a closer reading of the scriptures we gain new insights into the real flesh and blood Joseph who was far different than we have imagined. We see a man who was compassionate. He did not want to make a public spectacle of Mary because of the skepticism as to her explanation of her pregnancy. He favored a quiet divorce. But, he changed his mind after hearing from an angel from the Lord who told him not to divorce his wife. Therefore, he was obedient to God. Unlike many modern-day absent fathers, current live-in boyfriends, or uncaring stepfathers, Joseph loved and cared for his family as shown by a day's journey back to Jerusalem and a three-day search for the missing twelve-year-old Jesus. Joseph was also a man who obeyed the laws of the land (he paid his taxes) as well as the laws of God (he took his child to the temple and presented him unto the Lord). Joseph protected his family as evidenced by their sojourn in Egypt.

Humble, compassionate, obedient to God, law-abiding, honest, concerned parent, protector, provider—all paint a picture of Joseph as a righteous (virtuous) man and loving husband and parent. What better set of adjectives could a man ask for when describing his life? However, for most people in this self-obsessed modern world, Joseph does appear to be a man whose life was lived in the shadows. But in God's account book, a man's worth is not measured by his popularity, bank balance, worldly success, or fame as evidenced by a pile of press clippings. When God looked at Joseph the shadows disappeared because the righteous "shine like the sun in the kingdom of their Father." [Matthew 13:43. RSV]

Creative Evolution – Screwtape's science for Christians

Part I (1-16-15)

In the early days of World War II the survival of Western civilization hung in the balance. With memories still fresh in their minds of the horrific carnage and sacrifice caused by the Great War that ended a mere twenty years earlier, the British people were in danger of being overwhelmed by a sense of foreboding and self-doubt as to the defense of their civilization and its values.

James Welch, Director of Religious Broadcasting at the British Broadcasting Corporation (BBC), described the religious climate of Britain at the time. "Two-thirds of BBC listeners…were living without any reference to God. God was simply not a factor." They were either unresponsive or openly hostile to Christianity.[1]

The British government saw the necessity of keeping their people from becoming demoralized amid the destruction of English cities by German bombs, massive loss of life, and threatened invasion by the German army. Welch believed the church acting through BBC broadcasts could be a major factor in giving the British people a reason for hope and answers to their questions of why this was happening and what they were fighting for.

> In a time of uncertainty and questioning it is the responsibility of the Church – and of religious broadcasting as one of its most powerful voices – *to declare the truth about God and His relation to men*. It has to expound the Christian faith in terms that can be easily understood by ordinary men and women, and to examine the ways in which that faith can be applied to present-day society during these difficult times.[2] [emphasis added]

To accomplish this task, Welch called upon an Oxford don who was not only an academician and superb writer but also a Christian apologist who had the essential quality that Welch sought: a remarkable ability to explain profound truths of God and the universe to ordinary men and women seeking answers to the basic questions of life. C. S. Lewis's series of war-time talks from 1941 through 1944 were eventually published as *Mere Christianity*. The major themes of

Lewis's talks were "Right and wrong as a clue to the meaning of the universe," "What Christians believe," "Christian behavior," and "Beyond personality – The first steps in the doctrine of the Trinity." In his talks on the BBC (and later in *Mere Christianity*), Lewis's goal was to defend the beliefs that had been common to nearly all Christians for almost two thousand years.[3]

The reason for this rather lengthy back story to the subject of this article is to demonstrate the *utmost importance of getting it right with regard to what Christians believe*. Christians dare not experiment with new theories of divine truth, the biblical understanding of creation, and the origin of man by introducing extra-biblical philosophies that fuel speculations and suppositions which undermine faith in the commonly held beliefs of Christians since the time of Christ. More specifically, the church must not undermine and weaken an understanding of the truthfulness of the Christian message by incorporating into Christian theology the tenets of the false and anti-God philosophies of materialism (humanism) in hopes of opening the doors for dialogue and witness to non-Christians.

One of the most alarming examples of this mixing of Christian and anti-Christian beliefs is the re-emergence of creative evolution which has spread rapidly since 2007 and which is being given a measure of legitimacy and respect by the leadership of many Christian colleges, organizations, and churches. The driving force behind creative evolution is the nonprofit BioLogos Foundation which is promoting a significant and well-funded effort to "...*change the way Christians understand Genesis and the origin of man*."[4] [emphasis added] Dr. Francis Collins, founder of BioLogos in 2007, was the former director of the Human Genome Project. In 2009, he was appointed by President Obama as director of the National Institutes of Health.[5]

When one begins to read the listing of beliefs of BioLogos, one may think he is reading the tenets of faith of the most conservative churches in America. Its beliefs are sprinkled with many phrases familiar to conservative Christians: "We believe the Bible is the inspired and authoritative word of God...We believe that all people have sinned against God and are in need of salvation...We believe in the historical incarnation of Jesus Christ as fully God and fully man. We believe in the historical death and resurrection of Jesus Christ..." So far, so good. But as the reader continues he arrives at the essence of BioLogos beliefs that create spiritual heartburn for most Christians.

> We believe that the diversity and interrelation of all life on earth are best explained by the God-ordained process of evolution with common descent. Thus,

evolution is not in opposition to God, but a means by which God providentially achieves his purposes. There, we reject ideologies that claim that evolution is a purposeless process or that evolution replaces God.

We believe that God created humans in biological continuity with all life on earth, but also as spiritual beings. God established a unique relationship with humanity by endowing us with his image and calling us to an elevated position within the created order.[6]

Three of the core commitments of BioLogos reveal its purposes which are to "...affirm evolutionary creation, recognizing God as Creator of all life over billions of years...seek truth, ever learning as we study the natural world and the Bible...strive for humility and gracious dialogue with those who hold other views."[7]

From the language of these core commitments we see that BioLogos views creative evolution as an established or accepted fact (as we are frequently reminded by evolutionists of all stripes). For BioLogosians, all other truths and interpretations must bow to the absolute truth of creative evolution when studying the natural world and the Bible. In other words, if creative evolutionists deem truth to be one thing but the beliefs based on the Bible that have been common to nearly all Christians for two thousand years deem truth to be something else (or the Bible is silent on the subject), then BioLogosians must choose the truth as dictated by creative evolution.

Proponents of creative evolution are devoted evangelists for their cause, and their technique for evangelism is dialogue as described on the BioLogos website. "Evolution and Christian Faith supports *projects and network building* among scholars, church leaders, and parachurch organizations *to address theological and philosophical concerns commonly voiced by Christians about evolutionary creation.*"[8] [emphasis added]

The bait of dialogue is particularly appealing to the academically inclined, seminarians, and many in church leadership. Following the obligatory disclaimers that the views of BioLogos do not necessarily represent the views of the participants (and likewise, the views of participants do not necessarily represent the views of the BioLogos), the BioLogos website lists a surprising array of respected and influential participants which include: Fuller Theological Seminary, Calvin College, Bethel University, Westmont College, Oxford University, Trinity Western University, Wheaton College, Northwest Nazarene University, Gordon College, and Oral Roberts

University. The stated purpose of some of the BioLogos projects is "to engage in meaningful and productive dialogue to reduce tensions between mainstream science and the Christian faith."[9] The John Templeton Foundation is the funding source for the missionaries of creative evolution and their willing participants. Dialogue takes the form of projects funded by Templeton grants ranging from $23,000 to $300,000. Thirty-seven projects have been funded to date.[10]

As the bait is consumed, many of the academicians, seminarians, and pastors carry the heresies back to their unsuspecting students and congregations. Even if the participants don't buy into creative evolution, their joint-participation with BioLogos lends an air of creditability and respectability to creative evolution and its emissaries.

Written by Lewis in 1941, *The Screwtape Letters* brilliantly satirize the tactics of Satan used to undermine faith and biblical truth. In this fictional but all too true account, Screwtape is a senior demon that is mentoring his nephew Wormwood, a Junior Tempter. Screwtape offers detailed advice to his nephew with regard to various methods of undermining faith and promoting sin in a British man known as Patient. Let's peek over the shoulder of Wormwood as he reads portions of the first of his uncle's letters.

> I note what you say about guiding your patient's reading and taking care that he sees a good deal of his materialist friend. But are you not be a trifle *naïve?*...Your man has been accustomed, ever since he was a boy, to have a dozen incompatible philosophies dancing about together inside his head. He doesn't think of doctrines as primarily "true" or "false", but as "academic" or "practical", "outworn" or "contemporary", "conventional" or "ruthless". Jargon, not argument, is our best ally in keeping him from the church. Don't waste time trying to make him think that materialism is *true*! Make him think it is strong, or stark, or courageous—that it is the philosophy of the future. That's the sort of thing he cares about...[11]

Through the enticement of dialogue creative evolutionists implant doubt about the common beliefs of Christians which have been sustained by the biblical narrative for almost two thousand years. When doubt has taken root in the heart of Christians, they are prepared to accept the lie. Heresies clothed in the soothing words of "meaningful and productive dialogue" and reduction of "tensions between mainstream science and the Christian faith" are still heresies.

Evolution may be considered by many as accepted fact and presented as the face of mainstream science, but it is still the creation story of the false philosophy of humanism (aka materialism or naturalism). Creative evolution stands firmly in the camp of this false philosophy and no amount of "meaningful and productive dialogue" can bridge the abyss that lies between Christianity and evolution.

In Part II we shall briefly examine the mechanics of creative evolution and how BioLogosians and many other Christians have succumbed to Satan's tactics as they attempt to paint a Christian face on mainstream evolution.

Part II (1-23-15)

C. S. Lewis's World War II radio broadcasts came almost immediately on the heels of publication of *The Screwtape Letters*. When Lewis's broadcasts were published as *Mere Christianity*, he added a footnote on creative evolution which he labeled the "In-between" view that attempts to navigate a path between the religious and the materialist views of creation.

> But to be complete, I ought to mention the In-between view called Life-Force philosophy, or Creative Evolution, or Emergent Evolution...People who hold this view say that the small variations by which life on this planet "evolved" from the lowest forms to Man were not due to chance but to the "striving" or "purposiveness" of a Life-Force. When people say this we must ask them whether by Life-Force they mean something with a mind or not. If they do, then "a mind bringing life into existence and leading it to perfection" is really a God, and their view is thus identical with the Religious. If they do not, then what is the sense in saying that something without a mind "strives" or has "purpose"? This seems to me to be fatal to their view.[12]

In spite of Lewis's assertions, BioLogos Foundation still attempts to plant one foot in each worldview—the religious and the materialist. BioLogos Foundation did not invent creative evolution as it has been around for over one hundred years. The Foundation merely took it off the shelf, dusted it, adjusted its mechanisms, painted a new face on it, and presented it as a culture-friendly version of creation to a wavering, powerless church struggling for survival in a post-Christian and post-modern world.

Origin of man according to the gospel of BioLogos

In an attempt to weave a path between Lewis's stark take-it-or-leave-it choice between godless materialism and the young-earth implications of Genesis, the modern proponents of creative evolution introduced a series of options as to how God might have used evolution to create man.

The first option offered by creative evolutionists is to view the biblical Adam and Eve as *archetypes* of humanity, that is, historical figures chosen to represent mankind living about 10,000 years ago. A second option presents an *allegorical* Adam and Eve that merely symbolize a large group of man's ancestors who lived 150,000 years ago. The third option is to treat Adam and Eve's story as a *parable* of each person's individual rejection of God. BioLogos does not bet the farm on any one view as being the correct model for man's origin but simply "...encourages scholarly work on these questions."[13] Irrespective of how God may have accomplished the creation man, BioLogos firmly rejects Adam and Eve as the *first* man and woman created by God by reducing them to a mere symbol for a larger existing population of humans.

BioLogos staffers such as program director Kathryn Applegate believe that miracles did not play a role in the earth's natural history but that the evolution process worked on its own without special intervention from God. "I don't think there's evidence from the science that He supernaturally zapped something into existence."[14] But, in its statement of fundamental beliefs, evolution is "...a means by which God providentially achieves his purposes."[15] Other words for providential are pre-ordained, God-given, and heaven-sent. On the one hand, BioLogosians deny God's interference in the process of evolution. On the other hand, BioLogosians believe the evolution process was pre-ordained to produce a specific outcome. These assumptions raise additional questions for creative evolutionists. Did God just assemble the parts needed, give the universe a spin to jumpstart the process, and then leave it for evolution to work its magic? More specifically, was man created by chance through the highly improbable evolution process or did God somehow rig the system so that man as we know him had to be created in His image through evolution? BioLogosians appear to answer yes to both questions.

In the center of all the speculations of BioLogos, questions remain as to the appearance of three essential ingredients necessary to explain mankind: the divine imprint, freewill, and original sin. Were these ingredients implanted before, during, or after this multi-billion year evolution process? Whenever these essentials were imparted to man, seemingly insurmountable conflicts and problems arise for the purveyors of creative evolution as an explanation for the creation of mankind.

Origin of sin

When, why, and how did sin enter the supposed evolutionary chain of events in mankind's development? Sinful man is a fact. The Apostle Paul's letter to the Romans states that, "For all have sinned and come short of the glory of God." [Romans 3:23. KJV] For creative evolutionists, original sin refers to the *current* state of humanity. They agree that all men have sinned, but they cannot answer the question as to when the first sin occurred and permanently infected mankind's gene pool. Although creative evolutionists claim the sciences of evolution and archeology can provide some insight, they conveniently punt the question of original sin into the theological arena which has many possible answers, some of which they claim correspond to scientific evidence currently available.[16]

Both creative evolutionists and their opponents must agree that man cannot have evolved as *inherently* sinful. Otherwise, we negate the fundamental belief that there was a point when man was sinless and then became sinful. The Apostle Paul agrees. "Wherefore, as *by one man sin entered into the world*, and death by sin; and so death passed upon all men, for that all have sinned." [Romans 5:12. KJV] [emphasis added] If Paul is correct, then BioLogosians must agree that man (and not pre-man) was fully evolved before he sinned. Otherwise, we must assume Paul meant well but got it wrong because he didn't have benefit of the modern creative evolutionists' correct understanding that Adam and Eve were only historical or allegorical placeholders to mark the group appearance of our first ancestors. But, if there was not an historical first couple through whom sin entered the world, what then?

Freewill

And what of the appearance of freewill in man, that sure-fire sin generator? Was man given freewill before, during, or after the evolution of man? Freewill can't have arrived by chance for it is an essential ingredient in the grand meta-story of the creation, the fall, and redemption. Therefore, we must believe that freewill entered man after he was fully formed. If freewill entered mankind long before man was fully man, then so too would original sin have entered. As we have previously determined, that cannot be.

Whether by miracle or through the unaided evolution process, BioLogosians can do little more than say that, "God gave us our spiritual capacities and calls us to bear his image."[17] It also appears that original sin and freewill must have entered mankind through God's miraculous magic—or not.

It's time we push speculation aside and read the words of Jack Collins who leads us back to sanity with regard to man's origins.

> The actual historicity of Adam and Eve is extremely important as a fundamental Christian doctrine... Christian doctrine is best understood as the true story of who we are and how we got to be where we are...It will come apart if we don't tell the story with the proper beginning...The Bible leads us to expect a special creation of humankind...If we take the idea of a purely natural process from molecules to mankind, then I think that is very difficult to square with the Bible...It might even be impossible.[18]

Creative evolutionists offer only flawed science and no biblical validation for their theories. They must rely on man's puny reason, speculations as to what the Genesis story really means, and their faith in the accepted fact of evolution. This is hardly the stuff to win over skeptical anti-God evolutionists let alone Christians.

The Apostle Paul wrote to the Romans of the deplorable condition of the Gentiles. Paul stated that even though the Gentiles did not have the revelation of the Hebrews, they were guilty of violation of God's laws *evident in His eternal power and deity as revealed in nature.*

> For what can be known about God is plain to them, because God has shown it to them. Ever since the creation of the world his invisible nature, namely, his eternal power and deity, has been clearly perceived in the things that have been made. So they are without excuse; for although they knew God they did not honor him as God or give thanks to him, but they became futile in their thinking and their senseless minds were darkened. Claiming to be wise, they became fools, and exchanged the glory of the immortal God for images

resembling mortal man or birds or animals, or reptiles.
[Romans 1:19-23 RSV.]

Prior to the rise of humanism (aka naturalism or materialism), nature was viewed as an imperfect imitation of divine reality. However, modern man has been taught that he need only "...to reason correctly upon evidence from nature."[19] But man's effort to explain the nature of God through creative evolution is both unnecessary and impossible. It is unnecessary because God's invisible nature is already plainly understood by man's perception of the things He created. It is impossible because imperfect nature cannot add clarity to the picture of divine reality as revealed by the Bible. The biblical record brought clarity to nature, not the other way around. This is the fundamental error of BioLogos when it attempts to humanize religion by embracing creative evolution to give a better understanding of divine reality through the workings of imperfect nature.

As was the case in the early days of World War II, the fate of Western civilization in the twenty-first century hangs in the balance. And once again the outcome may be determined by how well we *get it right with regard to what Christians believe.*

I'm so ashamed! I was a member of a hate group and didn't know it. (4-30-13)

They say confession is good for the soul, and after the shocking news I received a few days ago, I must somehow make amends for my life of hate. It's a sordid story that began in my childhood. I can't take all of the blame. Maybe it was peer pressure or parent pressure. Who knows? But I was molded, shaped, and destined for a life of hate. What's worse, I am responsible for corrupting my own children with that hateful lifestyle. They say ignorance is not an excuse, but I really didn't know that what I was doing was wrong. Actually I looked at my beliefs and activities as a badge of honor and felt that I was doing good works for my family and the country.

The news came a few days ago as I was browsing through my emails. There it was, the Family Research Council email warning us that our cover had been blown (it was only then that I realize that FRC is an avowed enemy of the state, a hate group organization with whom I'm associated, unofficially of course).

It seems that a certain military officer, Lieutenant Colonel Jack Rich, discovered that a number of groups in America "did not share our Army values."[1] This shocking discovery prompted him to send an email to thirty-eight of his fellow officers and NCOs (non-commissioned officers) to educate them that "when we see behaviors that are inconsistent with Army values—don't just walk by—do the right thing and address the concern before it becomes a problem."

Well, I can tell you his warning sent chills down my spine! I lay awake several nights knowing that LTC Rich and the Army were not ignoring my behavior while wondering how they would address my problem. And I just can't take it any longer so I'm confessing. I'm an evangelical Christian. And worse yet and to my undying shame I have been a member or fellow traveler of several subversive, hate-filled organizations including the American Family Association and the Family Research Council.

I know I can do nothing to atone for my sin other than to throw myself on the mercy of LTC Rich and the U.S. Army. Yet, I think there are some circumstances that might mitigate whatever punishment I receive. First, I blame the Army for not doing more to re-educate me before I was too deeply immersed in my life of hate. I was young and impressionable when I received the letter from President Johnson informing me of his invitation to join the military in 1967. If they had done the proper background checks, they would have known of my hateful tendencies and radical Christian associates and could have dealt with them then. I hadn't intended to violate Army values. Heavens, I didn't know there were any Army values other than to do what I was told by anyone with more than one stripe on their sleeves or they would kick my you-know-what to @#%! and back. (Sorry for the language but "Heavens" has been a part of my vocabulary for many years, and old habits are hard to break.)

But I've thought a lot about those days long ago since my discovery last week that I was deeply involved with domestic hate groups. Perhaps the Army realized back in 1967 that I didn't share their values and that they did the right thing by sending me to Vietnam as a way of dealing with my issues before they became a problem. Certainly, a lot of people with those issues didn't return from Vietnam to cause problems. Oh well, who knows?

I'm so glad to get this off my chest. I'm feeling much better already. I wonder if they will give me probation and allow me to join HA (Haters Anonymous). Perhaps I could be a group leader and go to some of those organizations identified by LTC Rich and show them the error of their ways:

- The Christian Right
- Various Racist Skinhead groups
- American Family Association
- Ku Klux Klan
- Family Research Council
- Various Neo-Nazi groups[2]

These are just a few of the organizations identified by LTC Rich with the aid of the Southern Poverty Law Center.[3] As the old saying goes, "The fields are white unto harvest!" I could be sort of a missionary spreading Army values across the land. Oops, sorry for the biblical language again.

It's good to know there are other true patriots in the Army in addition to LTC Rich who have implemented a number of initiatives to expose or root out hate group activities in the military:

- A War Games scenario at Fort Leavenworth that identified Christian groups and Evangelical groups as being potential threats;
- A 2009 Dept. of Homeland Security memorandum that identified future threats to national security coming from Evangelicals and pro-life groups;

- A West Point study released by the U.S. Military Academy's Combating Terrorism Center that linked pro-lifers to terrorism;
- Evangelical leader Franklin Graham was uninvited from the Pentagon's National Day of Prayer service because of his comments about Islam;
- Christian prayers were banned at the funeral services for veterans at Houston's National Cemetery;
- Bibles were banned at Walter Reed Army Medical Center – a decision that was later rescinded;
- Christian crosses and a steeple were removed from a chapel in Afghanistan because the military said the icons disrespected other religions;
- Catholic chaplains were told not to read a letter to parishioners from their archbishop related to Obamacare mandates. The Secretary of the Army feared the letter could be viewed as a call for civil disobedience.[4]

Well, this just goes to show those who think the country's going to the dogs are wrong. There is hope for America with patriots such as LTC Rich out there spreading Army values!

With deep and sincere remorse,

An older but wiser—Larry G. Johnson.

Part II – Worldview

Why I believe (8-29-14)

A child-like faith

    I became a Christian as a child of six. Owasso was a tiny little hamlet of about 250 people, barely four blocks long and two blocks wide straddling a two-lane concrete highway meandering southward towards Tulsa through the perennially-flooding bottom lands and across an old bridge over Bird Creek. This little wide spot in the road had two or three churches, a grocery or two, a school, a collection of small houses, and not much else. Our children's church teacher and her husband (a nonbeliever) were dairy farmers as were my parents and as my mother's parents had been. Our teacher helped with the milking and some of the farm work, but on Sunday mornings after chores, she would pick up her grandchildren and any other neighbor kids that were so inclined and take them to church. I still remember well those Sunday mornings when she taught us flannel graph stories from the Bible including Noah, Moses, Joseph, David and Goliath, and Daniel in the Lion's Den. She mixed in her own stories of "Barney in the Barrel," "The Little Red Hen," and others, all reflecting the truth of Christ's love for each of us.

    One Sunday morning she asked if any of us (probably about eight or nine in attendance that morning) would like to accept Jesus into their heart. I moved from the back row of three homemade benches and came to the front and accepted Him as my Lord and Savior. Why did I *believe?* Some will say my child's faith was mere emotional manipulation. Others will say it was the Christian influence of family and friends to conform. But the Bible gives the real reason. *I believed because my child-like faith responded to the gentle wooing of the Holy Spirit*. Luke recorded Christ's words as He described the utmost importance of a child-like faith, "Truly, I say to you, whoever does not receive the kingdom of God like a child shall not enter it." [Luke 18:17. RSV]

Reason

As we grow physically and mentally, our child-like faith must not remain static. Since that day I moved from the back bench to publicly profess my belief, my faith has grown and continues to grow *because of reason*. Right reason applied to my observations and experiences in the light of the biblical revelation and divine guidance increases my faith and helps me in my everyday life's walk of faith. Life happens, and bad things happen to people who are faithful to God. How should Christians respond when they experience the trials of life such as when a spouse unexpectedly files for divorce, the death of a child or spouse, loss of job, betrayal by friends, and agonizing pain or loss of health? Here, right reason helps sustain faith in times of adversity. The believer continues to believe because he or she knows the truth of God's word and because their life's observations and experiences substantiate the truth upon which their faith rests. All the while the world shouts that there can be no faith in a God who would allow such tragedies, but the world only sees the natural and temporal. Faith transcends the natural to the realm and reality of the supernatural. The Apostle Paul wrote of how Christians should deal with the difficulties of life in their faith walk.

> For we know that if the earthly tent we live in is destroyed, we have a building from God, a house not made with hands, eternal in the heavens. Here indeed we groan, and long to put on our heavenly dwelling, so that by putting it on we may not be found naked. For while we are still in this tent, we sigh with anxiety; not that we would be unclothed, but that we would be further clothed, so that what is mortal may be swallowed up by life. He who has prepared us for this very thing is God, who has given us the Spirit as a guarantee. So we are always of good courage; we know that while we are at home in the body we are away from the Lord, for we walk by faith, not by sight. [2 Corinthians 5:1-7. RSV]

Is Paul saying that faith is blind and denies reason? Absolutely not! Paul is speaking of the eternal hope of the Christian in spite of present circumstances. Faith is not an abandonment of reason. C. S. Lewis challenged the widespread assumption that there is a battle between faith and reason, "It is not reason that is taking away my faith: on the contrary, my faith is based on reason. It is my imagination and emotions [that attack faith]. The battle is between faith and reason on one side and emotion and imagination on the other."[1]

Reason is an ally of faith. Our observations and experiences of life aided by right reasoning lead us to belief in the truth of Christianity and all upon which it rests in spite of circumstances. In one sense reason leads us to the door of Christianity, but faith invites us in and holds our hand as we continue the faith journey. However, reason was not left at the door. As we move along our faith journey, we encounter life—all sorts of thoughts, ideas, things, situations, difficulties, trials, struggles, disappointments, opportunities, and so forth. At that point reason continues to assist and guide within the framework of truths we hold and have incorporated into our faith walk. In this sense, reason helps us to accept the seemingly unreasonable as we search the Bible, pray for Divine guidance, and work out our own salvation.[2]

Lewis captures well the linkage between faith and reason when he wrote that faith "...is the art of holding on to things your reason has once accepted, in spite of your changing moods."[3] It is not blind faith but a faith that is supported and increased through right reason. In time faith grows to be more important to our belief in the God of the Bible than our reasoning ability. Faith never abandons reason for it continues to play a secondary and supporting role. As faith grows and reason diminishes, reason has helped us come full circle once again to a child-like faith, and through faith we can withstand changes in our moods, our failures, our doubts, our circumstances, or any other of life's challenges.

I *believed* because of a child-like faith. I *continue to believe* and my faith grows as right reason filters my observations and experiences in life in the light of the biblical revelation and divine guidance. However, there is a third reason I believe.

Best evidence

We humans have an insatiable thirst for truth about the meaning and purpose of life. Man has always recognized a divine order in the universe, nature, and human relationships. The more science reveals about the earth's exquisite and complex order, the greater the evidence for a supernatural creator of that apparent order. Those that deny a supernatural creator continue to search for an over-arching theory of everything. For them the universe is nothing more than a cosmic box full of puzzle pieces in which each piece must to be analyzed in its minutest detail. Once understood, the pieces can be fitted together to answer the basic questions of life, all of which is to be accomplished without help from a mythical God. In their attempts to fit the pieces together, often forcing un-natural and harmful configurations, they focus on the minutia, constantly arranging and rearranging, and end with meaningless patterns which reveal neither truth nor offer satisfactions demanded. Richard Weaver diagnosed modern man's affliction which he described as a "...severe fragmentation of his world picture...which leads directly to an obsession with isolated parts."[4]

The Bible is a book of history, poetry, prophecy, parable, and allegory in which God reveals Himself and paints the grand mural of the creation, the purpose of man, our present sorrow, the means of redemption, and our eternal destination.[5] It is the unifying picture on the puzzle box which in one grand sweep makes sense of everything in man's experience since his creation. However, the picture is not enough for it is prescriptive and must be applied by each human being in order to fit the pieces together in a way that gives meaning, purpose, and satisfaction in this life and the next.

In spite of all the protestations of humanists, Darwinists, atheists, intellectuals, pundits, false religions, and others, the long view of man's sordid history on this planet and the heart-breaking immediacy of the world's pain and suffering revealed by today's 24/7 news cycle point to man's failed efforts to answer the basic questions of life with false philosophies and religions that deny the God of the Bible. It is the biblical revelation that gives the best explanation and evidence of who we are, what went wrong with the world, and how we can get out of the mess we are in. This is the third reason why I believe.

What is your purpose in life?

Part I (8-23-13)

Some may suggest this is a silly or trivial question. For those that attempt to answer, the variety of responses will likely be as numerous as the number of people responding. Many consider life meaningless (and by implication hopeless). Others focus their answers on themselves, e.g., their purpose is to survive whether in a primitive society (kill or be killed) or the modern (the 8 to 5 so-called rat race of working to provide the necessities of life). But these answers are inadequate and do not speak to the fundamental question that every one of us must answer.

Man is a special being, if for no reason other than he is the only creature to ask why he is here. That very question presupposes his denial that he owes his existence to some fantastically improbable celestial *and* biological crap shoot. Man senses his specialness and cannot abide nothingness as the reason for his existence. He looks at himself and sees faint images of something far greater, and he is compelled to search for answers as to the meaning and purpose of his life. He yearns to be something above what he sees in the natural world. Unique to the earth and its living creatures, man thinks, verbalizes, and symbolizes his quest for connection to some greater purpose.[1]

Alexis de Tocqueville's words of 180 years ago confirm these sentiments when he wrote: "…the imperfect joys of this world will never satisfy his heart. Man alone of all created beings shows a natural disgust for *existence* and an *immense longing to exist*; he despises life and fears annihilation."[2] Tocqueville's words elevate man's quest for purpose from the mundane level of survival and the minutia of life. Man *must* seek answers to that fundamental question of life…what is our purpose?

Each individual's quest for purpose will be profoundly affected by his or her worldview. Worldview deals with *basic* beliefs about things—ultimate questions with which we are confronted; matters of general principle; an overall perspective or perception of reality or truth from which one sees, understands, and interprets the universe and humanity's relation to it. Simply put, a worldview is a person's beliefs about the world that directs his or her decisions and actions.[3] And it is these beliefs (worldview) from which we answer the question, "What is our purpose?"

But not all worldviews are created equal. The beliefs one holds tend to create a pattern, design, or structure that fit together in a particular way. This structure or order (worldview) generally must have a coherence or consistency which is necessary to give orientation and direction for living life. If a person's decisions, actions or outcomes are not consistent with their beliefs, the conflict must be resolved or over a period of time that person's integrity and mental health will be diminished. Therefore, a person must discover what is true and live a life compatible with that truth. Also, if one has a false worldview that does not align with objective reality, then that person's answer to our *purpose of life* question will not be correct, and they climb the ladder of life with the ladder leaning against the wrong wall.

In America, there are two competing worldviews which give differing views on man's purpose in life. One is the biblical worldview of Christianity upon whose principles the nation was founded and governed for 150 years. The other is what an acquaintance of mine calls the official religion of America—humanism. So how do these competing worldviews define man's purpose?

Humanists hold that the preciousness and dignity of the individual person is a central humanist value in which individuals should be encouraged to realize their own creative talents and desires and exercise maximum individual autonomy *consonant with social responsibility*. As to the individual, humanists promise a freedom from the mores, norms, tradition, and distant voices of the past. The freedom espoused by the humanists gives unbridled control to the self and senses. However, one must read the fine print in the humanists' promises, i.e., individual autonomy must be *consonant with social responsibility*. Therefore, humanists harness an individual's dignity, worth, and freedom to the principle of the greatest-happiness-for-the-greatest-number which is hitched to the humanist belief that the highest moral obligation is to humanity as a whole. The obligations of the individual are subservient to his obligations to the larger society, and those obligations are determined and defined by the humanist intellectual elite, i.e., God is replaced by man as the authority.

In the Christian worldview, each individual was created for a personal and loving relationship with God and each other. Because man is born with the mark of sin that was transmitted to him down through history from his first ancestor, the relationship remains broken. The Christian worldview recognizes the fallen condition of humankind and that God has provided a means whereby man can return to Him through repentance and living in a proper orientation to His laws and plan. A personal (individual) relationship with God is possible only through recognition of who God is and obedience to his precepts. That relationship is restored through the acceptance of God's son, Jesus Christ, as the individual's Lord and Savior.

From these two descriptions of worldviews we see a fundamental difference in the purpose of man that form one of the bases for the culture wars in America. One is based on exaltation of the individual and the other is based on relationships. One is inward looking and the other is outward looking. As America has moved from the biblical to the humanistic worldview, the pathologies in American society have exploded as the false worldview of humanism contradicts the innate God-given nature of man. In Part II we will take a closer look at these differences.

Part II (8-30-13)

In Part I we described man's purpose in life from the perspective of the two dominant combatants in the culture wars. One is the biblical worldview of Christianity upon whose principles the nation was founded and governed for 150 years. The other has been described as the official religion of America—humanism. So how do these competing worldviews define man's purpose? The humanistic vision of the purpose of man is based on the exaltation of the individual, is inward-looking, denies the role of God in man's purpose, and whose centerpiece is a vague, undefined egalitarianism focused on equality of outcome. Christianity's view of man's purpose is rooted in relationship, is outward-looking, and is defined by those timeless truths which are revealed in the Bible.

The exaltation of the individual and denial of the Creator are found in the elemental tenets of humanism, and we need only look to *Humanist Manifesto II* for affirmation. "The ultimate *goal* should be fulfillment of the potential growth in each human personality…We can discover no divine *purpose* or providence for the human species."[4]

The battle between the humanistic and biblical worldviews is not new. Its beginnings are recorded in the third chapter of Genesis. The ancient Greeks judged "man the measure," and its humanistic roots continued down through centuries until its flowering in the Renaissance and Enlightenment. It was the egalitarian notions of the French philosophers that became the framework for the disaster of the French Revolution. However, this radical, mystical egalitarianism remains the center piece of the modern humanistic philosophy. By egalitarian is meant a belief in human equality with special emphasis on social, political, and economic rights and privileges and a focus on the removal of any inequalities among humankind. This focus is a forced leveling of society and ultimately results in socialism.

If one reflects on the various descriptions of humanism through its definition, philosophy, application, and worldview, one can see the emphasis on the horizontal (leveling of society) and the sharp contrast with the vertical (hierarchical) with regard to relationships in all spheres of family and society. Humanism's exaltation of self over family, denial of patrimony, emphasis on the present and the experiential, flexible and interchangeable values, life lived for the moment for there is nothing beyond, and deference to the senses represent a detachment from any hierarchical bonds of duty, obligation, patrimony, and the permanent things. There is no heaven above nor hell below and therefore no hierarchy, only an everlasting march to an unattainable and unknowable horizon that continually recedes into the distance.[5]

Richard Weaver superbly contrasts the humanists' obsession with the individual and a society leveled by radical egalitarianism with the truth of the opposing biblical concept of relationship and fraternity.

> The comity of peoples in groups large or small rests not upon this chimerical notion of equality but upon fraternity, a concept which long antedates it (equality) in history because it (fraternity) goes immeasurably deeper in human sentiment. The ancient feeling of brotherhood carries obligations of which equality knows nothing. It calls for respect and protection, for brotherhood is status in family, and family is by nature hierarchical. It demands patience with little brother, and it may sternly exact duty of big brother. It places people in a network of sentiment, not of rights..."[6]

In the Christian worldview, God did not create man out of need. Rather, it was a will to love, an expression of the very character of God, to share the inner life of the Trinity (i.e., relationship). Man's chief end is to glorify God by communing with God forever. Being God, He knew the course and cost of His creation. But creating man with a free will meant the possibility of rejection of God and His love. In other words free will and the potential for rejection of God was the penalty for the possibility of love. So it is on the earthly plane, to risk love is to risk rejection. Rejection was not a surprise to an omniscient God. Before creation, God knew the cost would be the death of His Son, and this is hinted at in Revelation 13:8, "...Lamb slain from the foundation of the world." God's infinite love exceeded the cost of that love at Calvary. We were created for relationship!

The primary reason a culture fails is because it loses its cohesiveness or unity. If human relationships mean order in society, then equality as defined by the humanists is a disorganizing concept. Therefore, this radical egalitarianism may be the greatest pathology and greatest threat to the survival of America and the rest of Western Civilization.

Our worldview defines our purpose in life. Lost in the fast pace and minutia of life, few stop to consider the importance of knowing their purpose in life or that there is even a purpose apart from themselves. But as Americans increasingly embrace the humanistic worldview with its cult-like focus on equality and the freedom of the individual from the mores, norms, traditions, and voices of the past, the resultant pathologies are eroding the central cultural vision of the nation. We have become a nation of individuals consumed with self as opposed to relationship.

In twenty-first century America, a majority of its citizens still hold the biblical worldview, but most of the leadership of American institutions have abandoned it for the humanistic worldview. For America to survive, we must rediscover that our *purpose* in life (both individual and national) is tied to those permanent truths as revealed in the biblical record and not the disintegrating concepts of humanism. Only then can we restore unity under the central cultural vision of the Founders upon which the nation was founded.

Thrill killers, the ACLU, Benjamin Spock, and C. S. Lewis (9-13-13)

Two young men and their driver (all ages 15 to 17) residing in a small rural town in southern Oklahoma allegedly killed a twenty-two year old college student from Australia by shooting him in the back while he jogged down a road. The only motive mentioned by one of the alleged perpetrators was "boredom". Within a week another random attack killed an 88-year-old World War II veteran in Spokane, Washington. The two 16-year-old killers' only motive was robbery. The man was only slightly above five feet tall and died of severe head injuries. What threat could this diminutive 88-year old man have posed to cause the 16-year-olds to beat him to death? These are but two instances among hundreds if not thousands occurring in the United States each year.

Few people in America are unaware of the recent spate of so-called "thrill killings" in various parts of the country. Headlines blaze and talk shows buzz. People shake their heads and use adjectives such as "senseless, heartless, and soulless." The first reaction to these irrational takings of human life is incomprehension, then anger. We wonder why all of this is happening with increasing frequency and heinousness. Then a quiet sense of unease casts a pall over our minds as we see the evil that is rooted in our being, that indelible hereditary sin stain that has passed down to us from our first ancestor. Either as victim or perpetrator, we wonder if "There but for the grace of God, go I." Pundits and experts search for motives and causes that can be addressed and treated, or they attempt to fix the blame on some failure of society or some perceived culpable villains (i.e., the perpetrator becomes the victim). The solutions come in all shapes and sizes including more laws, more regulation, or added layers of social engineering. But the real culprit is the domination of American institutions and popular culture by those holding the humanistic worldview. Always ready with excuses, reasons, and solutions, the humanists with humanistic answers merely exacerbate the trauma inflicted on a society whose central cultural vision is no longer anchored to the biblical worldview.

It has been a half century since prayer was allowed in American schools. The posting of the Ten Commandments in schools and on our public buildings is now illegal. Young people are not taught the values upon which this nation was founded. In fact, they are taught that there are no absolutes, no right or wrong, and all religions and belief systems have equal value. Unrestrained by tradition or other moral force, popular culture denigrates the central cultural vision upon which the nation was founded. Tradition, by itself, can only maintain a central cultural vision for a time as the moral capital accumulated from adherence to that vision is eroded. If a society's central vision is corrupt or false, that rebellion may be a good thing if one assumes that there are moral absolutes of right and wrong, truth and falsity. But a popular culture that misreads and wars against the validity of a morally sound central cultural vision will cause that culture to disintegrate.[1]

Oklahoma's State Capitol is seventy miles north of the little town of Duncan where three bored youths allegedly shot Chris Lane who died in the ditch where he fell. On the grounds of the State Capitol stands a monument paid for with private funds and inscribed with the Ten Commandments. The sixth commandment reads "You shall not murder." [Deuteronomy 5:17. NKJV] Six days after the murder of Chris Lane, the American Civil Liberties Union filed suit against Capital Preservation Commission of the State of Oklahoma, seeking removal of the monument. The suit states that, "This piece of public property, placed upon public property, conveys an explicit religious message that supports and endorses the faiths and creeds of some churches and sects." Brady Henderson, Legal Director with the Oklahoma ACLU, stated "Our constitution makes it clear you cannot use state property and state resources to support a particular religion and this monument does just that."[2]

In answer to Mr. Henderson's interpretation of the Constitution, we once again return to the words of Supreme Court Justice Joseph Story (appointed by James Madison, reputed to be the father of the Constitution which speaks volumes about Story's understanding of the Founders' meaning with regard to the Constitution and its Amendments).

> …We are not to attribute this prohibition of a national religious establishment to an indifference to religion in general and especially to Christianity which none could hold in more reverence than the framers of the Constitution…Probably at the time of the adoption of the Constitution and of the Amendments to it, the general, if not universal, sentiment in America was that Christianity ought to receive encouragement from the State…An attempt to level all religions, and to make it a matter of state policy to hold all in utter indifference,

would have created universal disapprobation (condemnation), if not universal indignation.[3]

One wonders if any of the killers in Duncan, Oklahoma and Spokane, Washington would have had second thoughts about their actions if at some point during their school years a copy of the Ten Commandments had been posted on their school room wall and a teacher had taken the time to explain what each commandment meant.

Even prominent humanists recognize the loss of our fundamental values in American society. One such was Benjamin Spock, famous for his best-selling baby care book. His life's work and influence greatly advanced the humanistic worldview in America. He remained a champion of humanism throughout his life, and his efforts were recognized when he was named Humanist of the Year in 1968. In 1994, four years before the end of his life at age ninety, Spock wrote *A Better World for Our Children – Rebuilding American Family Values*. In the book Spock expressed considerable concern as he viewed the harmful effects of society on American children.

> "I am near despair. My despair comes not only from the progressive loss of values in this century, but from the fact that present society is simply not working. *Societies and people who live in them fall apart if they lose their fundamental beliefs, and the signs of this loss are everywhere.*"[4] [emphasis added]

Amazingly, Spock remained oblivious to humanism's disintegrating effects and did not see that the ills of society are a direct result of well over a century of humanism's dominance in American life as it stripped away our fundamental beliefs instilled by a biblical worldview. In his book *The Abolition of Man*, C. S. Lewis captured the essence of this cultural madness brought about by the unwitting soldiers in the army of the "knowledge class" having been indoctrinated with a humanistic worldview.

> It is an outrage that they should be commonly spoken of as Intellectuals. This gives them a chance to say that he who attacks them attacks Intelligence. It is not so. They are not distinguished from other men by any unusual skill in finding truth...It is not excess of thought but defect of fertile and generous emotion that marks them out. Their heads are no bigger than the ordinary: it is the atrophy of the chest beneath that

makes them seem so. All the time...we continue to clamour for those very qualities we are rendering impossible...In a sort of ghastly simplicity we remove the organ and demand the function. We make men without chests and expect of them virtue and enterprise. We laugh at honour and are shocked to find traitors in our midst. We castrate and bid the geldings be fruitful.[5]

America is losing its fundamental beliefs. America's original central cultural vision is held together by the moral capital banked decades ago but is near depletion. Faced with a hostile popular culture and leadership in our American institutions that embrace the humanistic worldview, we are in critical danger of forever losing the central cultural vision established by the Founders—those men with chests.

Acts of God or Acts of Man? (8-8-14)

The phrase "an act of God" is typically associated with destruction, loss, pain, and suffering beyond the control of man. Many property and casualty insurance policies contain exclusions of coverage on losses attributed to "acts of God" because certain massive acts of nature can't be controlled such as earthquakes, floods, and hurricanes. However, other less pervasive natural and therefore insurable occurrences such as tornadoes, hail, storms, high winds, and ice may be covered. War, although man-made, is often included in these exclusions. Then there are other uninsurable catastrophes such as famine, pandemic disease, and pestilence that kill millions each year. For many, the biblical God of love has a lot to answer for if these actions are truly His responsibility.

It seems that God gets blamed for most if not all of the evil in the world. If He is not blamed for causing it, then He is blamed for not preventing it. For several well-known individuals, a good God cannot exist if He allows such pain and suffering. The last vestiges of Charles Darwin's Christian faith evaporated upon his daughter's painful death. Likewise, billionaire Ted Turner became an outspoken unbeliever upon his sister's death from a painful disease. "I was taught that God was love and God was powerful, and I couldn't understand how someone so innocent should be made or allowed to suffer so." Former well-known evangelist Charles Templeton wrote *Farewell to God* in 1996. The reason for his rejection of belief in God is revealed by his question, "How could a loving and omnipotent God create such horrors as we have been contemplating?"[1]

So how could a good God allow a world full of pain and suffering to exist? It is a legitimate question, especially for those who deny the existence of God or who reject the biblical answer for mankind's pain and suffering.

Before we require God to explain the reasons for the existence of pain and suffering in the world, we ought to be in agreement as to the definition and meaning of two words necessary to understand God's answer: *love and freedom*. When we speak of love, we refer here to interpersonal relationships (as opposed to the impersonal "I love pizza!"). Our friend Webster describes love as "affection," "devotion," "warm attachment," and "adoration."[2] But love can be one directional and rejected by the intended recipient. Love cannot be commanded, only accepted and returned or rejected. Here we see that love is a matter of choice. One is free to accept or reject love. The popular mantra that "love is all that is necessary" is wrong. We may love the terrorist, but that won't stop him from maiming and killing innocent people. Even if the terrorist is won over by our love and renounces his terrorist activities, the pain and suffering caused by mindless natural forces can't be stopped. So, we must agree that love requires freedom for both the giver and recipient.

With this understanding of love and freedom, we are able to comprehend God's answer for the existence of pain and suffering in the world. To do so we must step back and take in the entire breadth and height of the biblical meta-story of creation including man who was God's special creation.

> God existed before the universe was created, and then God created the universe and all that is within it including the laws that govern that creation. Unlike all of the other elements of His creation, man was created with a free will. This part of the Christian worldview is called Creation. Mankind's free will allowed man to think and act in ways that were contrary to God's plan and will for His creation. When man acted in ways contrary to God's laws (truths), such disobedience to God's laws was called sin, and as a result decay and death entered into God's creation. This is called the Fall, and it affected not only man but all of God's creation. But as God is a loving God, He created a way through His son, Jesus Christ, which allows man to bring order to the chaos he created. This is called the Restoration. There you have the basic elements of the Christian worldview: the Creation, the Fall, and the Restoration. No other worldview recognizes the true nature of the human condition and provides a means whereby man can return to a proper orientation to God's laws and plan. It answers the questions of where we came from and who we are, what went wrong, and how we get out of the chaos and restore order to our souls.[3]

God's creation of man with a free will meant the possibility of rejection of God and His love. In other words free will and the potential for rejection of God was the penalty for the possibility of love. So it is on the earthly plane, to risk love is to risk rejection.[4] Pain and suffering entered the world through man's rejection of God. But man was not the only victim of his rebellion.

> Even natural evil—involving earthquakes, tornadoes, floods, and the like—is rooted in our wrong use of free choice. We must not forget that we are living in a fallen world, and because of this, we are subject to disasters in the world of nature that would not have occurred had man not rebelled against God in the beginning (see Romans 8:20-22).[5]

Humanism is the great competing meta-story and stands in stark contrast on every major point to that of Christianity with regard to man's creation, purpose, and destiny. The humanistic philosophy denies the existence of all forms of the supernatural, proposes that nature is the totality of being and exists independently of any mind or consciousness. Man is the evolutionary product of Nature, and man has no conscious survival after death due to the unity of body and personality. Humans are masters of their own destiny, and human values are grounded in this-earthly experiences and relationships.[6]

Humanism presents the problem of suffering as the greatest objection to the existence of God. But humanism stands convicted by its own arguments in its denial of the existence of a supernatural God. If there is no supernatural God, and if humans are masters of their own destinies, what is the source of evil that has led to universal pain and suffering in the world? Its worldview has no logical, realistic, or compelling answers. Christian apologist William Craig Lane expresses the humanist's dilemma.

> Paradoxically, then, even though the problem of suffering is the greatest objection to the existence of God, at the end of the day God is the only solution to the problem of suffering. If God does not exist, then we are locked without hope in a world filled with pointless and unredeemed suffering. God is the final answer to the problem of suffering, for He redeems us from evil and takes us into the everlasting joy of an incommensurable good: fellowship with Himself.[7]

As the world is increasingly awash in unfathomable sorrow, pain, and suffering, those who are redeemed by God through the sacrifice of His Son Jesus Christ can take comfort in the words of Christ to His disciples just before His betrayal and death on the cross.

"These things I have said to you, that in me you may have peace. In the world you have tribulation; but be of good cheer, I have overcome the world." [John 16:33. RSV]

Statistics: Facts often used to replace truth (9-12-14)

Leonard Pitts' recent syndicated column was provocatively titled "If GOP is so right, why are red states so far behind?" Pitts raised the question because of the results of a recent study by two Princeton economists that found the economy has grown faster under Democratic presidents. From President Kennedy to and including President Obama the economy grew at 4.35 percent as compared to 2.54 percent growth under Republican presidents during the same period. He also pointed to a statistic supplied by Occupy Democrats, a left-wing advocacy group, that of the ten poorest states, nine are red states and of the poorest 100 counties, ninety seven are in red states. Based on the report's statistical revelations, Pitts asked several questions, "If Republican fiscal policies really are the key to prosperity, if the GOP formula of low taxes and little regulation really does unleash economic growth, then why has the country fared better under Democratic presidents than Republican ones and why are red states the poorest states in the country?"[8]

To be fair, Mr. Pitts does note that the ability of presidents to influence the economy is "vastly overstated." He even cites the Princeton researchers who stated that their study does *not* support the idea that Democratic policies are responsible for greater economic performance under Democratic presidents. Further, he concedes that red states and counties tend to be more rural and likely to have modest incomes while at the same time may enjoy greater spending power than wealthier states and counties. Yet, Mr. Pitts can't resist the assumption that the fiscal economic policies of the Republicans are inferior to those of the Democrats. He states that, "…the starkness and sheer preponderance of the numbers are hard to ignore." After comparing the true blue state of Connecticut's first place in per capita income of $56,000 with red-state Mississippi's last place at $32,000, Pitts says that, "At the very least, stats like these ought to call into question GOP claims of superior economic policy…"[9]

"There are three kinds of lies: lies, d**n lies, and statistics." Mark Twain popularized this quote in America but attributed it to former British Prime Minister Benjamin Disraeli. How does one lie with statistics? One way is to erroneously *assume* a correlation between two variables and simply imply that one causes the other. Although Mr. Pitts agrees that the study's findings do *not* support the idea that there is a correlation between the economic policies of Democratic presidents and the above-mentioned superior economic statistics, that is, one does not cause the other, he does believe that, *given the sheer magnitude of the numbers*, we must assume there is some correlation between the economic policies of Republican presidents and the lesser economic growth experience thereunder.[10]

Mr. Pitts has not lied (in a manner suggested by Twain), but he has been seduced by the power of statistical "facts" and as a consequence has "...drawn a mathematically precise line from an unwarranted assumption to a foregone conclusion."[11] To summarize, Mr. Pitts' conclusion is that, although the statistics provide no correlation between superior economic performance and the economic policies of Democrat presidents, the statistics must almost certainly provide correlation between the Republicans' lesser economic results and their economic policies. Therefore, Republican economic policies are linked *in some unexplained manner* with the poorer results and consequently must undermine Republican claims of superior economic policies. Calling the Republican claims of superior economic policies as "overblown, at best," Mr. Pitts ends his column with a challenge. "If that's not the case, I would appreciate it if some Republican would explain why."

If Mr. Pitts had done his homework, he would have found the explanation given by another nationally syndicated columnist less than ten days earlier. Robert Samuelson has written about business and economic issues since 1977. He is the author of three books on the American economy, a columnist for the *Washington Post*, and formerly was a columnist for *Newsweek* magazine for twenty-five years. Like Pitts, Samuelson also wrote a column about the Princeton study which he titled "Do Dems run the economy better? Nope."[12]

Samuelson's interpretation of the results of the Princeton study was very different than that of Pitts. Samuelson stated that "Democrats would no doubt like to attribute the large...growth gap to macroeconomic policy choices, but the data do not support such a claim." Samuelson called about half of the gap that favored Democrats attributable to their "good luck" with regard to outside events or trends beyond their control. Three of those events and trends that dominated (and whose timing favored Democrats) were the global oil shocks that hurt Republicans more than Democrats, productivity gains, and military buildups that boosted economic growth.[13]

To the Princeton researchers the cause of the remaining half of the gap favoring the Democrats is a mystery. But for Samuelson the reasons were obvious and contrary to what the study's statistics seem to suggest. He explained that, "Democrats focus more on jobs; Republicans more on inflation. What resulted was a cycle in which Democratic presidents tended to preside over expansions (usually worsening inflation) and Republicans suffered recessions (usually dampening inflation)." Without thoughtful interpretation, the surface implications of the Princeton study suggest that the "...economy's performance during a president's tenure in office is a good test of the soundness of policies." Samuelson disagreed and explained that there is a long lag between the adoption of policies under a current administration and their true effects over time (usually after the administration has left office). He points out that expansive policies that feed an economic boom spawn hurtful consequences (e.g., inflation and overconfidence resulting in financial crises) that must be addressed with more painful policies, usually during the next administration. However, those painful policies can (and generally do) result in long-term dividends.[14]

Samuelson's diagnosis of America's economic roller coaster is somewhat akin to the analogy of visits of grandchildren to permissive, over-indulgent grandparents. It's party time for the grandkids: high sugar diets, new toys, fun and games, and few rules. A good time was had by all. However, when mom and dad pick up the kids, they have to deal with the belly aches, renew and enforce rules and restraints, and re-establish the connections between work-reward and rebellion-consequences. In other words, the kids must return to the real world under mom and dad's rule. For close to six decades Americans have ridden the economic roller coaster, alternately driven by Democratic children and their Republican parents. Hopefully, the American electorate will eventually understand the cause of much of America's economic ups and downs. If so, there is hope for Republican economic prescriptions.

In the information age, facts have grown exponentially. We have become a fact driven society. Richard M. Weaver wrote, "One notes that in everyday speech the word *fact* has taken the place of *truth*...And the public is being taught systematically to make this fatal confusion of factual particulars with wisdom...The acquisition of unrelated details becomes an end in itself and takes the place of the true ideal of education."[15] The myopic acquisition of unrelated details by a society results in fragmentation through loss of wisdom. Such societies retreat from the glorious heights from which one can clearly see truth and descend into a forest of facts—minutiae that hide truth and ultimately destroy in men's minds that even the concept of truth exists.

Part III – Conflict of Worldviews

Liberalism explained (5-2-14)

To understand the origins of the pervasive humanism and secularization that blankets modern America, particularly as it affects government, we must examine the rise of liberalism. Liberalism is the political legacy of the Enlightenment, a skeptical and revolutionary cultural tradition that emanated from eighteenth century Western Europe and "...promoted the belief that critical and autonomous human reason held the power to discover the truth about life and the world, and to progressively liberate humanity from the ignorance and injustices of the past."[1]

This new understanding of what freedom meant and how it was to be achieved was more practical than idealistic and resulted in a major paradigm shift. The new freedom proposed that man should be happy on *this earth*, a new concept invented in the eighteenth century. However, the emphasis on this new freedom unhooked from tradition became an attack on the Church and then religion itself.[2] A fundamental difference between liberalism spawned by the Enlightenment and the Judeo-Christian ethic revolves around a disagreement on the end purpose of man. The Enlightenment's humanism says, "The end of all being is the happiness of man." But Christianity says, "The end of all being is the glory of God."[3]

Before we proceed, we must distinguish between what Robert George calls "old-fashioned liberalism" of the American Founding and the Constitution as opposed to "contemporary liberalism." Liberalism of the Founding era was one "...of religious freedom, political equality, constitutional democracy, the rule of law, limited government, private property, the market economy, and human rights."[4] Contemporary liberalism and liberals are of a wholly opposite variety which

> ...defend large-scale government-run health, education, and welfare programs. They support redistributive taxation policies. They favor affirmative action programs for women and minorities and call for the revision of civil rights laws to prohibit discrimination based on "sexual orientation." They

may support the legal redefinition of marriage to include same-sex relationships. They certainly support legalized abortion and the government funding of abortions for indigent women. They oppose the death penalty.[5]

Professor George's "old-fashioned liberalism" is one and the same as F. A. Hayek's "true liberalism" in the original nineteenth century sense and the opposite of the contemporary liberalism in which "...liberal has come to mean the advocacy of almost every kind of government control." As a result, many old-fashioned liberals began describing themselves as conservatives.[6] Conservatism will be examined in the next article. For our purposes, when we speak of liberalism we refer to a contemporary understanding of liberalism which emphasizes extensive state control in all aspects of society.

As the powerful forces of Enlightenment liberalism rolled across the Atlantic from Western Europe during the nineteenth century, the Protestant establishment and the nation experienced significant inroads of secularization between 1870 and 1930. Out of that struggle a tenuous compromise occurred between evangelical Protestant Christianity and Enlightenment liberalism. The American Christian church, already divided by denomination, region, race, ethnicity, and class, would split again into fundamentalists and modernists between the late nineteenth century and the mid-1920s. Amid the rising skepticism, positivism, and Darwinism emanating from Enlightenment liberalism, the new liberal and modernists Protestant leaders chose survival through accommodation with the adversary and their doctrines of Science, Progress, Reason, and Liberation. But this compromise would only forestall the approaching "...final dominance of Enlightenment moral order in the public square and the relegation of Christian and other religious concerns to private life" that has gained increasing momentum since the 1930s.[7]

By the 1930s, liberalism's eventual domination of the moral order was assured. As the nation wallowed in the depths of the Great Depression, liberalism used the economic crisis to advance its political agenda. Beginning in 1936, the Supreme Court's liberal interpretations of the "general welfare" clause of the Constitution have dramatically enlarged the powers of the federal government, diminished the rights of states, and encroached on fundamental property rights through its welfare programs.[8] This liberal interpretation significantly expanded what the legislature could do with regard to providing for the "general welfare" of the United States. The results of the liberal interpretation of the "general welfare" clause is an unprecedented assault on right of private property through imminent domain laws, a diminution of the right of contract and obligations thereunder, an oppressive income tax system, and the onerous limitations on the possession and use of property through regulation.[9]

To give a clearer understanding of liberalism's secular political ideology, we must examine its signature postulates.

> *Progress* - The liberal mantra is progress, ever onward and upward to a better society, perhaps even a utopia. Man is not fallen but basically good and therefore perfectible. Progress also implies movement, change, and challenge to the status quo. Yet, as the liberal marches boldly into the future, he has become a prisoner of time, perhaps more precisely a prisoner of the moment. Truth becomes relative. Search for an enduring order fails as one's worldview constantly changes bringing disquiet to the soul and society. Progress, being oriented to time, fails to apprehend those timeless truths that bring order to the soul.[10]
>
> *Change* - The liberal's chant for change is a matter of principle and reflects a doctrinaire hatred for permanence. But what is the liberal's answer as change upon change only compounds the lack of rootedness? Change requires movement, but movement doesn't always mean progression. The promises of progress ring hollow in light of rising social disorder.[11]
>
> *Individual* – Liberalism exalts the individual with a resulting self-centeredness; hence, selfishness becomes virtue. For the liberal, community is secondary to a pervasive individualism where individual, personal rights are supreme. Duty and obligation to clan and community are consigned to the dustbin of a foolish and irrelevant past. Yet, there appears a fundamental conflict in the statements of humanists with regard to the individual and the larger society, and such conflict cannot be hidden by fuzzy and euphemistic definitions extolling the dignity of the man and the cherishing of the individual. Under the humanist philosophy it is evident that the individual must be subordinate to the good of all humanity, and it is the leaders of the state that determine the definition of what is good. This

subordination of the individual is confirmed by terms such as "greater good of all humanity", "obligation to humanity as a whole", and "contribute to the welfare of the community." Ultimately the designated elite of society rule as they see fit and do so without regard to the individual.[12]

Liberty – Liberalism's new freedom centers on the individual and is superior to the other two requirements of a civil society—Justice and Order. As to the individual, humanists promise a freedom from the mores, norms, tradition, and distant voices of the past by which humanity has achieved a measure of civilization. The freedom espoused by the humanist is a freedom that gives unbridled control to the self and senses and ultimately leads to bondage. However, for all of man's time on this earth this personal license has been the path toward disaster. To believe that such personal freedom will lead to the greater good of mankind is folly for man is a fallen creature, and he cannot lift himself by pulling at his own bootstraps.[13]

Liberalism is the child of humanism, and the inevitable destination of liberalism is socialism. Socialism breeds disharmony and erodes the foundations of a civil society. Socialism leads to an enforced leveling of society with resulting declines in quality of life, standards of living, loss of trust in government and its institutions, and ultimately a loss of freedom.

Conservatism explained (5-9-14)

In "Liberalism explained," we said that liberalism is a philosophy that attempts to explain and direct the affairs of men based on the belief that "...critical and autonomous human reason held the power to discover the truth about life and the world, and to progressively liberate humanity from the ignorance and injustices of the past.[1] Liberals attempt to define the tenets of conservatism as opposites of the concepts and ideologies upon which liberalism rests. But unlike liberalism, conservatism is not an ideology encompassing a sociopolitical program of continuously changing claims, theories, and aims—a thing invented by the mind of man.

Rather, conservatism declares the existence of a transcendent moral order in which man attempts to order his soul and society. Therefore, the concepts and tenets of conservatism are not a product of man's design but recognition of transcendent, unchanging, and everlasting truth.[2]

Without question, the source of that truth was biblical Christianity in Western civilization and especially in the American experience since the arrival of the first colonists. It is in this central concept we see the ultimate distinction between conservatism's reverence for divine truth and that of liberalism's changing truth and its inherent relativism. And it is in man's deference to and defense of this divine truth and order from whence flows the *spirit of conservatism*. And from conservatism's spirit is birthed conservative thought and action. In this light we see conservatism as a defense of truth, not truth as a defense of conservatism.

If we are serious in our belief of conservatism's reverence for transcendent, objective, unchanging truth, we must be careful in describing the "principles" of conservatism when talking of conservative politics because a nation's politics is a product of its dominant religion, historic experience, and ancient customs. In examining political and social order, Russell Kirk lists six concepts or principles that are reflective of the conservative mindset.[3] Rather than "principles," perhaps a better word is "attitude" or even "inclination" that is reflective of conservative thought and action. The reader should note that none of the concepts are created by conservatism but rather *observed*.

Transcendent Moral Order – Meaning, value, purpose, and moral authority flow from a transcendent God who created the laws of nature and laws of human nature. We can know this moral order because universal truths are evident in His creation and through the revelation to the ancient Hebrews and first century Christians. Being created in His image, man bears the divine imprint of the Creator from which he derives his value and purpose.[4]

Social Continuity – Social continuity produced order, justice, and freedom over many centuries of long and painful social experience. However, rightly defined and applied, these concepts are seen as not of human construction but man's expressions of the transcendent moral order over time. Social continuity is not anti-change nor does it mean inflexibility of society. It does mean that interruption or disturbance of social continuity must be gradual, discriminating, and careful.[5]

Prescription – Conservatism relies on the principle of prescription—adherence to things established by immemorial usage including rights and morals. Habits, customs, and conventions of past generations stand tested and true and therefore are prescriptive as opposed to baseless innovations and tinkering of humanistic man regarding his morals, politics, and tastes.[6]

Prudence – By prudence is meant someone that is judicious, farsighted, and careful. It is the chief virtue of a statesman, and any public measure or consideration must be concerned with long-term consequences. Having weighed the consequences, the conservative tends toward caution, restraint, and reflection. Chronic reformers, liberals tend toward the quick fix for temporary advantage or popularity. Ignoring the prescriptive past and nature of man, liberals become casualties of the law of unintended consequences.[7]

Variety – Social institutions and modes of life long established are preferred over the "...narrowing uniformity and deadening egalitarianism" of liberalism. Conservatives recognize that healthy societies require hierarchy which implies orders and classes that reflect differences of skill, ability, possessions, and status. The variety valued by the conservative is not that of the liberal oxymoron of diversity and forced equality.[8]

Imperfectability – Conservatism recognizes the imperfectability of man and therefore the impossibility of creating a perfect social order. Evil, maladjustments, and suffering will be present in every society due to man's fallen nature. However, the conservative sees that these afflictions can be reduced in a rightly ordered, just, and free society if care is given to maintenance of established and time-tested institutional and moral safeguards and the observance of prudent reforms.[9]

Another means to contrast humanism's contemporary liberalism with conservatism is to look at truth and time. For the conservative, truth is absolute and therefore timeless, that is, things of the highest value are not affected by the passage of time.[10] Liberals often decry conservatives for being antiquarian, wanting to live in the past, or wishing to turn back the clock to a time from which mankind really wanted to escape. The liberal mantra is progress. Progress, being oriented to time, fails to apprehend those timeless truths that bring order to the soul and society. Conservatives search for those permanent things, those moorings to which one may cling as the river of time sweeps by toward an unattainable infinity.[11]

Men crave "...systematic and harmonious arrangements..." which we call order. There are two spheres of order necessary for any culture to survive in the long term. One is order of the soul by which we govern ourselves and is of first importance. The second is social order by which we organize how we live in relation to others.[12] In the political and other institutions of public life, liberals and conservatives present different avenues for civil social order and vie for preference. Faced with an increasingly humanistic worldview in a society that is ignorant of the nation's founding principles, some in American conservative circles question the necessity of an order of the soul in achieving a conservative order of society. In their hunger for victory at the ballot box, some conservatives wish to maximize certain conservative positions such as limited government, lower taxes, private property, and a market economy while at the same time minimizing or abandoning altogether the moral aspects of the conservative cause (e.g., opposition to abortion and same-sex marriage). However, without moral order of the soul, self-absorption looses passion and impulse which fragments any nation's unifying central cultural vision and disorders society. In its end, a disordered society inevitably leads to either anarchy or totalitarianism, a truth that is universally validated by an examination of the historical record.

Abandonment of the order of the soul is an abandonment of the conservative spirit—man's deference to and defense of divine truth and order. Those that abandon the conservative spirit in favor of selected conservative positions perhaps more palpable to the prevailing humanistic worldview are merely pseudo conservatives. In the words of C. S. Lewis, we see their end and possibly the end of conservatism in America.

> We continue to clamour for those very qualities we are rendering impossible…In a sort of ghastly simplicity we remove the organ and demand the function. We make men without chests and expect of them virtue and enterprise. We laugh at honour and are shocked to find traitors in our midst. We castrate and bid the geldings be fruitful.[13]

Mainstream Environmentalism – The Dark Side

Part I (7-11-14)

According to his website, Finland's Pentti Linkola is "...an ecological activist of the most serious kind: those who believe humans must set aside individual desires in order to preserve nature."[1] The 82 year old Mr. Linkola's eco-fascism includes extreme population control measures. His objectives and methods become clear when we read his thoughts on protecting the environment.

> What to do, when a ship carrying a hundred passengers suddenly capsizes and there is only one lifeboat? When the lifeboat is full, those who hate life will try to load it with more people and sink the lot. *Those who love and respect life* will take the ship's axe and sever the extra hands that cling to the sides. (emphasis added)

> If the present amount of Earth's population is preserved and is reduced only by the means of birth control, then...birth giving must be licensed. To enhance population quality, genetically or socially unfit homes will be denied offspring, so that several birth licenses can be allowed to families of quality.

> In this time and this part of the world we are heedlessly hanging on democracy and parliamentary system, even though these are the most mindless and desperate experiments of the mankind...In democratic countries the destruction of nature and sum of ecological disasters has accumulated most...Our only hope lies in strong central government and uncompromising control of the individual citizen.[2]

David Brower (1914-2000) is considered as the father of the modern environmental movement and whose message has helped recruit generations of environmental activists. He was the executive director of the Sierra Club from 1952 to 1969 and whose membership increased from 7,000 to 70,000 during his tenure. Later he founded Friends of the Earth and Earth Island Institute. A three-time nominee for the Nobel Peace Prize, his accomplishments are listed as fighting dams in the Grand Canyon and Dinosaur National Park, campaigns to establish ten new national parks and seashores, and significant work in passing the Wilderness Act of 1964 which restricted usage of millions of acres of public lands.[3]

Many may object to linking Brower's environmentalism with Linkola's brand of eco-fascism; however, most American's would be shocked that Brower's beliefs are remarkably similar to Linkola's in the callous disregard for the human element in environmentalists' efforts to advance their ecological agenda.

> While the death of young men in war is unfortunate, it is no more serious than the touching of mountains and wilderness areas by humankind.
>
> Childbearing [should be] a punishable crime against society, unless the parents hold a government license...All potential parents [should be] required to use contraceptive chemicals, the government issuing antidotes to citizens chosen for childbearing.
>
> Loggers losing their jobs because of Spotted Owl legislation is, in my eyes, no different than people being out of work after the furnaces of Dachau shut down.[4]

In Mr. Brower's world, war casualties, freedom to bear children, and loggers are the equivalent of touching mountains and wilderness areas, unlicensed childbirth, and death camp executioners. It is these statements we see the similar worldviews of Brower's mainstream and Linkola's radical environmentalism.

Based on Linkola and Bower's similarity of views as to the value of human beings in relation to nature, it becomes very difficult if impossible to distinguish between mainstream environmentalism depicted by Smokey the Bear and lovable dolphins as opposed to radical environmentalism. The foundation of both rests on a philosophy often called "deep ecology" which is "a movement or a body of concepts that considers humans no more important than other species and that advocates a corresponding radical readjustment of the relationships between humans and nature."[5] In reality, the kid-friendly icons and school programs offered by the environmental movement are mere cover for the real agenda of indoctrination of children into a worldview that leads to the enslavement of humanity to the god of nature and its humanistic enforcers.

One example of environmental activists' deep ecology that elevates nature over man is their efforts to have the federal government declare the greater sage grouse as an endangered species. The obscure chicken-sized bird is known for its mating dance. The government's proposal will have the effect of limiting hunting, energy exploration, and ranching on 165 million acres of the bird's habitat spread over eleven western states. This acreage is in addition to 400,000 acres that the federal government has already declared off-limits for development to protect the bird. Opponents state that the federal limits will cost between 5,000 and 31,000 jobs, but local and state efforts to protect the bird's habitat will avoid most of the job losses. Hinting at a much wider agenda, several environmental groups say the bird is a merely a stand-in as a means of preserving a vanishing Western ecosystem.[6]

The environmental movement's legal and regulatory demagoguery not only costs thousands of jobs but is so uncompromising in its eco-theology that it willingly sacrifices millions of taxpayer dollars to enforce its will even when their actions damage the very environment they profess to protect. One recent example is the Department of Defense and the Environmental Protection Agency agreement to end the Federal Excess Personal Property and Firefighter Property program which provides excess DOD vehicles to rural fire districts. Under the twenty-five year old program, 8,812 vehicles and pieces of equipment valued in excess of $150 million have been remanufactured and transferred to rural fire departments for use in wilderness areas. The U.S. Army stopped providing the vehicles in order to comply with a previously unenforced twenty-five year old agreement with the DOD and EPA originally aimed at the reduction of emissions for vehicles not meeting EPA standards. Rather than giving these to rural fire departments, these vehicles, ten years old or newer with fewer than 20,000 miles, *will be destroyed*. A spokesman for the Oklahoma Forestry services said the decision will expose those communities to increased risk of loss of life and property, and "The greenhouse gas emissions associated with the vehicles are marginal at best compared to emissions of an uncontrolled wildfire."[7]

These are just two recent examples of a vast array of laws, regulations, and restrictions generated over decades by activist environmental movements in which American citizens are being subjugated to the whims and beliefs of radical environmentalists and their humanistic worldview. They have captured much of the nation's political and regulatory machinery and insulated it from the will and wishes of the people.

The beliefs of environmental activists and the agendas of the organizations that support them have their roots in the humanism. In Part II, the foundational beliefs and tactics of the environmental movement will be examined in some detail.

Part II (7-21-14)

The unifying element between mainstream and radical environmentalism is the status or position of human beings in nature's hierarchy. In Part I we noted that this unifying belief is sometimes called "deep ecology" by which is meant "a movement or a body of concepts that considers humans no more important than other species and that advocates a corresponding radical readjustment of the relationships between humans and nature."[8] This false concept of the value of human beings has its roots in humanism, one of two worldviews contending for dominance in Western civilization and particularly America, the other worldview being Christianity.

Modern environmentalism and its humanistic worldview

This humanistic worldview offers two pillars upon which environmentalists rest their efforts. First, life is the product of a long evolutionary process of nature. Corliss Lamont was one of the twentieth century's leading humanists and author of *The Philosophy of Humanism*. Lamont brings together all of the variations and branches of humanist thought under the title of naturalism.

> Naturalism considers that human beings, the earth, and the unending universe of space and time are all parts of one great Nature. The whole of existence is equivalent to Nature and outside of Nature nothing exists. This metaphysics has no place for the supernatural, no room for superphysical beings or a supermaterial God, whether Christian or non-Christian in character, from whom we can obtain favors through prayer or guidance through revelation. But the adherents of Naturalism recognize and indeed rejoice in our affinity with the mighty Nature that brought us forth…[9]

It is from naturalism that springs forth the environmental movement's current adulation of "…mighty Nature that brought us forth…" and in which we "…are all parts of one great nature." But such beliefs require that we jettison belief in the supernatural and the specialness of man's creation. In other words, humans are no more important than other species which requires a new view of the relationship between humans and nature which is articulated in the numerous environmental laws, regulations, and restrictions to enforce the ordinariness of humans.

The second pillar of environmentalism is that man has the ability to solve his problems through science and reason and without help from God. Modern concepts of humanism emerged from eighteenth century Enlightenment which "...promoted the belief that critical and autonomous human reason held the power to discover the truth about life and the world, and to progressively liberate humanity from the ignorance and injustices of the past."[10] But Charles Colson has identified the singular riff in the humanist reverence for both progressivism and naturalism and has labeled them the optimistic and pessimistic sides of the same coin. With the rise of science and technology during the Industrial Revolution of the nineteenth century, humanist philosophy optimistically exalted the ability of humans to solve their problems without God. Human reason allowed man to control his own destiny.[11] However, any student of world history over the last two hundred years will agree that man's ability to solve his problems without God has failed miserably.

So what is the humanist to do? As humanist optimism fades to pessimism that man can fix his own problems through evolutionary progressivism, the humanist overlords intercede to save man and nature from man himself. Environmentalism is once again man's attempt to control all the variables without God or even knowing what the variables are or the impact of the unintended consequences resulting from their efforts. Man's solutions for the environment almost invariably come at great cost of time, money, and freedom to humankind and often at great cost to the ecosystem they propose to protect. "In today's clash between two forms of humanism, Christianity can offer a balanced alternative."[12]

Tactics of environmentalism's activists

The early history of the Sierra Club illustrates the tension between the worldviews of biblical Christianity and humanism with regard to nature and the environment. In 1864, Abraham Lincoln had originally set aside a portion of the Sierra Nevada mountain range in northern California in a public trust under the jurisdiction of that state. Efforts by naturalist John Muir to restrain local interests and curb development of areas in and around the Yosemite Valley led to a shift of control of the area to the federal government and the establishment of Yosemite National Park. Muir's successful efforts to bring the area under federal jurisdiction led directly to the founding of the Sierra Club in May 1892 with the expressed purpose to protect the new park. From the very beginning of the club there was a tension between utilitarian conservation as directed by Gilford Pinchot, the first director of the U.S. Forest Service, and the aesthetic preservation of Muir and the Sierra Club. This tension between the two dissimilar environmental philosophies and tactics would continue for decades.[13]

As Muir and the Sierra Club began promoting its philosophies and exerting its influence, the club's leaders learned two important lessons for successful environmental activism: first, the need to build a broad base of membership through the establishment of chapters far from local and even state boundaries, and second, "the need to elevate local or regional preservation issues to the national agenda to overcome the entrenched political power of local interests."[14] Over one hundred years later, we see the success of these tactics as the environmental movement has indoctrinated the federal government, academia, and science with its humanistic approach to the environment and has influenced the enactment of environmental policies and practices that fit its humanistic worldview.

Be it Smokey the Bear and fire prevention, recycling campaigns, or cleaning up trash at a local park, few elementary school rooms in America are devoid of worthwhile and reasonable instruction with regard to conserving and protecting the environment. These efforts are in agreement with the Christian worldview that we are stewards and conservators of the earth and its environment. However, these early efforts at stewardship and conservation are used by environmental activists to condition children to accept the larger and more radical message and agenda of environmental activists and their humanistic worldview. This normalization or reasonableness of what was once thought radical is a standard practice in the humanistic attack on the larger culture (e.g., acceptance of homosexuality, abortion, gay marriage, and co-habitation). This was a favorite tactic used by David Brower, the reputed father of the modern environmental movement. Brower described the increasingly radical direction of his environmental activism throughout his life.

> The Sierra Club made the Nature Conservancy look *reasonable*. I founded Friends of the Earth to make the Sierra Club look *reasonable*. Then I founded Earth Island Institute to make Friends of the Earth look *reasonable*. Earth First! now makes us look

reasonable. We're still waiting for someone else to come along and make Earth First! look *reasonable*.[15]

However, when one removes the façades of many of these seemingly *reasonable* environmental organizations, the deep ecology dark side is revealed. And however successful the environmental movement is in promoting the supposed reasonableness of its philosophy, its deep ecology dark side remains immersed in a false and destructive worldview, and its efforts will continue to fail as it has over the last one hundred years.

Charles Colson succinctly captures the dilemma of humanists and their environmental activist cohorts as well as the solution.

> The lesson is clear: Humanism in any form is not only arrogant but mistaken. We are not God and we cannot control the variables—or even foresee them. The solution to our environmental problems must be found elsewhere: in the biblical teaching that God made human beings to be stewards over creation. That means that God intended us to develop the potential in creation through industry and technology. But it also means creation is not ours to misuse for our own purposes. We are responsible to someone higher than ourselves for how we treat creation.[16]

From Colson's observations we see the fundamental difference between the biblical prescription of stewardship and conservation and the hammer of humanistic environmentalism that devalues and controls man through worship of the creation instead of the creator.

Progressivism's Fatal Flaw (8-16-13)

Liberalism as we know it came of age in the nineteenth century and was a product of the Enlightenment,[1] that skeptical and revolutionary humanistic cultural tradition that emanated from eighteenth century Western Europe which "...promoted the belief that critical and autonomous human reason held the power to discover the truth about life and the world, and to *progressively liberate* humanity from the ignorance and injustices of the past."[2]

For the humanist-liberal-progressive, man is continuously perfectible, a process whereby he will become *progressively* better and better. Progress is possible because man is not fallen and does not need redemption. Therefore, humanists assert there is no limit to the perfecting of the powers of man other than the duration of the globe upon which nature has spawned us.[3]

Progressives believe that through human reason alone, truth about life and the world can be discovered and pave the way to liberate humanity from ignorance and injustice. How is this to be achieved? Perfect justice, prosperity, and equality are possible if enlightened elites are given the power to organize and run society according to scientific knowledge about human nature and behavior.

Therefore, in the humanist worldview, the liberation of humanity from ignorance and injustice rests on three assumptions:

- Power must be surrendered to the elites to organize and run society. This is achieved through socialism and big government based on man's laws.
- Reliance on reason and scientific knowledge alone. There is no room for a supernatural God or His laws.
- Man's nature is basically good and therefore perfectible.

But the liberal chant of progressivism is a flight from reality. If reality is objective truth (and it is), then progressivism is a lie. The humanistic worldview's pillars of human reason, scientific advancement, flawed understanding of human nature, and organization of society contrary to man's innate thirst for freedom crumble under the weight of objective truth.

Denial of the progressive's assumptions does not mean that those with a Christian worldview are *un*progressive or deny the value of progress. They only assert that the source of that improvement must come from God and not man. And this improvement must first occur within the individual as he orders his soul by returning to a right relationship with God. For those that look to those universal truths revealed by the Creator in his creation and the biblical revelations to order their souls, they neither progress nor regress but move to the center. It is a matter of being, not becoming. As like-minded citizens order their souls accordingly, order comes to society.[4]

Those holding the biblical worldview focus on the eternal beyond time—not regressing nor progressing in an ever frustrating march to some unknown, unknowable, and unattainable destination. The progressive labors on the treadmill of time, always moving but never arriving at his destination for the goals of infinite progress always recede into the future and therefore are never attainable. In fact, the goals of such progress are not even identifiable apart from the pliable platitudes of the current conditioners of society. For the progressive, time and matter are paramount, but such are rudderless, temporal, and pass away. However, the things of the highest value rest with eternal truths, and without eternal truths man becomes purposeless.

The progressive may even equivocate that although the goal of perfectibility of the human condition will never be attained (something not admitted), the process of self-improvement is still worthwhile and thereby mankind will become better and better. However, an understanding of human nature and history defeats this assertion. Civilization is an intermittent process with some cultures descending from a high state of organization to dissolution. History is replete with societies that achieved great stature in past eras only to fall to ruin—Egypt, Greece, Venice, and Germany to name a few.[5]

In modern times the humanistic worldview in organizing society continues to fail—the greatest example being the socialistic variant of communism in the twentieth century. There is an intimate relationship between the communist ideology espoused by Karl Mark and humanism with regard to the nature of man, the non-existence of the Creator, and the need for a socialistic form of organizing society run by the elites. Both had their roots in the eighteenth century Enlightenment philosophy. Marx's ideas presented in *The Communist Manifesto* ultimately were responsible for the enslavement of a third of humanity for three-fourths of the twentieth century, the consequences of which were failure, misery, and death unparalleled in the history of mankind. So we see that regardless of the era examined, the humanistic philosophy fails to sustain its promise of infinite progress and perfectibility of man.

To summarize, the humanistic formula for the perfectibility of man is this: the innate goodness of man + progress over time = perfectibility of man. But the fatal flaw of progressivism in achieving perfectibility of man is that he has a *fallen nature*, and no amount of psychologizing or social engineering will change that truth.

Liberal Hypocrisy – The Hollywood Ten and the Friends of Abe (1-31-14)

One would have thought that when the IRS (and the Obama administration) got their tail feathers burned in the scandal over targeting conservative groups (through harassment and denial of tax exempt status) the IRS would use a little more caution or at least subtlety in promoting the liberal agenda. Rather, they have taken their cue from President Obama who ignores the constitutional separation of powers in favor of illegal executive orders, bureaucratic bullying, and legitimization of incompetence. And now the IRS need not worry about little things like criminal charges. According to the *Wall Street Journal* as reported by the *Chicago Tribune*, the FBI investigation of the IRS "…did not uncover the type of political bias or 'enemy hunting' that would constitute a criminal violation. The evidence showed a mismanaged agency enforcing rules it did not understand on applications for tax exemptions…"[1] So behind this shield the administration and the IRS have doubled-down on their attack on conservatives.

But subtlety is not the liberals' strong suit in their rush to change society into the image of a humanistic worldview. Given recent cover granted by FBI investigators, the IRS continues its storm-trooper tactics when dealing with conservative organizations. Another example surfaced in recent weeks. Friends of Abe is a relatively small conservative-leaning organization of 1,500 people in the entertainment industry who hold conservative values within the enormous and blatantly liberal industry. To be conservative in Hollywood is to risk marginalization, loss of work, and eventual banishment. Therefore Friends of Abe tends to be a secretive organization except for a few who have chosen to come out of the conservative closet. Quoting the *New York Times*, Friends of Abe "…keeps a low profile and fiercely protects its membership list, to avoid what it presumes would result in a sort of 21st-century blacklist, albeit on the other side of the partisan spectrum."[2]

For two years Friends of Abe has sought tax-exempt status under IRS 503(c)(3) regulations. Last week the IRS requested detailed information about meetings with conservative-leaning politicians such as Paul D. Ryan, Thaddeus McCotter and Herman Cain, as well as other matters. Previous demands by the IRS included access to the organization's security-protected website that included all members' names, but the organization refused the IRS's request. Tax experts said that giving the IRS enhanced access to the secured portions of its website would have meant access to the group's members list. The experts stated that the IRS already had access to the site's basic level which is usually all that is required. To demand access to Friends of Abe's security-protected site and by default the names of its members was unusual.[3]

Jeremy Boreing, executive director of Friends of Abe, said, "Friends of Abe has absolutely no political agenda. It exists to create fellowship among like-minded individuals." But for every conservative organization like Friends of Abe, there are a multitude of liberal organizations in the entertainment industry such as People for the American Way that spend millions of dollars a year directly or through affiliates on issue advocacy in Washington and elsewhere.[4]

Few Americans know the history of the late 1940s and early 1950s with regard to the extent of communist infiltration of American government and the rise of anticommunism. The political and cultural fallout of these events came to define the liberal-conservative riff in American life and foreshadowed the culture wars that began in the 1960s. One of the side-stories of that era was the investigation by the House Un-American Activities Committee (HUAC) of the influence of the Communist Party within the movie industry.

During the 1930s, the political preferences of people in the movie industry covered the entire spectrum, but there was a strong tendency to lean to the liberal and left. Within this liberal-left community was a strong and active Communist presence that contained several dozen screenwriters who were Communist Party members. Large amounts of money were raised by Hollywood Communists for Party approved political and social causes. Communist influence spread into various unions associated within the entertainment industry and Popular Front causes approved by the Communist Party. Numerous actors, screenwriters, and others in the movie industry were subpoenaed and called to testify before HUAC. Some were friendly and testified as to their observations and knowledge of Communist efforts in the industry. Others, upon advice of the Communist Party, were unfriendly and took a defiant stance toward HUAC. The hostile witnesses charged HUAC with preparing America for fascism and Nazi-styled concentration camps and claimed they had a First Amendment free-speech right to refuse to answer HUAC's questions. However, federal courts later upheld the right of Congress to subpoena witnesses and compel testimony.[5]

Following the hearings, Congress cited ten of the witnesses with contempt of Congress because of their refusal to answer questions (nine were members of the Communist Party USA and one a close ally). The ten could have avoided prosecution by invoking the Fifth Amendment and thereby refuse to give testimony that might be used against them in a criminal case.[6] The cited screenwriters became known as the Hollywood Ten and a *cause célèbre* for liberals to the present day.

As a result of the revelations about Communist infiltration and spying within the government and the emerging Communist threat worldwide, Americans were concerned. Mindful of public opinion and its effects on the box office, the major movie studios pledged to not employ Communists. Both Communist and non-Communist witnesses before HUAC who invoked the Fifth Amendment (estimated at 200 to 300) were swept up in the national backlash against Communism. Most of those witnesses who invoked the Fifth Amendment were or had been members of the Communist Party. However, others invoking the Fifth Amendment for whatever reasons became unwitting victims of the movie studios' blacklist that lasted until the late 1950s.[7]

Today, a great majority of the entertainment industry is fervently liberal but denies there is an informal but effective unwritten blacklist of conservatives in their industry just as the hierarchy of American universities will deny there is an omnipresent liberal bias that effectively operates as a blacklist of conservatives in academia.

However, we must not assume *moral equivalence* between the blacklist of Communists and fellow travelers in the entertainment industry of the 1940s and 1950s and the implicit blacklist of known entertainment industry conservatives of today. Nine of the Hollywood Ten were members of the Communist Party USA which was under the direct and dominating influence of the Comintern (Communist Party International) that trained and guided a network of Communist agents, party members, and spies bent on the overthrow of the American system of government. These were not heroes but traitors. Communism operating in America during the first half of the twentieth century was of the same political and social philosophy that was ultimately responsible for the enslavement of a third of humanity for three-fourths of the twentieth century, the consequences of which were the deaths of millions and misery unparalleled in the history of mankind. And of what are the Friends of Abe and other conservatives guilty? Their sin is to support traditional American values—those values prized by the Founders and woven into the Constitution. Liberals' targeting of conservatives for their beliefs exposes their pervasive hypocrisy.

Liberalism dominates American culture and the leadership and institutions of American life. But, the *end result* of liberalism stands in stark contrast to the beliefs of a majority of Americans and the principles upon which the nation was founded. And it is in the end result of liberalism that we find the humanistic worldview and its undeniable linkage to totalitarianism.

End of the Citizen-Soldier? (5-17-13)

Topical moments in media and culture are often of great debate and concern but are largely forgotten within a short time. Such moments command headlines and sound bites repeatedly play during the 24-hour news cycle. Yet, it is by the accumulation of such topical moments we give a face and direction to the culture in which we live. However, there are singular occurrences, often unrecognized or thought of as only of momentary concern, which starkly define the reasons for "why we fight" in the raging culture wars. One such singular occurrence happened within the last couple of weeks.

As he was traveling to Boston to take command of the Continental Army in June 1775, George Washington stopped to address New York's Provincial Congress. In that address he famously called attention to the inseparability of the citizen and soldier. "When we assumed the soldier, we did not lay aside the citizen."[8] In other words, when one becomes a soldier he does not lay aside his the responsibilities of citizenship nor the rights attendant thereto. But if the Pentagon has its way, we may see an end to our nation's historical admiration and respect for the citizen-soldier as the wedge of state is driven between the two. The Pentagon has proposed a policy to prosecute military personnel for promoting their faith. Specifically, the Pentagon stated that, "Religious proselytization is not permitted within the Department of Defense...Court martials and non-judicial punishments are decided on a case-by-case basis..."[9] For all military personnel the end result would be to virtually eliminate all expressions of faith, even on a one-to-one basis between close friends or merely social acquaintances. And for all practical purposes the military chaplaincy would cease to function.

It appears that the source of the anti-proselytizing agenda is former ambassador Joe Wilson, Larry Wilkerson, former chief of staff to Colin Powell, and Michael Weinstein, the head of the private Military Religious Freedom Foundation. The three men recently met with several generals to discuss religious issues. Wilkerson equates religious proselytizing to sexual assault, both of "which are absolutely destructive of the *bonds that keep soldiers together.*"[10] So what did the generals also hear from Mr. Weinstein? Perhaps it was something like what he wrote for the Huff Post:

I founded the civil rights fighting organization the Military Religious Freedom Foundation (MRFF) to do one thing: fight those *monsters* who would tear down the *Constitutionally-mandated wall separating church and state* in the technologically most lethal entity ever created by humankind, the U.S. military. Today, we face incredibly well-funded gangs of fundamentalist Christian *monsters* who terrorize their fellow Americans by *forcing* their weaponized and twisted version of Christianity upon their helpless subordinates in our nation's armed forces...If these fundamentalist Christian *monsters* of human degradation, marginalization, humiliation and tyranny cannot broker or barter your acceptance of their putrid theology, then they crave for your universal silence in the face of their rapacious reign of theocratic terror. Indeed, they ceaselessly lust, ache, and pine for you to do absolutely nothing to thwart their oppression.[11]

Well! Mr. Weinstein's rant does tend to leave one breathless. But, let's let one of our nation's former citizen-soldiers who also knew a little about the Constitution speak for the opposition. On July 4, 1775, General George Washington issued the following order from his Cambridge, Massachusetts headquarters:

> The General most earnestly requires and expects a due observance of those articles of war established for government of the Army which forbid profane cursing, swearing and drunkenness. And in like manner he requires and expects of all officers and soldiers not engaged in actual duty, a *punctual attendance of Divine services*, to implore the blessing of Heaven upon the means used for our safety and defense.[12]

A year later and five days after the Declaration of Independence was signed, the Continental Congress authorized the provision of chaplains for every regiment in the newly constituted army headed by General Washington. On that same day Washington issued his first general order to his troops:

> The General hopes and trusts that every officer and man will endeavor so *to live, and act, as becomes a*

> *Christian Soldier* defending the dearest Rights and Liberties of his country.[13]

In another general order issued at Valley Forge on May 2, 1778, General Washington implored his troops:

> While we are zealously performing the duties of good citizens and soldiers, we certainly ought not to be inattentive to the higher duties of religion. To the distinguished character of Patriot, it should be *our highest Glory to laud the more distinguished Character of Christian.*[14]

Unlike Wilkerson and Weinstein, Washington knew the real source of that which forged those *bonds that keep soldiers together*. That source was religion and in particular the Christian religion. However, if the Pentagon's civilians and military brass have their way *and* General Washington was alive today, he would be court-marshaled for (paraphrasing Weinstein) *forcing* his weaponized and twisted version of Christianity upon his helpless subordinates in the Continental Army in sharing his religious views.

Some will argue that we no longer have a military of citizen-soldiers but a professional army with no need of religious influences. Not so. Many are reservists and members of the National Guard. And those full-time members of the military didn't leave their faith behind at the induction centers. More importantly, whether a professional army or citizen-soldiers, our nation's Armed Forces without the Constitutionally-guaranteed freedom of religion will deteriorate into a palace guard loyal only to their masters and not to the Constitution or the people.

The Pentagon's anti-proselyting regulation is the culmination of dozens of anti-Christian regulations and initiates in the military that have arisen during the Obama administration. But it is this Pentagon regulation that is a singular occurrence which lays the ax to the root of our religious freedom of sharing one's faith. This marginalization of religious freedom reaches far beyond the Armed Forces. The agenda of the Obama administration to fundamentally change America encompasses every segment of the public square and is the culmination of decades of humanistic infiltration of American culture.

Those of the humanistic worldview have risen to leadership levels in all institutions of American life, and their humanistic policies, laws, and initiatives are being imposed on a nation whose citizens that still cling to the biblical worldview of the Founders. This is the cause of culture wars—the conflict for supremacy in the American cultural vision between those holding the humanistic and Christian worldviews. Christians who ignore or disengage from the battle place religious freedom and our nation at peril.

Part IV – Language

Liberal language and the trashing of truth (6-28-13)

Richard Weaver believed that "...a divine element is present in language. The feeling that to have power of language is to have control over things is deeply imbedded in the human mind." Throughout the ages language has been the means of achieving order in culture. Knowledge of truth comes through the word which provides solidity in the "shifting world of appearances."[1]

However, for humanist-liberal-progressivists, the shifting world of appearances is more important and useful than objective truth which they deem to be a fiction. Humanist writer-philosopher Paul Kurtz summarized this sentiment when he wrote that no man or group can claim to be infallible with regard to truth and virtue and that "...truth is often the product of the free give and take of conflicting opinions."[2] Therefore, truth is mere perception, shackled to time, and cannot be objective or eternal. But how is the humanist-liberal-progressive to highjack the power of language and cause truth to be relegated to a mere consensus of opinion?

The Obama administration has provided an excellent example in recent weeks. There has been much ado in the news about the administration's "talking points" regarding the 9-11-2012 attack on the U.S. Embassy in Benghazi, Libya. The attack which killed the ambassador and three other Americans threatened to be a major embarrassment to the administration only six weeks before the 2012 presidential election. Having portrayed Al-Qaeda beaten, it was very inconvenient to be proven wrong by such an incident. Even more tragic was the administration's inexcusable negligence in rescuing the besieged Americans at the embassy. Therefore, through the administration's talking points, blame was redirected toward an obscure anti-Islamic film circulating on the Internet rather than the truth that the orchestrated attack was the result of Al-Qaeda linked terrorists which was known immediately after the attack. Knowing the truth, the administration's talking points were an effort to cover up the real source and reason for the attack. An extensive account can be found on the Weekly Standard's website.[3]

There were several players in the tangled affair of the Benghazi talking points including the White House, Department of State, CIA,

National Security Council, and Office of the Director of National Intelligence. Through three iterations of the talking points, the cause of the Benghazi tragedy moved from "Islamic extremists with ties to Al-Qaeda" to an obscure YouTube video critical of Islam and from "terrorist attack" to "demonstration." For the Obama administration, the reality (truth) of what happened at Benghazi was ignored and replaced by the free give and take of conflicting opinions, that is, a manufactured truth through consensus.[4]

Writing about the larger issue of the decline of the American language, Paul Greenberg succinctly captured the essence of the Benghazi talking points in a recent column.

> They [modern political operatives] know that the way to win an election is to muffle unpleasant truths and soften hard principles. Besides, clarity is hard work. It's so much easier to fuzz the message and so write around any inconvenient facts that may disrupt the smooth flow of currently fashionable patter.[5]

In modern American politics dominated by the humanistic worldview, talking points have supplanted truth. But the Obama administration's Benghazi obfuscation is merely a minor tempest compared to the larger assault on language and ultimately truth.

In the battle of worldviews, certain words have gained power to obscure truth and history through the machinations of humanist redefinition. Modern politicians who obscure both truth and history have borrowed a page from V. I. Lenin, founder of the Communist party and leader of the Russian Revolution.

> We must be ready to employ trickery, deceit, law-breaking, withholding and concealing truth. We can and must write in the language which sows among the masses hate, revulsion, scorn, and the like, toward those who disagree with us.[6]

This is the technique or protocol of the humanist-liberal-progressive: *Deny* the existence of objective, eternal truth; *redefine* key concepts such as truth, freedom, justice, and equality; and *revise* history to promote the belief that America was created as a secular nation and thereby drive Christianity from the public square. Because of what humanist-liberal-progressives have sown, Americans who disagree with them are targets of hate, revulsion, and scorn. Thus, we have identified differing views as to the meaning of truth as the origin of the vast chasm separating the humanist and Christian combatants in the war for supremacy in the central cultural vision of America.

Weaver called words the storehouse of our memory. In our modern age humanists have effectively used semantics to neuter words of their meaning in historical and symbolic contexts, that is, words now mean what men want them to mean. By removing the fixities of language (which undermines an understanding of truth), language loses its ability to define and compel. As the meaning of words is divorced from truth, relativism gains supremacy, and a culture tends to disintegration without an understanding of eternal truths upon which to orient its self.

Who owns the language? (12-6-13)

Sarah Palin spoke to the Iowa Faith and Freedom Coalition on November 9th. Her views on the damaging effects of the burgeoning federal debt were well received by the conservative audience, but it provoked considerable hostility in the liberal media and in particular from MSNBC's Martin Bashir. What especially provoked Mr. Bashir was Palin's statement that the burgeoning federal debt would eventually result in a form of slavery for American citizens.

> Now you know coming up, the other side will offer more of the same, more false promises, more free stuff, and the media, for all too long, will go along with it and all of the deception. What will you counter it with? It's free stuff! It's seductive.
>
> Why is it marketers use free stuff to bring people in? Free Stuff. It's such a strong marketing ploy. The tool of free stuff is seductive.
>
> Didn't you all learn too in Econ 101 that there ain't no such thing as a free lunch? Our free stuff today is being paid for by taking money from our children and borrowing from China. Then that note comes due...and this isn't racist..try it, try it anyway...this isn't racist. But it's going to be like slavery when that note is due. Right? We are going to be beholden to a foreign master because there is no plan, no plan coming out of Washington, D.C. to stop the incurrence of debt is there? All we're hearing about is why we need to grow more debt. I believe that if you're in a hole and you don't want to be in that hole, quit digging.[1]

Apparently Ms. Palin's use of the word "slavery" in her analogy was judged to be incorrect as well as unauthorized by the speech police of the liberal establishment. Such was the magnitude of her offense that Mr. Bashir was compelled to respond a week later on his Friday MSNBC show's "Clear the Air" segment.[2]

Bashir called Palin America's "resident dunce" and that her remarks were "scraping the barrel of her long-deceased mind, and using her all-time favorite analogy in an attempt to sound intelligent about the national debt. Given her well-established reputation as a world class idiot, it's hardly surprising that she should choose to mention slavery in a way that is abominable to anyone who knows anything about its barbaric history."[3]

To correct Ms. Palin, Mr. Bashir attempted to contextualize the horror of slavery by quoting from the diary of Thomas Thistlewood, an 18th century British overseer of a Jamaican sugar plantation. Bashir explained that Thistlewood recorded his brutality in a diary which included stories of forcing slaves to defecate and urinate on each other as a form of punishment.[4]

Bashir ended his monologue by saying, "I could go on, but you get the point. When Mrs. Palin invokes slavery, she doesn't just prove her rank ignorance. She confirms if anyone truly qualified for a dose of discipline from Thomas Thistlewood, she would be the outstanding candidate."

After a firestorm of criticism over his remarks, Bashir apologized to Palin and his audience during his show on the following Monday.[5]

Kathleen Parker of the *Washington Post* thought Bashir's attack on Palin was vicious and unwarranted but agreed with Bashir that the comparison of slavery and debt was inappropriate. Parker wrote, "...slavery merits its own place in America's memory. To compare it to anything else, especially something as mundane as debt, is wrong on its face. Indentured servitude to China might have been a better choice for Palin...In Palin's defense, she obviously meant no offense and the attacks in response have been so vicious that the attacks themselves are beyond comparison."[6]

What Parker is saying is that some words are so unique or one of a kind that they shouldn't be used for comparison with other things. She includes words such as "slavery," "Nazi," and "Holocaust" in this category of untouchables when devising a simile—a comparison of two essentially unlike things with similar characteristics. But Parker's sentiments reveal liberalism's hypocrisy because liberals frequently do the same thing by affixing the label of "racism" to almost anything which opposes their egalitarian liberal agenda as defined by their humanistic worldview.

Well, let's follow Palin's analogy to its logical conclusion. Ultimately the free stuff funded by borrowed money must be paid for by someone—either now or in the future. If repayment is not made, the debt is restructured upon negotiated terms or foreclosure follows. When a nation nears default it attempts to renegotiate the debt with its creditors. This generally results in heavy taxation and significant curtailment of services to the citizens of the debtor nation. If a nation defaults on its debts, the population continues its slide into abject poverty over time resulting in life lived at or near subsistence levels.

So, may we not call excessive, onerous, and perhaps unpayable debt a form of slavery? One definition of slavery is that it is "drudgery, toil...submission to a dominating influence."[7] Ms. Parker would substitute servitude for slavery, but the dictionary lists servitude as slavery, "...the state of subjection to another that constitutes or resembles slavery or serfdom."[8]

Liberalism is the precursor of socialism. But the altruistic and lofty goals of liberalism (including the free stuff) become somewhat tarnished when one examines a society under the growing influence of socialism in which freedom gradually erodes into slavery. The European Union is a great example in which a number of its members are in severe economic straits (e.g., Greece and Spain) and beholden to the creditor nations. The solvent members of the EU now dictate the rules which have placed extremely painful financial burdens and restraints under which the profligate countries must live. In spite of protests and riots in Greece and other EU debtor nations, it certainly appears that, in the end, debtor members of the EU have submitted to the will of the dominating creditor nations, a situation which we have correctly defined as a form of slavery.

Therefore, it appears Sarah Palin accurately described the potential outcome of our growing national debt as analogous to slavery. But the Bashir-Palin war of words is merely a tempest in the cauldron of the culture wars.

Who owns the language?

Richard Weaver believed that "...a divine element is present in language. The feeling that to have power of language is to have control over things is deeply imbedded in the human mind." The symbols of language are words, singly and collectively, through which we assign meaning and truth, and it is inherent in man's nature to seek truth. This is frightening to liberals for in their worldview truth does not exist except as mere perception without fixed reference points. Thus, the liberal must harness, manipulate, and thereafter mold words to end polarity that arises from pursuit of objective truth which allows man to define what is right and wrong.[9] Hence, liberals attempt to *own the language* through imposition of politically correct concepts of *appropriateness* as well as *prohibitions* through "hate speech" laws as defined by the liberals.

In our modern age humanists have effectively used semantics to neuter words of their meaning in *historical and symbolic* contexts, that is, words now mean what men want them to mean. By removing the fixities of language (which undermines an understanding of truth), language loses its ability to define and compel. As the meaning of words is divorced from truth, relativism gains supremacy and a culture tends to disintegration without an understanding of eternal truths upon which to orient its self.[10] In the battle of worldviews, certain words have gained power to obscure truth and history through the intrigues of humanist redefinition. Again, Richard Weaver is a master at describing the humanist protocol with regard to corrupting the language.

> Just as soon as men begin to point out that the word is one entity and the object it represents is another, there sets in a temptation to do one thing with the word and another or different thing with the object it is supposed to represent; and here begins that *relativism* which by now is visibly affecting those institutions which depend for their very existence upon our ability to use language as a permanent binder.[11] [emphasis added]

Liberals (the vast majority of whom hold the humanistic worldview) attack language in its historic and symbolic contexts in an effort to dislodge the generally conservative biblical worldview from America's central cultural vision. Media shock troops are complicit in the efforts to discredit and immobilize the opposition (those holding the biblical worldview) through the devaluation of language. For those holding the biblical worldview, we must be vigilant in our endeavor to *free language from its enslavement by liberals.*

The *New* Ministry of Truth 2014 (3-7-14)

In 1949, George Orwell wrote *1984*, a grim novel about an omnipresent government set in Airstrip One, formerly Great Britain but now merely a province of Oceania, a super-state ruled by a political system called English Socialism. Oceania's leaders are the Inner Party, a privileged elite headed by Big Brother, the pseudo-divine party leader who uses mass media, propaganda, and a cult-like following to create his idealized, heroic, and god-like public image. Oceania is a land of constant war, omnipresent government surveillance, and public mind control. However, the oppressive nature of the regime is justified by Big Brother and the Party in the name of the supposed greater good.[1]

Control of the public's mind is achieved with the assistance of the *Ministry of Truth* which is responsible for propaganda and historical revisionism and controls the news media, entertainment, the arts, and publishing. The *Ministry* falsifies the historical record where necessary to conform it to the government-approved version of events. To assist in its propaganda and revisionist efforts, the government invented *Newspeak*, a language used to limit freedom of thought and other expressions of individualism and independent thinking which are considered thought crimes.[2]

In 2014, it appears that America's current version of Big Brother is attempting to develop his own *Ministry of Truth*. The Federal Communications Commission (FCC) hired Social Solutions International, Inc. in 2012 to develop a study and data gathering procedures which were scheduled for testing this spring in South Carolina.[3] The study is designed to:

> Identify and understand the critical information needs (CINs) of the American public (with special emphasis on vulnerable/disadvantaged populations).
>
> To provide a comprehensive analysis of access/barriers to CINs in diverse American communities.
>
> To determine what barriers to entry exist in FCC regulated market and to what extent these barriers have a negative impact.[4]

To put FCC's *Newspeak* into layman's language, the purpose of the Multi-Market Study is to uncover information from the daily operations of television and radio broadcasters, newspapers, and the Internet that will reveal the process used to select news stories for presentation, frequency of coverage of critical information needs, media bias, and media responsiveness to underserved populations as perceived by FCC.[5]

The FCC has already identified certain information that it considers as critical information needs of all Americans: health and welfare, education, transportation, economic opportunities, environment, civic information, political information, and emergencies.[6] Effectively, the FCC will control news content through imposition of content standards consistent with its own definition of CINs. Deviation from the FCC's CIN standards will be judged as broadcaster/print media bias and therefore subject to FCC regulatory oversight, censure, punishment, and correction.

Although the study has been labeled as voluntary, the Multi-Market Study is merely the door-opener for federal control of the content of broadcast and print news media. Broadcasters must obtain periodic license renewals, and once FCC-defined CIN standards are established, what is to prevent the FCC's power over broadcaster license renewals from being the hammer used to force broadcasters to accept FCC CIN content requirements? This is somewhat akin to a state or a local school district's "voluntary" acceptance of Common Core standards. If Common Core standards that are *acceptable* to the U.S. Department of Education are not chosen, funds will not be forthcoming.[7] Also, the FCC does not have regulatory authority over print media and the Internet *at present*. However, if FCC-defined bias is found by the study to exist in print media, such perceived bias will be justification for the federal government to expand the FCC's regulatory reach into newspapers, magazines, other print media, and the Internet.

For those that haven't been paying attention, this is the liberal formula for controlling American society: create a victim, elevate victim status to being deprived of an imaginary "right" and thus tantamount to discrimination, and finally impose a government solution to fix the discrimination. The perception by the FCC (a perception perhaps encouraged by the FCC's superiors) is that some Americans are being victimized, particularly the vulnerable and disadvantaged, by not getting the critical information they need from a "biased" media. All Americans have a "right" to critical information to which some are being deprived and therefore are discriminated against. The government's solution is to eliminate the perceived discrimination found by the FCC study by (1) requiring existing media to disseminate whatever the government determines to be critical information and (2) providing government licensing, support, special privileges, and sources of financing for new media outlets that will supply the critical information needs of the diverse but marginalized-vulnerable-disadvantaged communities presently unserved or under-served by the existing biased media.

Since the FCC's proposed insertion of monitors into newsrooms caught the attention of many Americans, there has been a firestorm of controversy surrounding the intrusion of big government into the newsrooms of America. Because of the massive negative publicity, the study has been shelved although not rejected at the present time.

Opposition to the FCC study has come from both within and without the media. Opponents have voiced a loud and long defense of First Amendment protections of a free press. But where are the First Amendment champions when religious freedom also guaranteed by the First Amendment is repeatedly trashed by the Obama administration? This administration has made it clear that wherever conflicts occur between religious freedom and its definition of equality, equality will be the victor every time. One need only look at the Affordable Care Act and the advancement of the homosexual agenda as just two of many examples of the trouncing of religious freedom in America.

The FCC's efforts to control the message through dictating CINs mimics the tactics of the *Ministry of Truth* in Orwell's fictional account of a totalitarian socialist state. However, the FCC has also become the real-life moral and de facto equivalent of Communist political commissars of the twentieth century who were assigned to military units to teach party principles and policies and to insure party loyalty. Non-military commissars were also used to attempt to *control public opinion or expression*.[8]

The FCC's latest attempt to inject themselves into the newsroom and thereby control the message is just one example of the over-reach of American government into the minutiae of the lives of all Americans. We see the same government intrusions into doctors' offices and hospitals, school rooms, businesses, local government, property rights and right of contract, religious organizations, and families to name just a few. Government intrusion ranges from serious violation of the Constitution through behavior and speech codes to ridiculous regulations on sugary drink sizes and light bulbs.

Massive government intrusion into the lives of its citizens began in the 1930s under new interpretations of the general welfare clause of the Constitution. Government expansion began in Roosevelt's New Deal Years of the 1930s and accelerated with Lyndon Johnson's

Great Society of the 1960s. However, the exponential growth during the last five years into the minutest detail of the daily lives of American citizens has become suffocating. Alexis De Tocqueville, in his 1835 *Democracy in America*, had a prophet's foresight into America's 2014 slide into a totalitarian Oceania.

> We forget that it is, above all, in the details that we run the risk of enslaving men...Subjection in the minor things of life is obvious every day and is experienced indiscriminately by all citizens. It does not cause them to lose hope but it constantly irks them until they give up the exercise of their will. It gradually blots out their mind and enfeebles their spirit ...

> The democratic nations which introduced freedom into politics at the same time that they were increasing *despotism in the administrative sphere* have been led into the strangest paradoxes. Faced with the need to manage small affairs where common sense can be enough, they reckon citizens are incompetent. When it comes to governing the whole state, they give these citizens immense prerogatives. They turn them by degrees into playthings of the ruler or his masters...[9] [emphasis added]

The most powerful weapon (8-22-14)

The terrorist will argue that the bomb is the most powerful weapon. Who can dispute the destructive power of a nuclear bomb? Others will declare the airplane or drone is the most powerful weapon because those deliver the bombs and without the means of delivery their explosive power would be dormant or ineffective.

Yet, others will say that the question of power overlooks the greater question of purpose. The target for which a weapon is used is the more important consideration than the power of the weapon itself. The assassin may prefer the thrust of a well-aimed stiletto, for the garrotter the seemingly innocuous cord is the weapon of choice, and for the timid or less-strong a few grams of cyanide in the victim's cocoa will suffice. And we must not forget the megalomaniac or neighborhood bully's invisible weapons of fear and intimidation.

A third group will submit that it is not a question of the powerfulness of a weapon or choosing the correct weapon to fit the target. Rather, the important thing is that a weapon is not inherently evil in itself but can be used for both good or ill. The laser used to destroy enemies can destroy the cataract that makes possible the improvement of one's vision. The poison of chemo-therapy kills the cancerous portions of the body in order to sustain the larger organism. The bullet that kills the dictator bent on genocide may save thousands of lives.

Weapons evolve over time. The first weapons were blunt instruments (fists, stones, or clubs) and still favored in some detective stories. The up-close-and-personal blunt instrument was replaced by the more impersonal projectile (the arrow, the bullet, and the bomb). Through man's ingenuity and industriousness, each generation of weapons provides new ways to oppress, maim, and kill. In time all weapons deteriorate and become ineffective. Even the bully's power fades, and he is replaced by a younger, stronger thug. Although weapons corrode or become obsolete and tyrants die, there is one thing that never loses its power and never grows old. It is the *word*.

The supreme importance of two things is shown by their existence in God's realm before He created the universe and all therein including man: the *word* and *love*. How is this possible? It is possible because God *was* the word and God *is* love. We know this from John's gospel. "In the beginning was the Word, and the Word was with God, and the Word was God. He (Jesus) was in the beginning with God..."

[John 1:1. RSV] We are told in 1 John 4:8 that, "...God is love." In the Revelation to John we also see that God's love for His special creation existed before creation itself, "And all mankind—whose names were not written down *before the founding of the world* in the slain Lamb's book of life—worshipped the evil creature." [Revelation 13:8, Living Bible] [emphasis added] God loved man before his creation. God did not need man's love, but rather it was a will to love, an expression of the very character of God, to share the inner life of the Trinity.

Language is unique to mankind. To compare the screeches, grunting, and howls of various species to that of human language is to compare mere recognition of night from day to that of a watch of intricate precision which can measure time to an accuracy of a fraction of a second. Richard Weaver wrote of the power of the word.

> [There is an]...ancient belief that a divine element is present in language. The feeling that to have power of language is to have control over things is deeply imbedded in the human mind. We see it in the way men gifted in speech are feared or admired; we see it in the potency ascribed to incantations, interdictions, and curses. We see it in the legal force given to oath or word.[1]

The author of the New Testament book of James called the tongue a small member of the body but which boasts great power. He compares it to a small fire that can set ablaze a great forest. James also speaks of the difficulty of taming the tongue and the great harm it can cause. "For every kind of beast and bird, of reptile and sea creature, can be tamed and has been tamed by humankind, but no human being can tame the tongue—a restless evil, full of deadly poison." [James 3:5, 7-8. RSV]

In the first chapter of Genesis we see that God *spoke* into existence the universe, the earth, and all therein, and a divine order was stamped on creation. Man was God's special creation and given dominion over the earth and the power of the word to name every creature. But man rebelled against God's order and was separated from a right relation with Him. Disorder now ruled man's life.

As Weaver has said, speech is a divine element for humans were made in the image of God. But man is a fallen creature, and the poet Ralph Waldo Emerson sums up the consequences, "The corruption of man is followed by the corruption of language."[2] In His revelation, God instructed man on how he ought to live life and included the right use of the word. Such was the importance of the word to God, His instruction to man as to the proper use of the word required two of the Ten Commandments, "You shall not take the name of the Lord your God in vain; for the Lord will not hold him guiltless who takes his name in vain…You shall not bear false witness against your neighbor." [Exodus 20: 7, 16. RSV]

For all of man's time on earth language has been the means of achieving order in culture. But in this modern age humanists have effectively used semantics to neuter words of their meaning in historical and symbolic contexts, that is, words now mean what men want them to mean.[3] We live in a world of increasing disorder sustained and propelled by the perversion of language in which the meaning of words and ideas are separated from truth. Weaver recognized the folly of such perversion, "…here begins that relativism which by now is visibly affecting those institutions which depend for their very existence upon our ability to use language as a permanent binder."[4] Words freed from the anchor of truth (reality) disorient and provide no clarity or direction regarding fixed, eternal values necessary for order that mankind craves and requires for living life.

The ordering and sustaining power of truthful words reverberates through history. Whether our words are a weapon of evil or an instrument of good is a matter of choice, and three thousand years ago Solomon identified the importance of that choice when he said there is power of life and death in the tongue. We must choose life, and life is found in biblical truths revealed to the ancient Hebrews and first century Christians.

Part V - Islam

Liberal defense of Islam (1-20-15)

Liberals and the governments and institutions they represent are having ever increasing difficulty in convincing their constituents that the atrocities of Islamic terrorists do not represent the supposedly peace-loving Islamic religion followed by moderate Muslims. The frequency, shrillness, and fervor with which liberals defend Islam grow proportionally with each announcement of a new Muslim terrorist attack regardless of its magnitude and vicious brutality.

Howard Dean is the former head of the Democratic National Committee and one-time candidate for the Democratic nomination for president. Following the murder of two policemen and ten employees of *Charlie Hebdo*, a satirical magazine that routinely criticized Islam's Muhammad as well as many other non-Muslim religious and political leaders, Mr. Dean refused to label the perpetrators as Muslim terrorists in spite of the three gunmen shouting "Allahu Akbar" during the killing spree. Allahu Akbar translates as "Allah is the Greatest" and is the opening declaration of every Islamic prayer as prescribed by the Prophet Muhammad.

> I stopped calling these people Muslim terrorists. They're about as Muslim as I am. I mean, they have no respect for anybody else's life, that's not what the Koran says. Europe has an enormous radical problem. I think ISIS is a cult. Not an Islamic cult. I think it's a cult.[1]

The Paris murderers shouted the same exaltations of Allah as Army Major and fellow Muslim Nadal Hasan did when he shot and killed fourteen and wounded thirty-two at Fort Hood, Texas in 2009. The American government conveniently ignored Hasan's motives and obvious connections with Islamic jihad while euphemistically mislabeling the murders as workplace violence.

Following an attack on the Canadian Parliament by a thirty-two year old Muslim convert who shot and killed a guard during the attack, liberal leader Justin Trudeau quickly reassured his friends and fellow citizens in the Muslim community that, "...Canadians know acts such as these committed in the name of Islam are an *aberration of your faith.* Continued mutual cooperation and respect will help prevent the influence of *distorted ideological propaganda posing as religion.* We will walk forward together, not apart.[2] [emphasis added]

In response to the Paris attack political columnist Michael Gerson wrote that the murders in Paris were, "...the exploitation of religious passions for political ends...It is important to separate this violent political ideology from the faith of Islam."[3] Although many Muslims do not agree with and reject the violence occurring in the name of Islam, the separation of Islam from the violence prescribed by the Qur'an is impossible. These so-called moderate Muslims are Muslim in name only and have no standing in defense of the Muslim faith. They may be Muslims by birth, conversion, products of a predominately Muslim culture, and give lip-service to the Qur'an, but they are not representative of Muslims faithful to the teachings of the Qur'an. In fact, the Qur'an labels them infidels for not fully embracing the teachings of Muhammad and the Qur'an.

> They but wish that ye should reject Faith, as they do, and thus be on the same footing (as they): but take not friends from their ranks until they flee in the way of Allah (from what is forbidden). But if they turn renegades, seize them and slay them wherever ye find them; and (in any case) take no friends or helpers from their ranks. [Surah 4:89. Qur'an][4]

The same analogy applies to Christians. True Christians accept Christ as their Savior and follow His teachings. Those that claim to be Christian by birth, upbringing, or culture or do not follow Christ's teachings are Christian in name only and live without the Christian creed. But unlike the followers of Islam, Christians cannot compel conversion nor punish those who do not convert.

With the explosion of Muslim-inspired violence in the West as well as in Muslim-dominated countries, liberals refuse to acknowledge the *elephant in the room*—the obvious truth as to the nature of Islam. That truth which is being ignored and not addressed is that violent proponents of the Islamic religion are acting in accordance with the words and directives of the Qur'an to spread Islam through aggressive individual, military, and political threats, intimidation, and actions in order to achieve world domination.

One wonders why the humanists and their political operatives are so adamant in the defense of Islam, a most authoritarian religion, given the fact that humanism denies the existence of a supreme being and denigrates "...traditional dogmatic or authoritarian religions that place revelation, God, ritual, or creed above human needs and experience..."[5] Two reasons are apparent for humanists' defense of Islam. The first is that Christianity has so dominated the history and worldview of Western civilization that Western liberals demand not only equal time for opposing views but give preference to various anti-Christian religions and none more so than Islam. The second reason for humanism's defense of Islam is adherence to two of its core beliefs—humanistically defined multiculturalism and tolerance.

Multiculturalism is one of the cardinal doctrines of humanism and has its roots in the denial of absolutes which translates into moral relativism. According to humanist dogma, such a values-free approach makes it impossible to judge one period or era in relation to another or to say that one culture's ethic is superior to another. The end result of this philosophy is that all belief systems are equally valid. But if all belief systems are *not* equally valid (as demonstrated by the followers of Islam and the Qur'an), then the tenets of humanism including its humanistically defined concepts of equality, diversity, and multiculturalism are *false and unsustainable*. The liberal defense of Islam occurs not because they care for and respect the tenets of Islam. Rather, to reject Islam based on its history as a scourge to mankind is to admit that their humanistic conceptions of multiculturalism and tolerance are fundamentally flawed with regard to a mankind's understanding of his nature and transcendent values.

There is a third reason for humanists' defense of Islam. The words of the Apostle Paul give insight into the mindset of seemingly intelligent people who are so obviously in denial of the Islamic threat to Western civilization.

> And even as they did not like to retain God in their knowledge, God gave them over to a *reprobate* mind, to do those things which are not convenient. [Romans 1:28. KJV] [emphasis added]
>
> Now as Jannes and Jambres withstood Moses, so do these also resist the truth: men of corrupt minds, *reprobate* concerning the faith. [2 Timothy 3:8. KJV] [emphasis added]
>
> They profess that they know God; but in works they deny him, being abominable, and disobedient, and unto

every good work *reprobate*. [Titus 1:16. KJV] [emphasis added]

In whom the god of this world hath blinded the minds of them which believe not, lest the light of the glorious gospel of Christ, who is the image of God, should shine unto them. [2 Corinthians 4:4. KJV]

Reprobate is a very old-fashioned, King-James-style word little understood by moderns but well describes the humanist abandonment of rational thought regarding Islam. Although Christ loves the sinner, the Apostle Paul does not mince words as to the spiritual *condition* of a reprobate by which he means unworthy, corrupt, rejected, and condemned.

Are Christianity and Islam morally equivalent?

Part I (4-17-15)

During his presidency, Barak Obama has been the chief American apologist for Islam in spite of a worldwide upsurge of terror conducted by its adherents. Open Doors ministry reported that of the fifty countries with the worst persecution, forty-one are Muslim.[1] Both the Vatican and the Center for Study of Global Christianity reported that 100,000 Christians died in 2012 because they were Christian—devout, nominal, or cultural. These statistics include Christians killed for their beliefs or ethnicity, killed while worshiping in a church, murdered because they were children of Christians, or killed because of their Christian witness.[2] Most of the deaths were at the hands of Muslims and committed in the name of Islam as dictated by the Qur'an. Given the substantial increase in Muslim violence against Christian minorities in the Middle East since 2012, the number of Christian deaths at the hands of Muslims most certainly will increase substantially.

The Obama administration refuses to accurately label the world's battle against terrorism for what it is—a religious war with radical Islamists. He states that, "...I think we do ourselves a disservice in this fight if we are not taking into account the fact that the overwhelming majority of Muslims reject this ideology."[3] That the "overwhelming majority" of Muslims in the United States reject the fundamental tenets of radical Islam is debatable. But, what is not debatable is that the forty-one governments of the top fifty countries in the world with the worst records of persecution are Muslim and *represent an overwhelming majority of all the world's Muslims.* And most of those countries are enforcing a rigid adherence to the commands of the Qur'an. The President's implied peacefulness of Islam is spurious when one sees the reality of the vast persecution of Christians in the Muslim world. Where statistics of persecution may seem minimal in some Muslim countries such as Saudi Arabia, it is only because Christianity is so suppressed as to be virtually eradicated and non-existent.

Because the President's defense of Islam is so obviously groundless, he endeavors to minimize Muslim persecution of Christians by claims of moral equivalence between Christianity and Islam as to their respective historical abuses. A recent example of this was at, of all places, the National Prayer Breakfast where the President attempted to equate certain supposed evils in Christian history to that of modern Islamic terrorism.

> But we also see faith being twisted and distorted, used as a wedge—or worse, sometimes used as a weapon... We see ISIL, a brutal, vicious death cult that, in the name of religion, carries out unspeakable acts of barbarism—terrorizing religious minorities like the Yezidis, subjecting women to rape as a weapon of war, and claiming the mantle of religious authority for such actions.
>
> And lest we get on our high horse and think this is unique to some other place, remember that during the Crusades and the Inquisition, people committed terrible deeds in the name of Christ. In our home country, slavery and Jim Crow all too often was justified in the name of Christ.[4]

Those using the moral equivalence argument attempt to equate two distinct and dissimilar things that are not, in fact, equal. In such cases, whether used in a positive or negative sense, the argument is erroneous because the two are dissimilar. In his Prayer Breakfast speech, President Obama used moral equivalence in a negative sense by effectively labeling the *supposed* crimes committed in the name of Christianity as equivalent to the modern-day atrocities committed in the name of Islam. By doing so, the Apologist-in-Chief for Islam attempted to turn the focus of religious persecution on Christianity instead Islam.

President Obama's comments at the National Prayer Breakfast were wrong on two counts. First, the President misreads the history of Islam and its conflict with Christianity and Western civilization. Second, the President, his administration, and most of the liberal establishment blatantly distort the true nature of Islam. In this series of articles we shall examine the origins and nature of Islam as compared to Christianity and Christendom's past response to Muslim aggression.

Origins of Islam

Unlike the Christian Bible that was the product of the revelation of God to a host of writers over a 1600 year period, the Qur'an was a product of the verbal utterances of Muhammad born about AD 570 of poor parents who were members of a minor clan of an important Bedouin tribe living in the harsh desert conditions of the Arabian peninsula. As a young man he preached a monotheistic God. Most Arabs of the era were polytheistic, but monotheism was not a new message for there were Christian Arabs before there were Muslims. A descendant of Abraham, Muhammad saw himself as a messenger of God who will judge all men. Salvation was to be obtained by following his will in their personal and social behavior as well as religious observances. Over a period of twenty-two years, these revelations were written down by his followers but not collected together as the Qur'an until after his death. Even though there had been other prophets before him including the last who was Jesus of Nazareth, Muhammad believed all of their revelations had been falsified by Jews and Christians. Now Muslims were to believe that through Muhammad God had spoken his last message to mankind.[5]

Islam was a religion invented and built upon the sword, conquest, and forced conversion. Salvation came through works, and its primary work was war against the infidel by which is meant any who were not followers of Islam. Beginning with the Muslim prophet's first successful caravan raid followed by twelve centuries of Muslim conquests, Islam was unequivocally linked with worldly success and power. In the first few decades of Islam's existence, Muslims conquered half of the lands of historic Christianity including Syria and Egypt. According to one medieval Muslim historian, the Mediterranean was quickly turned into a "Muslim lake" in which "the Christians could no longer float a plank..."[6]

Just before his death, Muhammad told his followers, "I was ordered to fight all men until they say 'There is no god but Allah.'" His words are confirmed by his previous instructions recorded in the Qur'an: "...then fight and slay the Pagans wherever ye find them. And seize them, beleaguer them, and lie in wait for them in every stratagem (of war); but if they repent, and establish regular prayers and practice regular charity, then open the way for them..." [Qur'an 9:5] Faithful to the Qur'an and Muhammad's final words, his followers set out to conquer the world, and that is the goal of faithful followers of Islam in the twenty first century.

Before he died in 632, Muhammad had unified the Bedouin tribes in Arabia. The first conquest by his followers was Syria in 635, then part of the Byzantine Empire (Eastern Roman Empire).

Palestine, then a part of Syria, was conquered by 638. At the same time the Arabs attacked western Persia (Mesopotamia known as Iraq today) and it fell to the Muslim invaders. Soon, eastern Persia (known as Iran today) was invaded and conquered. The Muslim invaders turned north and subdued Armenia and then traveled east to occupy the Indus Valley (modern Pakistan) and over the centuries expanded into India. In 641 all of Egypt surrendered to the Muslim invaders. During the last half of the 600s, Muslims conquered the North African coast all the way to the Atlantic Ocean, crossed the isthmus separating Africa and Europe, and captured Spain. Eventually the islands of the Mediterranean and southern Italy were defeated and brought into the Muslim empire.[7]

Because of Muslim dominance of the Mediterranean and the lands in between, the Latin West was effectively separated from the Greek East. Muslim conquests of Spain and dominance of the Mediterranean placed the entire European continent under threat of Muslim attack.[8] During the thousand years that followed, some of the conquered nations cast off their Muslim captors. But Muslim conquest and domination of much of the world continued for ten centuries until a shocking defeat in 1798 led to the demise of the Muslim empire for the next 150 years.

In Part II, the nature of Islam and its concepts, beliefs, and practices that are fundamental to the Muslim faith will be examined.

Part II (4-24-15)

To judge the moral equivalency of Christianity with Islam, we must have a general understanding of Islam and what its followers profess to be truth. This understanding comes as we briefly explore the nature of Islam and its concepts, beliefs, and practices that are fundamental to the Muslim faith.

Sources of Islamic belief and law

- Qur'an – The revelations of God (Allah) to his prophet Muhammad over a twenty two year period in the seventh century.
- Sharia law – the Islamic moral code and religious law which deals with the institutions and daily life of the ummah (Muslim community).
- "Hadith" – Other words and deeds attributed to Muhammad but not found in the Qur'an.
- The rulings of the Islamic legal authorities (the "ulema"—its scholars, sheikhs, clerics, and muftis—both past and present).
- Historical texts that document jihad against Christendom over the centuries.[9]

Anti-Christian nature of the Qur'an

Islam's ultimate authority lies in the words of Muhammad as recorded in the Qur'an,[10] purported to be revelations from Allah. The Qur'an is intrinsically anti-Christian as shown by the following verses:

> Christian Trinity – "They do blaspheme who say: Allah is one of three in a Trinity: for there is no god except One Allah." [Qur'an 5:76]

> Christ is not God – "In blasphemy indeed are those that say that Allah is Christ the son of man..." [Qur'an 5:19]

> Christians are infidels and enemies of Islam who must be subjugated – "...fight and slay the Pagans wherever ye find them. And seize them, beleaguer them, and lie in wait for them in every stratagem (of war)...[Qur'an 9:5] "Fight those who believe not in Allah nor the Last Day, nor hold that forbidden which hath been forbidden by Allah and His Apostle, nor acknowledge the Religion of Truth, (even if they are) of the people of the Book, until they pay the *Jizya* with willing submission, and feel themselves subdued. [Qur'an 9:29]

Jews and pagans were considered by Muslims as the most hostile to Islam and least likely to convert. However, Christians are supposed to have a greater affinity for the message of Islam and can be expected to convert. Therefore, defenders of Islam who claim that it is a religion of peace often point to a number of verses in the Qur'an that seem to be quite friendly to Christianity. [See: Qur'an 5:82-93]

However, such verses are misleading because of the doctrine of "abrogation" (an instance of repealing). There are many contradictory verses in the Qur'an. To handle the resulting confusion as to what the Qur'an actually meant, early Islamic jurisprudence determined that whenever contradictory verses were found, the verse from later revelations of Muhammad would abrogate or cancel out the verse from his earlier pronouncements. This is confirmed by the Qur'an itself. "None of Our revelations do We abrogate or cause to be forgotten but We substitute something better or similar : knowest though not that Allah hath power over all things? [Qur'an 2:106] Synonyms for abrogate are repeal, revoke, abolish, and nullify.

The Christian friendly verses were voiced by Muhammad early in his career when he had no power. Those verses were replaced by Qur'an 9:29 (see above) and many others verses that are exceedingly hostile and intolerant to Christians and which were voiced later in his career when he had attained power.[11] In accordance with the doctrine of abrogation, the earlier Christian-friendly verses were repealed and caused to be forgotten.

Jihad

One must understand that the ultimate goal of Muslims is to conquer and subject the world to Islamic rule. Jihad is the unending Muslim holy war designed to conquer the world by converting or subjugating infidels and eliminating those that stand in their way. In the *Encyclopedia of Islam*, jihad is required because the "...spread of Islam by arms is a religious duty upon Muslims in general...Jihad must continue to be done until the whole world is under the rule of Islam..."[12] If there is any doubt as to the purpose of jihad in Islam, Muslim scholar, philosopher, and historian Ibn Khadum has settled the issue.

> In the Muslim community, the holy war [jihad] is a religious duty, because of the universalism of the Muslim mission and the obligation to convert everybody to Islam either by persuasion or by force...The other religious groups did not have a universal mission...They are merely required to establish their religion among their own people...But Islam is under obligation to gain power over the nations.[13]

Jizya

In a Muslim dominated society, Jizya is tribute money required to be paid by People of the Book (Christians) "...with willing submission and feel themselves subdued." Again, we refer to Qur'an 9:29 (see above) to confirm this requirement. There are also many other verses that require infidels to be despised and systematically humiliated. Ibn Kathir further illuminates the heinous meaning of the Qur'an.

> Allah said, "until they pay the jizya," if they do not choose to embrace Islam, "with willing submission,"

that is, in defeat and subservience, "and feel themselves subdued," that is, disgraced, humiliated, and belittled. Therefore, Muslims are not allowed to honor the dhimmis or elevate them above Muslims, for they are miserable, disgraced, and humiliated.[14]

From the very earliest years following Muhammad's death, the particulars of how Christians were to be made to feel themselves subdued were spelled out in precise detail in a document called *The Conditions of Omar* (Omar bin al-Khattab who reigned from 634-644). These conditions and restrictions were intended to humiliate and degrade Christians in every aspect of their lives life under Muslim rule including religion, business, housing, public demeanor, speech, dress, and deference to Muslims.[15]

Caliphate

Under Islamic rule there is no separation of church and state. The Caliphate is a unified government that rules the *ummah*, which is the entire Muslim community. As Allah is the only lawgiver, there is no legislature, and Muslims consider the caliphate as the highest type of political organization. Where human governments rule in the Muslim world, they only exist to enforce Allah's law. From the very beginning of Islamic rule by caliphs, each would choose a location in which to base his empire. Prior Sunni caliphates ruled from Damascus, Baghdad, and Istanbul. The Ottoman Empire was the last Sunni caliphate and was ruled for 500 years by Ottoman sultans. The Turkish Grand National Assembly abolished the caliphate in 1924[16]

Caliph (Imam)

Allah's vicegerent on earth is the Caliph or supreme leader that governs the Muslim community. He is charged with administering and enforcing Sharia law by rendering "righteous judgement" between men. One of the puzzlements of non-Muslims is the reason for the incessant fighting between Muslims sects. Muhammad died in 632 but did not leave instructions as to selection of his successor. The Sunnis believe that any believer in Allah was eligible to fill the office of Caliph. The Shias believed that the Imams (their word for Caliph) must come from Muhammad's bloodline. Following Muhammad's death the first three caliphs were Sunnis but severely criticized as being wealthy tyrants. The fourth caliph was Ali, a cousin and son-in-law of Muhammad, considered to be the first caliph eligible to fill the office because he was of the prophet's bloodline. Ali was murdered and replaced by a Mu-Awiyah, a Sunni caliph who set up his capital in Damascus. This was the beginning of the schism in Islam that is as intense today as it was at its beginning in the seventh century.[17] About ninety percent of the world's one billion plus Muslims are Sunnis, and the remainder is Shiites[18] who reside mostly in Iraq, Iran, and Lebanon.

In Part III we shall examine the growth and subsequent decline of the Muslim empire and Christendom's response in the Middle Ages. Following that, we shall examine the modern misinterpretation of Muslim history and culture as well as the distortion of Christian history and the Crusades.

Part III (5-1-15)

Muslim conquests and demise of the Islamic empire

In Part I the origins and explosive growth of the Islamic empire in the seventh and eighth centuries were described. Muslim domination of its distant empires waxed and waned over the course of its twelve centuries of war on the world. In 1672, the forces of the Muslim caliph Mu-Awiyah (previously mentioned in Part II) ruling from his capital in Damascus decided to attack Constantinople, the capital of the Byzantine Empire (today known as Istanbul). Sailing from the Syrian coast, Muslim ships entered the Dardanelles and moved north through the narrow strait that connects the Mediterranean with the Marmara Sea. At the north end of the Dardanelles lay Constantinople, gateway to the Balkans from which a Muslim victory would have allowed the invaders to attack all of Europe. The defenders of Constantinople easily defeated the Muslims who were forced to cede recently conquered islands in the Aegean and pay tribute. In one of the world's most consequential battles, all of Europe was saved from Muslim domination. This was the first major defeat of Muslim forces. Soon the Muslim hold on Spain began to ebb, and they were driven from Sicily and Southern Italy.[19] True to their mission of world domination, Muslim conquerors driven out in one area would regroup, conquer, and subjugate other lands and occasionally reconquer lands once held but lost.

For a thousand years Muslims had conquered and subjugated non-Muslims on much of three continents stretching from Spain to portions of India. Their military victories and success in eventual subjugation and establishment of Muslim cultures reinforced their unwavering belief in and allegiance to Islam. The Muslim world's arrogant confidence rested on the power of the sword, but the sword was also expertly wielded by a short-in-stature infidel from the heart of Europe. In 1798, Napoleon Bonaparte struck a blow at the center of the Muslim world that eventually led to its historic collapse. The little French dictator easily conquered Egypt which quickly led to the defeat and colonization of much of the remainder of the Muslim empire by a number of European powers.[20]

Over the centuries, it was Muslim power that dictated what was to be considered right. But when Muslim power failed in the early nineteenth century, they began to imitate many Western ideas including politics, government, customs, outward appearance, and dress. Reeling from the catastrophic collapse of its empire, Muslims began to question their fidelity to the Qur'an and Sharia law. All things Muslim began to appear outdated relics of another age, and many countries such as Turkey began distancing themselves from their Muslim past. According to noted author and journalist Raymond Ibrahim, the Westernization of many countries in the former Muslim empire introduced what he called the "Christian Golden Age" during the colonial and post-colonial years of 1850-1950. Greater freedoms and reduced oppression by the Muslim majority resulted from the direct liberation and protection of Christians by the now dominate European overlords. More importantly, Ibrahim attributes the diminished subjugation and oppression of Christians to a growing Muslim rejection of their former Islamic identities, mentality, and ways of life.[21]

The Crusades

Provoked by four centuries of Muslim wars to conquer and colonize the West, the Crusades were Christian Europe's response to Muslim plunder, rape, murder, and brutalization from one end of the known world to the other to accomplish their stated goal of world domination under an Islamic caliphate. The Crusades were a series of campaigns that occurred between 1095 and 1291 and intended to end Islam's brutal control of the Holy Land. At the time of the first campaign, much of what once were Christian territories had been under Muslim domination for four hundred years: the Middle East, Egypt, all of North Africa, Spain, southern Italy, and the major islands of the Mediterranean.[22]

The first Crusade was prompted by a plea for help from Byzantium emperor Alexius Comnenus to Pope Urban II. The letter requested that Europe's Roman Christians send troops to aid their Eastern Orthodox brethren in repelling the Seljak Turks (recent converts to Islam) that threatened Constantinople. The letter also described the ghastly tortures, rapes, and murders of Christians on pilgrimage to the Holy Land and desecration and destruction of Christian churches and Holy sites. Although there were many disagreements on lifestyle and cultural heritage that separated the two branches of Christianity, they stood on common ground in their opposition to the marauding Muslim aggressors.[23]

On a day in late November of 1095, Pope Urban mounted a platform in a meadow outside the city of Clermont, France, to present the Byzantium emperor's request for assistance. The Pope gazed across the immense crowd that spread in all directions. With a powerful and expressive voice he began describing the conditions being experienced by their fellow believers at Constantinople and the persecutions of Christians on pilgrimage to the Holy Land. The crowd was stirred by the Pope's passionate words, and plans were made to set out the following year to avenge Muslim wrongs and reclaim the Holy Land.[24]

In the exuberance and excitement of the moment, many in the crowd may not have understood the difficulties and hardships that lay ahead. But many of the nobles and knights present that day were not foolish or naïve for a number had made pilgrimages to the Holy Land or had close relatives or associates that had made the journey. They knew of the difficulties, cost, perils, hardships, and bloody battles that such a venture would entail in defeating the ferocious and determined Muslim foe.[25]

The Crusades were led by heads of families at immense personal cost with little hope or expectation of material reward. For the most part, the kingdoms established and maintained by the Crusaders for two hundred years did not produce material gain. This is confirmed by the fact that the colonies required large subsidies from the Crusaders' homelands in Europe.[26]

How can one find moral equivalency between twelve centuries of Muslim conquest and domination with the five campaigns of the Crusaders? One cannot. It is more correct to say the heinousness of twelve centuries of consistent and concerted Muslim aggression over three continents *far outweighs* the sporadic Crusades over two centuries and which were confined to a relatively small area. This comparison is accurate and very illuminating but still seems unsatisfactory because it fails to speak to morality.

We must first clarify that *good motives do not in themselves excuse immoral actions*, but an examination of motives (good and bad) can determine if moral equivalency exists. Put another way, those with bad behavior that seek moral objectives are not morally equivalent to those with bad behavior that seek self-serving objectives. Therefore, to determine moral equivalency, we must look to the motives of the

Muslims and Crusaders. What were their central motives? What drove their aggression?

As with all military conflicts between peoples, the motivations for war are not all the same. Many wars are fought to gain lands, booty, power, and forced conversions. This was the undeniable motive of Muslims which rested on a militant theocracy bent on world domination. At the other end of the spectrum, motives for war may include fighting to defend one's homeland, to attain freedom, to advance a righteous cause (e.g., end slavery and suffering), or to achieve a host of other noble objectives that may still contain a degree of selflessness. It is only in examining motives for going to war that we can comparatively judge the morality of the combatants. The *execution and events of war* itself must be judged separately from the motives for going to war. Even when the motives for going to war are known, the acts of war itself may often cloud those motives in retrospect. Over the centuries the true motives of the Crusaders appear to have often become clouded in in the minds of modern historians.

It is in the failures of the Crusaders' actions, often unfairly judged by modern standards, as opposed to a right understanding of the principle motives driving the Crusades that has caused widespread denigration of Christianity and Western civilization over the last three hundred years. The Crusades began as a noble and holy mission, and many of the knights leading the expeditions viewed their endeavor as such. Their goal was to liberate the Holy Land and end the suffering and death being inflicted upon their fellow Christians. The Crusaders' actions frequently fell short of their higher purposes for going to war. In spite of these shortcomings and failures, the details of history present a compelling confirmation of the worthy motivations of most Crusaders.[27]

In Part IV, the efforts of those that use the Crusades to make Christianity the moral equivalent to Islam will be exposed as falsehoods aimed at denigrating Christianity and Western civilization. More importantly, we shall present the moral superiority of Christianity over Islam through a comparison of the contributions of each for the betterment of the world.

Part IV (5-8-15)

Modern trashing of the Crusades, Christianity, and Western civilization

We began Part I with President Obama's description of ISIL (Islamic State of Iraq and Levant) as a distorted and deviant form of Islam. But he immediately suggests a moral equivalency of Christianity with ISIL, slavery in America, and past racism in the South.[28] But the President's denigration of Christianity and the Crusades are not a new phenomenon.

The historical explanations of how and why the first Crusade began have been perverted by historians, academia, liberal politicians, and others hostile to Christianity for three hundred years. Their new interpretation is much more sinister and contemptuous. This cynical view of the Crusades has been widely disseminated by the progressive education movement in America which wrested education from the influence of the church in the late 1800s. The progressive educational establishment is a bitter enemy of the biblical worldview and much of Western civilization in general. The tenets of progressive education stem from the Enlightenment and its humanistic influence. Therefore, the Crusades have become a convenient tit-for-tat when defending Islam and denigrating Christianity through claims of moral equivalency.

Typical of the charges against the Crusades are that they are the cause of modern Muslim bitterness and Islamic fury at their mistreatment by the Christian Crusaders. The Crusaders were motivated by lands, spoils, and power, not piety and safety of Christian pilgrims going to the Holy Land. Crusaders were barbarians that attacked, brutalized, and destroyed "the enlightened Muslim culture." Even the *New York Times* compared the Crusades to Hitler's atrocities. Others charge that the Crusades were "...an expression of Catholic bigotry and cruelty." These recurrent themes flow from the halls of academia, media, liberal politicians, and an assortment of humanist intellectuals, and their stanzas have been condensed to a single chorus by Rodney Stark, "...during the Crusades, an expansionist, imperialistic Christendom brutalized, looted, and colonized a tolerant and peaceful Islam."[29]

Although time does not allow a point by point refutation of the charges *against Christianity and the Crusades*, the remainder of this article summarizes and overwhelmingly exposes the absurd claims of the cultural and moral equivalency between Christianity and Islam.

Comparison of the tenets of Christian and Islamic Faiths

When one compares the tenets of Islam with those of Christianity, the two religions are worlds apart in their treatment of humanity. Islam is a militant theocracy with a stated purpose of subduing the entire world under an Islamic caliphate. But Christians obedient to the Bible cannot compel conversion nor punish those who do not convert as do the faithful followers of Islam. Numerous verses in the Qur'an speak of the subjugation or killing of non-Muslims. Perhaps the most telling difference between the tenets of Christianity and Islam is their respective records of persecution. Forty-one of the top fifty countries with the worst records for persecution are headed by Muslim governments substantially ruled or heavily influenced by Islamic theocracies. When one compares the tenets and the resultant actions of the faithful followers of the Qur'an compared to the faithful followers of Christ and the Bible, the superiority of the Christian faith is irrefutable.

Geographical extent, duration, and severity of Muslim aggression as compared to the Crusades

Disregarding motive and morality, there is a remarkable disparity in time, extent, and severity of conquest and brutality when comparing Muslim and Crusader aggression. In Part III it was noted that the twelve centuries of consistent and concerted Muslim aggression over three continents far outweighs the sporadic Crusades that occurred over two centuries and confined to a relatively small area. The historical record reveals that Muslim aggression lasted a millennium longer than the Crusades. Widespread accounts from various lands invaded and conquered reveal a consistent pattern of Muslim conquest and brutality that was far more frequent and harsh than the misdeeds of various Crusaders during the five campaigns to free and protect the Holy Land.

Motives and morality of Christians and Muslims

As stated in Part III, we must first clarify that *good motives do not in themselves excuse immoral actions*, but an examination of motives (good and bad) can determine if moral equivalency exists between Christianity and Islam. Stated simply, the motives of Muslims faithful to the Qur'an are to ultimately subdue the entire world under an Islamic caliphate. But in accordance with Christ's command, the principle motive of Christians is to share their relationship with God as they interact with humanity. Perhaps the best description of a Christian's motivation is described in that well-known verse found in John's gospel, "For God so loved the world, that he gave his only Son, that whosoever believes in him should not perish but have everlasting life." [John 3:16. RSV] This message is based on freedom to choose Christianity as opposed to Muslim coercion to convert to Islam. From the perspective of morality and motive, the superiority of Christianity is undeniable when compared to Islam.

Cultural superiority of Christianity over Islam – Making a better world

Not only do history's revisionists attempt to find moral equivalency between the Crusades and Muslim aggression, they also attempt to elevate Muslim culture in comparison with Western civilization. Arab claims of a sophisticated and superior culture are not the result of Arab development but are the result of what they learned from the cultures of peoples subjected to Arab rule, the *dhimmi* populations which included the Byzantium (Judeo-Christian-Greek cultures); Egyptian (the Copts and Nestorians), Persian (Zoroastrian), and Hindu. Most Arab science and learning was originated with and translated into Arabic by these assimilated *dhimmis*.[30]

Claims of a superior and advanced Muslim culture were enhanced by comparison with a supposed backwardness of Christendom as a result of the Dark Ages. Moderns often describe the Dark Ages as a time of intellectual darkness and barbarity during the five or six centuries following the fall of the western half of the Roman Empire during the fifth century.[31]

From the Enlightenment of the seventeenth and eighteenth centuries to well-known historians of the twentieth century, Western intellectuals consistently describe life in Europe during this era as a time of "…barbarism, superstition, [and] ignorance…" (Voltaire 1694-1778). Rousseau (1712-1778) stated that, "Europe had lapsed into the barbarism of the earliest ages." Historian William Manchester (1922-2004) labeled the period as an era "…of incessant warfare, corruption, lawlessness, obsession with strange myths, and an almost impenetrable mindlessness…The Dark Ages were stark in every dimension."[32]

Only recently has the myth of the Dark Ages been recognized. This recognition was noted in the Fifteenth Edition of the *Encyclopedia Britannica* (1981). The "Dark Ages" are no longer recognized as "… a period of intellectual darkness and barbarity." This period is now acknowledged as "…one of the great innovative eras of mankind" in which Europe's technological advances placed it well ahead of the rest of the world.[33]

In spite of the humanists' fiction of intellectual darkness and barbarity during Christendom's first five centuries in Europe, the influence of those Christian refugees from fallen Rome would ultimately influence and change the world as no other people ever had. But this story is little known or acknowledged in the midst of a hostile humanistic and secular culture that has ascended within America over the last three generations. We are indebted to Alvin Schmidt for giving us a definitive and unapologetic understanding of the unparalleled importance of Christianity in the history of the world. The following is merely a brief mention of the major themes outlined in Paul Maier's Foreword to Professor Schmidt's book, *How Christianity Changed the World*.

> ...many of our [America's] institutions and values reflect a Christian origin.
>
> Not only countless individual lives but civilization itself was transformed by Jesus Christ. In the ancient world, his teaching elevated brutish standards of morality, halted infanticide, enhanced human life, emancipated women, abolished slavery, inspired charities and relief organizations, created hospitals, established orphanages, and founded schools.
>
> In the modern era, Christian teaching, properly expressed, advanced science, instilled concepts of political and social and economic freedom, fostered justice, and provided the greatest single source of inspiration for the magnificent achievements in art, architecture, music, and literature...
>
> No other religion, philosophy, teaching, nation, movement—whatever—has so changed the world for the better as Christianity has done.[34]

The fiction of moral equivalency between Christianity and Islam has been utterly demolished by the facts as shown in these four articles. However, Christians and others who revere truth must understand that such attempts to find moral equivalency by President Obama and others is but one small battle in the much larger war of ideas and worldviews occurring between humanism and Christianity in America. It is in this battle that Christians must continually be engaged and vigilant for its outcome will determine if we, our children, and our grandchildren will live in freedom or slavery.

"Workplace violence" comes to Canada (11-21-14)

The Occupational Safety and Health Administration (OSHA) defines workplace violence as "...violence or the threat of violence against workers. It can occur at or outside the workplace and can range from threats and verbal abuse to physical assaults and homicide, one of the leading causes of job-related deaths. However it manifests itself, workplace violence is a growing concern for employers and employees nationwide." The OSHA website also tells us that workplace violence can strike anywhere and anyone...people in homes, pizza delivery persons, gas meter readers, psychiatric evaluators...literally anywhere work is or can be done.[1] But OSHA's definition is so broad that it is meaningless. Almost any violence can be classified as connected to the workplace however tenuous that connection might be. Not only does OSHA mask the real reasons for much of the violence, but it magnifies the level of workplace violence by equating minor non-violent and non-criminal occurrences with violent crimes such as physical assault and murder. Effectively, a large segment of general societal violence is jury-rigged to the workplace and made the responsibility of employers. The assumptive language of OSHA's workplace violence regulations is that all such violence is workplace related.

OSHA's workplace violence rules were written long before November 5, 2009, when Army Major Nidal Hasan shot to death thirteen people (fourteen including the unborn child of one of the victims) and wounded thirty-two others at Fort Hood, Texas. Major Hasan committed these crimes after years of open and verbal support of Islamic jihad while serving as an Army officer. Hasan is an American-born Muslim who had exchanged emails with a leading Al-Qaeda personage in which Hasan asked if those attacking fellow soldiers were considered martyrs.[2] Hasan fired over 200 rounds in the killing spree while shouting "Allahu Akbar," which means "Allah is the Greatest" and is the opening declaration of every Islamic prayer as prescribed by the Prophet Muhammad.

Only four days after the shootings at Fort Hood, General George Casey, Chief of Staff of the Army, appeared on several Sunday news talk shows and expressed concern regarding the speculation as to the cause or motivation behind the shootings. "We have to be careful because we can't jump to conclusions now based on *little snippets* of information that have come out. As great a tragedy as this was, it would be a shame if our diversity became a casualty as well." [emphasis added] Not only was the general more concerned with protecting diversity than exposing the truth regarding the attack, he deliberately switched the focus of what happened when he said that he did not think there was currently discrimination *against* the estimated 3,000 Muslims who served in the Army at that time. Implicit in the General's unwarranted statement was that if Hasan had acted because of his religious beliefs, it would have been because of discrimination against Muslims within the Army.[3]

Forty-six people were killed or wounded just three days earlier on an Army base whose supreme commander was General Casey. The perpetrator was a Muslim who shouted "Allahu Akbar" and had a well-known history among his military peers and superiors of being in sympathy with and vocally supporting Islamic jihad. However, the general's greatest concern was for discrimination *against* Muslims in the military and not the families of the dead and those wounded by Hasan. It is incredibly naïve for anyone to believe the general did know the complete story of Nidal Hasan within hours of the killings and not just little snippets of information.

So the United States government saw to it that Hasan's crimes were labeled "workplace violence" as opposed to what it really was…an act of terror whose motivation was to advance the beliefs and purposes of a false religion. Workplace violence may describe the *location*, but it does not reveal the *cause or motivation* of the violence. Government leadership committed to the philosophy of humanism must at all costs defend its humanistic concepts of diversity and multiculturalism in which *moral relativism* rules and all belief systems are coexisting and *equally valid*. Thus, we can all rest well tonight because diversity has been defended and OSHA is churning out even more rules and regulations to combat "workplace violence" such as committed by Major Hasan.

Recently, Michael Zehaf-Bibeau, a thirty-two year old Muslim convert, shot and killed a ceremonial guard on his way to attack the Canadian House of Commons and was subsequently killed by guards. Humanism in Canada is even more advanced than in the United States, but Canadian Prime Minister Stephen Harper had the courage to call the assault on the House of Commons a terrorist attack. However, true to liberalism's humanistic roots, liberal leader Justin Trudeau quickly reassured the Muslim community.

> And to our friends and fellow citizens in the Muslim community, Canadians know acts such as these committed in the name of Islam are an *aberration of your faith*. Continued mutual cooperation and respect

will help prevent the influence of *distorted ideological propaganda posing as religion.* We will walk forward together, not apart.[4] [emphasis added]

According to Muslim tradition, the Qur'an was verbally spoken to Muhammad and is the mother document upon which Islam rests. One wonders how Zehaf-Bibeau's actions are a deviation from the Islamic faith when the words of the Qur'an repeatedly justify his actions. Two examples of many similar verses that justify Zehaf-Bibeau's attack are found in the Qur'an.

They but wish that ye should reject Faith, as they do, and thus be on the same footing (as they): but take not friends from their ranks until they flee in the way of Allah (from what is forbidden). But if they turn renegades, seize them and slay them wherever ye find them; and (in any case) take no friends or helpers from their ranks. [Surah 4:89. Qur'an][5]

Remember thy Lord inspired the angels (with the message): "I am with you, give firmness to the believers: I will instil [sic] terror into the hearts of the unbelievers, smite ye above their necks and smite all their fingertips off them.[6] [Surah 8:12. Qur'an]

Are these verses, which are consistent with the actions of Zehaf-Bibeau, distorted ideological propaganda as Trudeau would have us believe? The Qur'an either does or does not define Islam and direct the actions of its followers? If they are reflective of the Qur'an's instruction for conduct of the followers of Islam, the verses cannot be distorted ideological propaganda. If the verses are not reflective of proper conduct for the followers of Islam, how does a follower of Islam determine which verses of the Qur'an are to be followed and which must be considered distorted ideological propaganda?

The philosophy of humanism would have us believe that all belief systems are equally valid. If all belief systems are *not* equally valid, then the tenets of humanism are fundamentally flawed including humanistically defined concepts of diversity and multiculturalism which are embraced by General Casey and most of the leadership of the institutions of American life. When common sense and thousands of years of human experience expose the falsity of the humanistic worldview, its defenders use the power of office and meaningless language such as "workplace violence" and bogus definitions of diversity and multiculturalism to mask its failings.

> Humanism's diversity is a close kin of multiculturalism and focuses on the differences within society and not society as a whole. With emphasis on the differences, mass culture becomes nothing more than an escalating number of subcultures within an increasingly distressed political framework that attempts to satisfy the myriad of demands of the individual subcultures. There is a loss of unity through fragmentation and ultimately a loss of a society's central cultural vision which leads to disintegration. Humanism's impulse for diversity is a derivative of relativism and humanism's perverted concept of equality.[7]

> ...the humanist multicultural agenda reveals that multiculturalism is not intended to supplement but rather to supplant Western culture that is so steeped in Christianity. The attack on Western civilization comes through a dismissal of American religious values as they intersected with and made possible the rise of the American political system...The essence of multiculturalism has its roots in the denial of absolutes, one of the cardinal doctrines of humanism, which translates into a moral relativism. Such a values-free approach, according to the humanists, makes it impossible to judge one period or era in relation to another or to say that one culture's ethic is superior to another.[8]

The American experience since the first Europeans set foot on its eastern shores has been centered on a Christian understanding of the world. America became the greatest nation in the world because it was founded upon principles based upon that understanding.

FINDING TRUTH IN THE MAZE OF FREEWILL

Part I – Marriage & Family

Marriage

Part I – Two Views of Human Relationships: Christianity and Humanism (10-4-13)

This is the first of a five-part series on marriage. In Part I we shall examine the underlying worldviews of Christianity and humanism as it applies to humankind's relationships in the broader sense. Part II will more specifically examine the origins of marriage. In Part III we turn our attention to the nature of marriage under the Christian and humanistic worldviews. In Part IV we will examine the pathologies of marriage and relationships under the dominant humanistic worldview in America. In Part V, we will examine the assault on the divine concept of marriage and the consequences to society under the humanistic worldview of marriage and relationships.

The reader is cautioned to not consider Parts I and II as merely an academic and therefore optional exercise in understanding the radical assault on marriage in twenty-first century America. Rather it is a fundamental and integral prerequisite in understanding marriage and the conflict regarding marriage in the battle of worldviews in the twenty-first century.

Much of the material for this series has been excerpted from *Ye shall be as gods* and succinctly frames the opposing Christian and humanist worldviews with regard to human relationships in general and marriage specifically.[1]

The Trinitarian relationship is a picture of God's fundamental nature or being. Under the Judeo-Christian ethic or beliefs, man was specially created for relationship with God. We are also made for relationship with one another. These Judeo-Christian beliefs are supported by a thoughtful reflection on the history of humankind in which those permanent things and universals stand as unrelenting testimonies of the truth of this special relationship with God and with each other. This history also points to the hierarchical nature of the relationships of God, humankind, and nature.

The distinction between the respective worldviews of humanism and Christianity regarding relationships can be visualized in positional terms, i.e., vertical versus horizontal. For Christians, the primary nature of those relationships is vertical (hierarchical)—God's being is shown by the Father-Son relationship and the relationship of Christ with the Church of which He is the head and we are the body. Because man was created in God's image, the hierarchical pattern of relationships is evident in various entities throughout history—marriage, family, community, nations, and the Kingdom of God. Hierarchy implies authority, superior and subordinate, order, and rank. Furthermore, if society is to be understood, it must have structure, and structure requires hierarchy which implies distinctions.[2]

Richard Weaver called the "steady obliteration of those distinctions" the most significant omen of our time. Modern society embraces the humanistic perversion "...that in a just society there are no distinctions", but this leads to a loss of cultural center and ultimately disintegration. And the most dangerous idea of modern society is an undefined equalitarianism which pretends to be the champion of justice but is the opposite.[3] In reality, humanistic equalitarianism is a thief of status, property, patrimony, and ultimately freedom. In such is not found justice.

Codes of behavior upon which cultures and societies must rest rely on fraternity and not equality. Fraternity resonates through history as it is the offspring of the seminal purposes of man—relationship with God and other men. The object of fraternity is other-directed and speaks of duty, congeniality, cooperation, and sense of belonging whereas equality focuses attention on self and results in egotism. Equality, rightly applied, is equality before God and the law. But under the humanistic worldview, equality has become a rapacious egalitarianism that imposes regimentation and leveling of circumstance which results in unnatural social groupings. One senses the relentless gravity of the humanistic worldview pulling society downward from hierarchy into a flat (horizontal) social plain and consequential mediocrity. Such humanistic regimentation and leveling of condition result in loss of a sense of belonging and place which leads to suspicion and resentment.[4] From this we see the humanistic definition of equality as "...a disorganizing concept in so far as human relationships mean order."[5]

If one reflects on the various descriptions of humanism through its definition, philosophy, application, and worldview, one can see the emphasis on the horizontal (egalitarian) and the sharp contrasts with the vertical (hierarchical) with regard to relationships in all spheres of family and society. By egalitarian is meant a belief in human equality with special emphasis on "social, political, and economic rights and privileges" and a focus on the removal of any inequalities among humankind. An examination of just a few of humanism's principles will assist in developing this mental picture.[6]

Chief among these leveling principles is humanism's insistence on *denial of God*, a severance that encompasses both time and authority. In other words, God does not now exist nor existed before the appearance of the universe. Creation was a random process of nature; therefore, we are not subject to the authority of some creator.[7]

A second example of the horizontal nature of relationships (and denial of hierarchy, rank, and order) in the humanistic worldview regards the *nature of man*. There are no giants upon whose shoulders we stand. Quite the contrary, contemporary man is the latest and greatest model that evolved from the slime pits of the past. As a product of evolution, humankind cannot be fallen nor have need of redemption. If man is not fallen, then there cannot be right and wrong, only different points of view. Man is his own master and owes nothing to a mythical God or the ancients. Humanism's exaltation of self over family, denial of patrimony, emphasis on the present and the experiential, flexible and interchangeable values, life lived for the moment for there is nothing beyond, and deference to the senses represent a detachment from any hierarchical bonds of duty, obligation, patrimony, and the permanent things. There is no heaven above nor hell below and therefore no hierarchy, only a progressive and everlasting march to an unattainable and unknowable horizon that continually recedes into the distance.[8]

In contrast to the humanistic worldview, Weaver described the hierarchical nature of family and its bond with fraternity.

> The ancient feeling of brotherhood carries obligations of which equality knows nothing. It calls for respect and protection, for brotherhood is *status* in family, and family is by nature *hierarchical*...It places people in a network of sentiment, not of rights...[9]

With this understanding of the contrast between the two worldviews regarding human relationships, we are now able to move into a more specific examination of the origins of the marriage relationship.

Part II – Origin of Marriage (10-11-13)

In Part II we will examine the origins of the marriage relationship. As one reflects on how humans have organized themselves over time, there is and has been a great diversity of societal forms in various cultures and periods of history.[10] However, underlying this variety is a structured order or arrangement that reflects the "creational givens." One of these givens is that the family structure is a societal institution established by the creator. "That the family structure consists of at least a father, mother, and children living together in bonds of committed caring is not an arbitrary happenstance; nor is it mere convention that can be dismissed when it has outlived its usefulness." This ordered family structure is a part of the human constitution and is ingrained in man's nature in all of its facets—biological, emotional, social and moral. This structure allows for variety but sets definite boundaries, i.e., lines that cannot be crossed without being in opposition to the divinely structured order of the family.[11]

The ordered family structure flows from God and is described in Genesis 1:27 which states, "God created man in his own image...male and female he created them..." Their characters and roles are distinct, but both are created in His image. Therefore, the roles of husband and wife and father and mother (monogamous married couple living with their children) are not societal constructs from which we are to be liberated. True human fulfillment is attained when men and women are faithful to the foundational principles of family.[12]

Through the millennia the molding and shaping of marriage and family progressed, not with changes to the basic structure but in the fleshing out of its bones. By our very nature, men and women are a "pair-bonding" species. From such comes reproduction and nurturance. Parents shape the moral understanding, behavior, feeling, and worldview of their children. Most importantly, "The family is where 'socialization'—the generational transmission of moral and cultural values—takes place." The home was the basic organizing unit of humankind—a father, mother, and children living together in bonds of committed caring. The home became part of the extended family, then village, community, and ultimately state. Society arose from the success of the home, and without the stable home a civilized society would have been impossible.[13]

The cultural universals of marriage and family provide for the needs of society, and across the millennia economic and political considerations played a major role in selection of marriage partners.[14] Society grew and stabilized through marriage and family and a network of extended family (relatives and friends) in which there are reciprocal expectations, obligations, and responsibilities. In this larger sense, marriage was more than just commitment between two people. It is a ceremonious and formal union in which two families celebrate the marriage and the consequent "entanglement" of the families. Each family rises in status or affinity with the other as well as having reciprocal claims on each other. With status and affinity comes the motivator to right conduct by not bringing dishonor to the family.[15]

Another basic need of society is the establishment of rules for sexual conduct. The family supports monogamy between the husband and wife. To such is born children that have status as family. Without monogamy the family tends to dilution and disintegration through "...loss of legitimacy, social identity, legal recognition, cultural tradition, and an estate." In both the nuclear and extended families, marriage provides the best arrangement for the nurture and protection of children, the impartation of respect for the authority of parents, and the recognition of obligations to the elder members of family. In other words, the cultural universals of marriage and family are the means whereby generational transmission of moral and cultural values is most effectively achieved.[16]

The seedbed of what are considered to be many of the ethical qualities of the modern nuclear family that were critical to its development in Western civilization lay in the tribal society of ancient Israel, but the nuclear family as we know it was not a product of that society. Characteristics of ancient Israel that are in conflict with definition of the modern nuclear family include polygamy and the keeping of concubines among certain classes and the wealthy, arranged marriages (for economic, political, and social reasons), and the lack of legal and property rights and status for women. However, from the Hebrews we received two outstanding contributions to the development of the modern nuclear family: their commitment to family life and making marriage the focus of human sexuality (and opposition to infidelity and homosexuality). Where the Hebrews opened the way, Christianity would continue the moral refinement of marriage and family. As Western civilization was Christendom, we must recognize the importance of Christianity and its inestimable impact on our understanding of marriage and family.[17]

In Christianity, the marriage relationship was of such importance that it is described in terms of Christ's relationship with the church (His bride). With the new definition of marriage and family in the New Testament came a remarkable elevation in the status of women. In the first century world, women were of low social standing in virtually all cultures. They were considered inferior to men and responsible for sexual sin. But, Jesus' attitude and example during His earthly ministry became the definitive model for our understanding of male-female relationships, marriage, and family life. Paul's teachings on the relationship of men and women, marriage, and family added texture and detail to Jesus' ministry. Both men and women were held accountable to the same standards of morality. The vows of marriage were meant to be permanent with divorce allowed under very limited circumstances.[18]

With Christianity the understanding of the divine concept of marriage and family came into full view. But it would take another 1,500 years before "...permanent, monogamous marriage had triumphed, and home was more comforting and more private."[19] In Part III we turn our attention to the nature of marriage under the Christian and humanistic worldviews.

Part III – Contract or Covenant? (10-19-13)

In Part III we turn our attention to the nature of marriage under the Christian and humanistic worldviews. Throughout history the marriage ceremony has been a ritualistic and solemn occasion between a man and woman—a highly public profession of commitment to the most private of relationships. The solemnity of the occasion arises from the enormous magnitude and significance of the commitments—to take the marriage partner as wife or husband, to have and to hold, for better or for worse, for richer or poorer, in sickness and in health, to love and to cherish; from this day forward until death do them part. This ceremonial language resonates with powerful sentiments that link us with prior generations since time immemorial and to an enduring and exclusive commitment to union while facing the uncertainties of life to come. The ritualism symbolically binds the families of the man and woman and attests to the importance of the unbreakable commitments of which God is both witness and participant.[20]

The reasons for such commitments arise from human nature which is rooted in creation—the need to give love and receive love, a deep longing for sexual intimacy and emotional attachment, and a desire for a home and children. The humanist will argue that these things can be attained without requirements of marriage, monogamy, commitment to the permanency of relationship, and God.[21] But such humanistic counterfeits are a weak, unsatisfying, and an imperfect imitation of the biblical view of marriage, "... the honorable estate, instituted by God."[22]

Marriage orders the soul whereas sexual intimacy outside of marriage, co-habitation, divorce (apart from infidelity and willful desertion), and homosexuality (with or without benefit of a civil union) are illegitimate and therefore not heirs to that honorable estate. History and human nature attest to these assertions for according to researchers, heterosexual married life as opposed to all other similar social arrangements provides greater financial security, better health and sex, and a longer and better life.[23] Bennett called marital love that rests upon a foundation of unconditional commitment as "...safer, more enduring, and more empowering that any sentiment yet discovered or any human arrangement yet invented." He credits these attributes to the basic complementarity of man and woman joined together as one in marital love. The complementariness of the relationship is based on the differences, not just the physical but also the emotional and psychological. As the physical differences make sexual union possible, so too do the emotional and psychological differences of the marriage partners complement and complete each other.[24] The union becomes stronger than its parts.

Do non-marital heterosexual relationships have the potential to be as strong? No, for such commitments are in conflict with human nature and cultural universals which God formed at man's creation. Such conflicts result in disorder of the soul. However, couples that do not hold the Judeo-Christian worldview but whose marital relationships are based on the cultural universal of monogamy and commitment to the permanency of the marriage relationship between a man and woman will achieve an order of the soul and a better life insofar as it relates to their marital relationship.[25]

Let us examine the mindset of modern marriage partners which typically falls within one of two camps. First, the vast majority view marriage as a contract which is reflective of the humanistic (horizontal or egalitarian) worldview regarding marriage. The contract mindset focuses on marriage as a mutually beneficial relationship and getting as opposed to giving. When the benefits stop flowing or hard times arise, the relationship is easily broken through divorce.[26] The contract mentality in marriage emphasizes the details, e.g., "If you do that for me, I'll do this for you." In other words, the marital ledgers must always be balanced, but marriage partners often have differing views of the value of what is given and received. These differing perceptions in a marriage often result in growing resentment, hurt, anger, and ultimately divorce.[27]

The second view is that marriage is a covenant relationship. Like a contract, a covenant is an agreement between two or more parties, but that is where the similarity ends. The nature of a covenant agreement is very different from that of a contractual agreement, and the key difference is *motive*. The covenant relationship is the essence of the cultural universal of marriage and is uniquely expressed in Christianity. God is a covenant maker and the importance of covenant relationships is illustrated by His covenants with Moses, Abraham, David, and others throughout the Bible. Jesus Christ fulfilled the old covenant and initiated the new covenant. Rather than to receive something in return, covenants are initiated for the benefit of others, that is, to minister to another person as opposed to manipulating someone to get something. In a covenant marriage, the motive is a commitment to the well-being of the spouse.[28]

However, it would be naïve to believe that most young couples would possess that motive and level of maturity at the time of the marriage ceremony. Rather, covenant marriages are grown and strengthened through the years. If couples commit to covenant marriages and recognize the covenant relationship requires nurturing during the difficult times, those marriages will far more likely endure than contract marriages based on a cash register/accounts receivable ledger mentality.[29] In a covenant relationship, the promises made are not conditional but open-ended, that is, the promise or commitment is not conditioned on reciprocal behavior. There are no "If...then" clauses in covenant marriage vows.[30]

Part IV – The Pathologies of the Humanist Worldview of Marriage (10-25-13)

Traditional marriage is in serious jeopardy in twenty-first century America. In Part IV we will examine the assault on the divine concept of marriage and the resulting pathologies of the humanist worldview of marriage and relationships.

As a result of the ascending humanistic worldview, the concept of marriage as known and practiced in Western civilization since its inception has been done great damage. In the liberal view, the importance of marriage has been diminished in at least two ways. First, the humanistic worldview is based on *exaltation of the individual person*. The individual should be encouraged to realize his or her own creative talents and desires and exercise maximum individual autonomy. In such a worldview, marriage is far less important, a mere choice that may or may not be evidenced by a contractual relationship. And humanistic man's laws are crafted to reflect the reduced status of marriage, e.g., no-fault divorce.

The ideal of romantic love inextricably linked with individual happiness *devoid* of the covenantal commitment is of recent origin and rests on the tenets of the humanist philosophy and worldview. When one examines the humanist view of marriage, it may surprise many that humanist writings have little to say with regard to marriage for the emphasis is not on a matrimonial bonding of a man and woman but the liberation of the individual.[31] Two of the common principles of *Humanist Manifesto II* clearly elevate the individual as opposed to the two who shall become one flesh. These principles are:

Fifth: *The preciousness and dignity of the individual person* is a central humanist value. Individuals should be encouraged to realize their own creative talents and desires. We reject all religious, ideological, or moral codes that denigrate the individual, suppress freedom, dull intellect, dehumanize personality. We believe in maximum individual autonomy consonant with social responsibility... (emphasis in original)

Sixth: In the area of sexuality, we believe that intolerant attitudes, often cultivated by orthodox religions and puritanical cultures, unduly repress sexual conduct. The right to birth control, abortion, and divorce should be recognized. While we do not approve of exploitive, denigrating forms of sexual expression, neither do we wish to prohibit, by law or social sanction, sexual behavior between consenting adults. The many varieties of sexual exploration should not in themselves be considered "evil."...individuals should be permitted to express their sexual proclivities and pursue their life styles as they desire...[32]

The second way humanism deconstructs Western civilization's concept of marriage is *to redefine and marginalize traditional marriage*. Marriage is no longer a union between a man and woman but now includes marriage between homosexuals in some states. Further deconstruction is on the horizon. Both houses of the 2012 California state legislature passed a bill that would allow a child to have three legal parents. The governor vetoed the bill so more time would be allowed "...to consider all implications of the change." Other advocates are calling for the legal recognition of multiple partner relationships (polygamy).[33]

To the average twenty-first century American, covenant marriage (See Part III) may appear impractical if not impossible amidst the swirl of a humanistic popular culture that idealizes romantic love inextricably linked with individual happiness. Most moderns hope to sail the seas of marital bliss in the flimsy craft built of fleeting emotion and temporal happiness. Marriages based on this false ideal will soon crash on the rocky shores of reality. Rather, covenant relationships are centered on steadfast or spiritual love which is far stronger and deeper than fleeting, emotion-driven romantic love. When the storms of life rage, the deep keel of a covenant marriage will keep the marital ship afloat. Certainly steadfast love contains emotional and romantic elements, but steadfast love is a choice, a way of thinking, a mindset and is best expressed in 1 Corinthians 13:4-8, "Love is patient; love is kind. Love does not envy; is not boastful; is not conceited; does not act improperly; is not selfish; is not provoked; does not keep a record of wrongs; finds no joy in unrighteousness, but rejoices in the truth; bears all things, believes all things, hopes all things, endures all things. Love never ends."[34]

This last phrase brings us to our next point. The covenant marriage is intended to be a permanent relationship. We can enter into a contract with anyone. The contract may involve sex, security, status, or a hundred other clauses and may or may not include love. However, we enter into covenant relationships only with those we love.[35] Therefore, to achieve the fullness of its promise, love must be an ingredient in the covenant marriage. In Paul's description of love in his letter to the Corinthians the careful reader will note an absence of the words important to proponents of the humanistic worldview—autonomy, independence, growth, and creativity. Faithful adherence to the words of 1 Corinthians 13 bring forth the fruit of a covenant marriage relationship. Such fruit is harvested only after the hard work of planting, weeding, and watering which is all wrapped up in one word—nurturing. Covenant marriages will involve its share of difficulties, trouble, and pain, but the harvest is worth the effort.[36]

For humanists and their feminist fellow travelers, extolling the virtues and provisions of a covenant marriage relationship may elicit howls of contempt. As has been noted, the focus of the humanists is on the "I" and not the "we", a message constantly conveyed and reinforced by media, government policies, the educational establishment, and popular culture. And this prevailing humanist worldview is carried into the great majority of male-female relationships regardless of type—marriage, cohabitation, or sexual promiscuity. We need not belabor these conclusions with additional explanation of the differences that are readily evident between the Judeo-Christian and humanist worldviews regarding marriage and family.[37]

Part V – The Consequences of the Humanist Worldview of Marriage (11-1-13)

Part V examines the consequences of the decline of traditional marriage in American society as a result of the ascending humanist worldview. The family and societal carnage that occurred in America during the twentieth century and thereafter as a result of the domination of the humanist worldview is monumental and recounted in numerous studies and reports. The statistics reflecting the precipitous decline of marriage and the American family are incontrovertible and coincide almost exactly with the emergence of the Boomer generation in the mid-1960s and the rapid and accelerating ascendancy of the humanist worldview.[38] Perhaps the signal statistic highlighting the collapse of marriage and the traditional family is the high level of births to unmarried mothers as reported in 2006: 68 percent of all black children, 45 percent of all Hispanic children, and 25 percent of all white children.[39]

The collapse of the traditional family is even more evident when one examines the population of women with and without spouse present. Of particular note is the dramatic twelve-fold percentage increase between 1960 and 1990 of women with children under the age of eighteen who have never married. This accounts for almost a third of all women with children under age 18 with no spouse present. For eighty years between 1880 and 1960, this figure *declined* from slightly over 12 percent to 2.6 percent in 1960 before the dramatic escalation to 31.6% in 1990. By the end of the first decade of the twenty-first century, four out of every ten births in America were to unwed mothers.[40]

What is also remarkable and further highlights the impact of the humanistic view of marriage is the decline in the percentage of women with children under eighteen who have a spouse present. For eighty years between 1880 and 1960, this figure was very stable at or near 90 percent before dropping to 76 percent in 1990.[41]

In their flight from marriage, humanists promised women emancipation and fulfillment; however, the big lie produced only bondage, drudgery, and exhaustion—poverty, long hours of daily separation from their children, and the drudgery of low-paying jobs in the workforce. The seeds planted by the those promoting the humanist worldview over the decades prior to the 1960s and thereafter have born bitter fruit—illegitimacy, cohabitation, fatherlessness, divorce, and a large number of single parent families with children who are locked in a continuing cycle of neglect and poverty.[42] When compared to homes where children were raised by married parents, children raised in homes by single parents are more likely to encounter emotional and behavioral problems, drink, smoke, use drugs, be physically abused, exhibit poor school performance and drop out, and exhibit aggressive, violent, and criminal behavior.[43] And in such an environment the memory of what once was or might have been is lost, and the transmission of the central vision of American culture to another generation is in peril.

Daniel Patrick Moynihan retired from the United States Senate (Democratic Senator from New York) in 2000. Near the beginning of his career he was an assistant Secretary of Labor in Lyndon Johnson's presidency. At the time of his retirement, the senator was asked to describe the biggest change he had seen in his forty years of government service. Articulate and intellectual, the distinguished public servant, having served both Democratic and Republican presidents, replied, "The biggest change, in my judgment, is that the family structure has come apart all over the North Atlantic world" and had occurred in "an historical instant. Something that was not imaginable forty years ago had happened." Author of the 1965 Moynihan Report officially known as "The Negro Family: The Case for National Action", Moynihan knew that of which he spoke.[44] Enormously controversial at the time of its release, the report continues to be a topic of debate in the twenty-first century. The report characterized the instability of the black families in America and the importance of the family unit in providing that stability.

> At the heart of the deterioration of the fabric of Negro society is the deterioration of the Negro Family. It is the fundamental source of the weakness of the Negro community at the present time…The role of the family in shaping character and ability is so pervasive as to be easily overlooked. The family is the basic social unit of American life; it is the basic socializing unit. By and large, adult conduct in society is learned as a child…the child learns a way of looking at life in his early years through which all later experience is viewed and which profoundly shapes his adult conduct.[45]

Writing shortly after Moynihan's perceptive summation of the condition of the family structure, William Bennett noted the deep concern of Americans with regard to the family. Bennett pointed to the general instability of the American family and the contributing factors such as the decline in the status and centrality of marriage in society, substantially greater percentage of out-of-wedlock births, and the significant increase in co-habitation. With the decline of social perception and necessity of matrimony, children are less valued, more neglected, more vulnerable to non-family influences, and have less resources devoted for their care and benefit. Bennett wrote that, "Public attitudes toward marriage, sexual ethics, and child-rearing have radically altered for the worse. In sum, the family has suffered a blow that has *no historical precedent*—and one that has enormous ramifications for American society."[46]

Another decade has elapsed since Moynihan's diagnosis of the disintegration of the family unit as the major modern affliction of the Western world and Bennett's reporting of Americans' purported concern for the survival of the family. It is no longer the problem of the black population. The deterioration of the family unit is pervasive and crosses all ethnic, socio-economic, and religious lines although the poor and disadvantaged bear a greater portion of the misery. Yet, there has been no concerted public outcry to reverse the decline, no urgency or sense of crisis in dealing with the problem, no new series of government studies explaining the situation, and no investigative reporting or meaningful media attention regarding the most profound change in society that has had no historical precedent. Why is this so? The answer is that the solutions to reverse the decline and devastation of marriage and the family unit stand as polar opposites of the prevailing and pervasive humanistic worldview.[47]

Love and Commitment (2-7-14)

It seems that in our modern world that the image of "commitment" has taken on a dubious persona. Evidence of the disdain for commitment is found in every facet of our society. "No commitment" is a hot seller in advertising these days. One need only do a quick Internet search of "no commitment" to discover pages of web sites offering everything from no commitment phone services to no commitment dating services. In the spirit of no-fault divorce, wedding vows that once included the supposed straightjacket of "until death do us part" have conveniently substituted the noncommittal "until love is no more." But in this non-committal world that we live, perhaps it is in an understanding of the real meaning of love that we find the value of commitment. In love and much of life, commitment is not only important but indispensable.

I was reminded of this indispensable connection between love and commitment by a story that I recently heard. The story was told by a Christian minister who had officiated at a large wedding in India at which 2,000 people were in attendance. The marriage was arranged by the Indian families of the groom, a brilliant young man with a Ph.D. in chemistry, and the bride, a beautiful, articulate, and well-educated young lady. The families had met, discussed the couple, and agreed the bride and groom would make a great marital union. Being an arranged marriage, the bride and groom did not know each other and had never met. Even as the bride came down the aisle and stood beside her husband-to-be, the groom did not look at her. As was the custom, the groom made a speech at the reception following the ceremony. He began by thanking his parents. He thanked the bride's parents and others. He ended by thanking his bride for loving him. The minister and others were surprised and intrigued by his statement. What did he mean? How could she love him for they had not met nor talked to one another? What the groom meant was his bride loved him because she was willing to commit herself to him even before they met. Although marriage is an experiential relationship, commitment is an indispensable component. Bring a commitment to your love and you'll reap the rewards of love. If you are not committed in love, you will not reap the rewards of love.[1]

As we examine the importance of commitment in love, we see a reflection of God's nature that is stamped on mankind. This nature is evident in the Apostle Paul's letter to the Ephesians, "...even as he chose us in him before the foundation of the world, that we should be holy and blameless before him. He destined us in love to be his sons though Jesus Christ, according to the purpose of his will." [Ephesians 1:4-5. RSV] God did not create man out of need. Rather, it was His will (commitment) to love, an expression of the very character of God, to share the inner life of the Trinity. Man's chief end is to glorify God by communing with God forever.[2]

Here we also see that commitment in love or the lack thereof is compatible with God's grant of freewill to man. By creating man with a free will meant the possibility of man's rejection of God and His love. In other words free will and the potential for rejection of God was the penalty for the possibility of love. So it is on the earthly plane, to risk love is to risk rejection. Rejection was not a surprise to an omniscient God. Before creation, God knew the cost of His will to love man would be the death of His Son and is revealed in Revelation 13:8, "...Lamb slain from the foundation of the world." God committed to love man before He created him, but God knew man would reject Him. Here we see the value of that infinite love exceeded the cost of that love at Calvary.[3]

Throughout much of history marriage has been a ritualistic and solemn occasion between a man and woman—a highly public profession of *commitment* to the most private of relationships. The solemnity of the occasion arises from the enormous magnitude and significance of the *commitments*—to take the marriage partner as wife or husband, to have and to hold, for better or for worse, for richer, for poorer, in sickness and in health, to love and to cherish; from this day forward until death do us part. This ceremonial language resonates with powerful sentiments that link us with prior generations since time immemorial and to an enduring and exclusive *commitment* to union while facing the uncertainties of life to come. The ritualism symbolically binds the families of the man and woman and attests to the importance of the unbreakable *commitments* of which God is both witness and participant.[4]

William Bennett called marital love that rests upon a foundation of *unconditional commitment* as "...safer, more enduring, and more empowering that any sentiment yet discovered or any human arrangement yet invented." The reasons for such commitments arise from human nature which is rooted in creation. The humanist will argue that these things can be attained without requirements of marriage, monogamy, commitment to the permanency of relationship, and God. But such humanistic counterfeits are a weak, unsatisfying, and an imperfect imitation of a man and woman bound by unconditional commitments in marriage, "... the honorable estate, instituted by God."[5]

The story of the young Indian couple reminded me of commitments my wife and I made almost forty-two years ago. I had watched the young woman for several months. She was as advertised—attractive, vivacious, and had a winning personality. I was almost twenty-six, and she had just turned nineteen when I summoned the courage to ask her for a date. Three months later we were engaged. But what did I know about this young woman that would cause me to commit a lifetime to her? More importantly, what did she know of me to make such a similar commitment?[6] At our wedding a few months after our engagement, we confirmed our unconditional commitment to love each other until death do us part.

Love infused with commitment will survive the inevitable trials of life, faded youth, and cooled passions. And such love will yield bountiful rewards.

Did father really know best? (7-25-14)

Father Knows Best was a late 1950s television program that depicted an idealized typical middle class family composed of a wise and loving father Jim Anderson, housewife and mother Margaret who was a voice of reason and patience, and three good kids (two teenagers and one pre-teen) whose comedic trials and troubles while growing up provided the basis for most of the weekly plotlines. In the end, Jim with Margaret's help, would provide the needed sage advice and words of encouragement to whichever of his three children needed it.

Over a half century later, the iconic Anderson family portrayed a different time in America and is considered quaint if not laughable by a modern culture overwhelmed by a humanistic interpretation of the world as it should be. Now, the entertainment media consistently portrays the father figure as an inept buffoon of marginal importance if not irrelevant to the family. In spite of the modern belief in the fiction of the typical 1950s Anderson-type family, it is the humanistic view that is an anomaly, abnormality, or even a perversion that is a stain on the pages of the history of marriage and family.

Stephanie Coontz wrote in her book *Marriage, a History*, that the male breadwinner/full-time housewife marriages that were the standard in America and Western Europe of the 1950s and 1960s were *not* a brief historical oddity. Coontz argues that such male-female role characterization was the culmination of a trend that had been growing since the late eighteenth century. For over 150 years there had been continuous movement toward and development of the once radical concept that love should be the basis for marriage and that the marital decision process should be controlled by the couple considering marriage.[1] These dramatic changes began in the eighteenth century and were embraced by both the humanistic and Christian worldviews. However, the *meaning and implementation* of these changes would become a battleground in the war between the humanistic and Christian worldviews.[2]

The roles of men and women throughout history remained relatively unchanged. Generally, men in all cultures and times have been the defenders of and providers for the family whereas women have been the nurturers and care givers for husband and children. Whether civilizations are modern or ancient, advanced or primitive, the complementary roles of husbands and wives along the lines just described will be present. Although those roles may or may not have finite and sharp distinctions (depending on the culture and time in history), the basic defender-provider/nurturer-care giver dichotomy remains a constant.[3]

The disappearance of the roles of men and women

The roles of men and women were defined and enhanced by the marriage relationship and made possible the enduring nuclear family unit. During the age of the Enlightenment and in particular the eighteenth century, advances toward the modern nuclear family would also bring dangers that would threaten its survival. These dangers included a more secular view of marriage and sexual relationships propagated by the tide of humanist thought and influence that swept through the nineteenth century.[4] By the 1960s and for the first time in history, the ideal of marriage came under direct attack by social engineers who "...believe a lifelong vow of fidelity is unrealistic or oppressive, especially to women...[and] marriage and family ties were...potential threats to individual fulfillment as a man or woman. The highest forms of human needs, contended proponents of the new psychologies, were *autonomy, independence, growth, and creativity*," and marriage was considered a hindrance to fulfilling these human needs.[5]

In 1963 Betty Friedan wrote *The Feminine Mystique* whose theme centered on the supposed alienation and meaninglessness experienced by the typical housewife.[6] Friedan's shot across the bow of traditional marriage and family eventually led to the establishment of the National Organization of Women three years later. NOW's 1966 Statement of Purpose was clear in its efforts to redesign the role of women in American society (and by implication the roles of men and children).

> NOW is dedicated to the proposition that women...must have the chance to develop their *fullest human potential*...it is no longer either necessary or possible for women to devote the greater part of their lives to child-rearing...True *equality of opportunity and freedom of choice* for women requires such practical, and possible innovations as a nationwide network of child care centers, which will make it unnecessary for women to retire completely from society until their children are grown...We reject the assumptions that a man must carry the sole burden of supporting himself, his wife, and family, and that a woman is automatically entitled to lifelong support by

a man upon her marriage, or that marriage, home and family are primarily woman's world and responsibility—hers, to dominate—his to support...We will seek to open a *reexamination of laws and mores governing marriage and divorce*...We are similarly opposed to all policies and practices—in church, state, college, factory, or office—which, in the guise of protectiveness, not only deny opportunities but also foster in women self-denigration, dependence, and evasion of responsibility, undermine their confidence in their own abilities and foster contempt for women.[7] [emphasis added]

At its core, the feminist view of the roles of men and women in marriage and family is essentially humanistic which differs markedly from the Christian worldview.

Humanistic worldview

The humanistic worldview and its values focus on the individual person and his/her independence, freedom, self- actualization, autonomy, growth, and creativity. Hence, marriage becomes secondary to the individual and is at best a contractual arrangement devoid of the requirements of covenantal "self-giving" as it interferes with humanistic values...Further, marriage is only one of several relational choices open to the individual. Marriage is not central or necessary for nurturing and the transmission of moral and cultural values to children. The pair-bonding elements of monogamy and permanency are individual decisions and not cultural universals.[8]

Christian worldview

The supreme reflection of God's image in humankind is in the marriage relationship followed by family. The roles of husband and wife and father and mother (monogamous married couple living with their children) are not societal constructs. The surface *patterns* and *functioning* of family may vary markedly in various cultures and societies down through the ages. However, the divinely ordered family *structure* is intrinsically a part of the fundamental identity of the family in every society and for all time. It is one of those universals or permanent things that are imbedded in the foundation of creation.[9] [emphasis in original]

Essentially, feminists view marriage as a zero-sum game in which gain by one person or side results in a loss by another person or side. In life there are only winners and losers—takers or givers. This is the humanistic worldview in which self is exalted at the expense of relationship. But life is not a zero-sum game. The ordered marital and family structure as reflected in the Christian worldview is a universal which focuses on giving, other-directedness, and relationship.

Not only is life not a humanist zero-sum game, playing the game leads to loss for the whole of society. When humanists and their feminist followers attempt to change the roles of men and women through a change of rules and mores regarding marriage, they discover the inflexibility of the marriage universal. Such changes have led to illegitimacy, cohabitation, divorce, fatherlessness, single-family households, and poverty in which the children face a rootless quest for meaning in life.

Did Jim Anderson always know best? No. But together Jim and Margaret Anderson usually got it right when it came to marriage, family, and life in general. In the Christian worldview, the complementariness of the roles of men and women in the marriage relationship is based on differences. Just as the differences make sexual union possible, the emotional and psychological differences of the marriage partners complement and complete each other, and the union becomes stronger than its parts. It is when the humanists attempt to erase the complementary and unique roles of men and women that marriage, family, and society suffer.

Part II – Abortion

Postcard from Hell (4-12-13)

"It would rain fetuses. Fetuses and blood all over the place...I felt like a fireman in hell. I couldn't put out all the fires."[1] These are the words of Steven Massof, one of the employees in an abortion clinic operated by Dr. Kermit Gosnell, describing the busy times when the women were given drugs to induce contractions all at once. Gosnell is on trial this week for killing seven children and a young mother in a filthy, blood-splattered clinic near Philadelphia.

The babies had the misfortune to be born live in Gosnell's clinic staffed in part by teenagers posing as licensed anesthetists. The bodies of the tiny victims were stored in a freezer in the basement of the clinic. Massof admitted that killing babies born alive was standard procedure at the clinic. He estimated that at least 100 babies were born alive in the clinic and had their necks snipped, but the beheadings were so routine that no one could determine the exact number.

Generally, such stories of horrific tragedies would be meat for the media grinder. However, you probably have not heard much if any reports from the great majority of news media. But thanks to the Family Research Council[2] and other conservative organizations and leaders, the story which the media have ignored or censored is gaining some attention.

Sherry West was another long-time employee of the clinic. She testified that she called the babies specimens "because it was easier to deal with mentally." West recalled one incident of a "screaming baby that really freaked me out...I can't describe it. It sounded like a little alien." She estimated the baby to have been between 18 and 24 inches long, one of the largest she had seen during abortion procedures at the Women's Medical Society clinic operated by Dr. Gosnell at that time.[3]

Perhaps you will recall President Clinton's statement that abortions in America should be "safe, legal, and rare." But his statement is just political sop to pacify the squeamish. The same sop to hide abortion's grisly reality was used by Alisa LaPolt Snow, the Florida Alliance of Planned Parenthood Affiliates lobbyist, in her testimony regarding a bill before the Florida legislature that would require abortionists to provide medical care to an infant who survives an abortion. In response to being asked what would Planned Parenthood do if a live baby were born on a table as a result of a botched abortion, Snow replied, "We believe that any decision that's made should be left up to the woman, her family, and the physician."[4]

Effectively, Planned Parenthood would leave the life or death decisions to the Dr. Gosnells of the world with regard to babies born alive after a botched abortion. Certainly the mother is in no emotional or physical shape to make a thoughtful and rational decision, and it is extremely unlikely that the doctor would consult the mother's family (generally not present anyway) as the baby is lying on the table and struggling for life. Apart from lack of sanitation and improper licensing, it appears that Planned Parenthood would have little to no issues with Dr. Gosnell's methods and decision-making process with regard to killing a live baby.

After January 22, 1973, the lives of unborn babies were no longer sacrosanct in America but placed in the hands of the deciders following the dictates of man's law. It is estimated that over fifty two million abortions have fallen victim to man's law in America from January 1973 through the end of 2008. These estimates came from direct surveys of abortionists by the Guttmacher Institute, once a research affiliate of Planned Parenthood. The number of abortions *per day*, if an average were calculated for the entire thirty-six year period, is over 3,900. This average number of abortions *per day* exceeds by over one thousand the number of lives lost in the terrorist attacks on September 11, 2001.[5]

Numbers and statistics are sterile things and do not convey the horror of a single abortion as shown above. Euphemisms, platitudes, and legal arguments about rights, privacy, and choice attempt to soften the picture or divert our attention from the horror surrounding the abortion of an unborn child.

Legalized abortion was the wedge used to split open the historic Western commitment to the dignity of human life. Now the humanist defenders of abortion continue attempts to drive the wedge deeper by sanctioning the taking of innocent life which effectively dispenses with concerns as to when human life begins. Thus, the abortionists' coveted right of choice is attempting to move across the line from abortion to infanticide. Doubters only need to listen to the testimony of Planned Parenthood spokeswoman Alisa LaPolt Snow.

Many scientists and academics would not stop at aborting babies born alive as the result of a botched abortion. Some such as Francis Crick, Nobel Prize winner for discovering the double helix in DNA, support screening newborns. For Crick, those that fail to meet certain health standards would be euthanized. Peter Singer, Princeton's

DeCamp Professor of Bioethics, believes that parents ought to be allowed to kill their disabled children. His reasoning is "...that they are 'nonpersons' until they are rational and self-conscious." Singer extends his reasoning to the "...killing of incompetent persons of any age if their families decide their lives are 'not worth living'."[6] Some would scoff that Crick's and Pinker's opinions are extreme and would never gain cultural acceptance. However, legalized abortion in America was also once thought extreme by most Americans.

Under the aegis of a majority of nine people on the United States Supreme Court, abortion became a choice in 1973, and unborn babies suddenly became mere fetal tissue with potentiality for human life. Contrast the Supreme Court's decision and humanism's convoluted defenses of abortion through fictitious rights and irrational moralizing about choice with the words of the Psalmist:

> You made all the delicate, inner parts of my body, and knit them together in my mother's womb. Thank you for making me so wonderfully complex! It is amazing to think about. Your workmanship is marvelous—and how well I know it. You were there while I was being formed in utter seclusion! You saw me before I was born and scheduled each day of my life before I began to breathe. Every day was recorded in your Book! [Psalm 139:13-16. Living Bible][7]

Oh!? It's a matter of sanitation and not murder. (5-10-13)

You may have followed the information (if you were able to find it in main stream media) flowing from the trial of Dr. Kermit Gosnell, the Philadelphia abortion clinic operator accused of murdering a woman and seven babies born alive. I have previously written about Gosnell and Planned Parenthood "Postcard from Hell." In that article I referred to the testimony of Alisa LaPolt Snow, the Florida Alliance of Planned Parenthood Affiliates lobbyist, regarding a bill before the Florida legislature that would require abortionists to provide medical care to an infant who survives an abortion. In response to being asked what would Planned Parenthood do if a live baby were born on a table as a result of a botched abortion, Snow replied, "We believe that any decision that's made should be left up to the woman, her family, and the physician."[1] With regard to her callus comment I said that, "Apart from lack of sanitation and improper licensing, it would appear that Planned Parenthood would have little to no issues with Dr. Gosnell's methods and decision-making process with regard to killing a live baby."

Referring to the heart-breaking and disturbing facts that occurred at the Philadelphia abortion clinic, Senator Mike Lee (R-Utah) attempted to have the Senate pass a sense of the Senate resolution that would have condemned illegal abortion practices. The resolution stated:

> Congress has the responsibility to investigate and conduct hearings on abortions performed near, at, or after viability in the United States, public policies regarding such, and evaluate the extent to which such abortions involve violations of the natural right to life of infants who are born alive or are capable of being born alive, and therefore are entitled to equal protection under the law.[2]

Given the facts coming out of the Philadelphia trial, it would appear that no reasonable person could object to Senator Lee's resolution. However, Senators Barbara Boxer (D-Calif.) and Richard Blumenthal (D-Conn.) have found a way. A favorite ploy of Congressional Democrats is to resort to obfuscation in blocking solutions for problems when those solutions are in conflict with their interests and agenda and those of their allies. The issue is effectively muddled by enlarging the problem and then seeking "comprehensive" solutions instead of addressing the pressing issue of the moment. One example of this Democratic obfuscation is illegal immigration in which securing America's borders is ignored or marginalized in favor of making it a part of a larger solution in dealing with "undocumented aliens."

Senator Blumenthal employed this tactic to defeat Senator Lee's resolution and propose his own resolution which states that *all* "incidents of abusive, unsanitary, or illegal health care practices should be condemned and prevented and the perpetrators should be prosecuted to the full extent of the law."[3]

Senator Lee sees clearly that the problem is immediate and of such compelling nature as to require Congressional action…it is about murdering born alive babies. But Notice Blumenthal's subtle footwork. For the Senator, it is not about murder but "abusive, unsanitary, or illegal *health care practices*." Yes, murder is abusive and illegal, but it can never be labeled a health care practice. It appears that Congressional Democrats, like their ally Planned Parenthood, cannot distinguish between abusive, unsanitary, or illegal health care practices and murder of born alive babies. While Congressional Democrats obfuscate and dither, little human beings are being killed.

Triage is a medical term. It means the sorting of and allocation of treatment to patients and especially battle and disaster victims to reflect the urgency of the patient's need in order to maximize the number of survivors. The culture wars rage and both born and unborn babies are battle victims dying in America's abortion mills. Senator Lee's proposal pointed to the urgency of the need in order to maximize the number of survivors. But for Congressional Democrats, murdering born alive babies does not rise to the level requiring triage. It is part of a larger problem that must be investigated, mulled, discussed, considered…ad infinitum. Meanwhile, millions of little babies will never see their first birthday.

Part III – Homosexuality

Equality – The homosexual agenda's Trojan horse in its battle for cultural acceptance (3-6-13)

"Trojan Horse" is a term used to refer to someone or something intended to undermine or subvert from within. The term derives from a tale of the Trojan War in which the Greeks built a giant wooden horse and hid forty soldiers inside. Then, the Greeks, appearing to have abandoned the fight and wooden horse, sailed their ships over the horizon. The unsuspecting Trojans pulled the horse into their city as a victory trophy. That night the hidden soldiers crept out of the horse, opened the gates for the Greek army that had returned under cover of darkness. The Greeks invaded and destroyed Troy, decisively ending the ten-year siege.

America is in the midst of a battle for supremacy in the central cultural vision of the nation. The battle between the biblical worldview and the humanistic worldview (under the guise of secularism, liberalism, and progressivism) is popularly known as the culture wars and has been ongoing far longer than ten years. One of those battles centers on the homosexual agenda's quest for legitimacy, respect, recognition, acceptance, and affirmation by American culture. The battle has escalated, and the homosexual agenda now requires the removal of all bans against gay marriage.[1]

This past week President Obama, citing the principle of equality that drove the nation's founding, spoke out against California's ban on gay marriage and said that the Supreme Court should strike it down.[2] This tactic has been very effective and successful is casting the proponents of homosexuality and same-sex marriage as commanding the moral high ground. They present themselves and their cause as morally superior to their opponents who are cast as villains in the morality play widely disseminated in popular culture. To oppose homosexuality is deemed the moral equivalence of racism, bigotry, ignorance, and homophobia. Those persons who are not accepting of homosexuality are labeled as intolerant.

But William Bennett identifies the humanists' perversion of the concept of tolerance. He calls it "...the disfigurement of the idea of tolerance at the hands of the agenda-pushers of our day...that would brand as bigots those of us who exercise our elementary responsibility…to make firm moral judgments in matters touching on marriage and the raising of our children." The humanists would force all to worship at the shrine of tolerance, but their price of admission is a tolerance rooted in moral relativism with no room for finding truth or judging something based on the concept of right and wrong. For those that fail to enter the humanist shrine, they become the objects of intolerant harassment through restrictions on free speech (speech codes), coercion, and intimidation. To the proponents of homosexuality, tolerance means forced acceptance, and such acceptance necessitates "normalization, validation, public legitimation, and finally public endorsement."[3]

Effectively, the advocates of gay marriage are using the Trojan horse of equality as a means to breach the gates of American culture built on the foundation of a biblical worldview. But the case against homosexuality entails far more than just the argument that it is contrary to the cultural traditions upon which America was founded. The accumulated weight of history speaks loudly against the homosexual agenda.

The ordered family structure is part of the human constitution, a universal truth, one of the permanent things, and exists in every known society. The family attains status within society—legitimacy, social identity, legal recognition, cultural tradition, and an estate. Humans have fashioned numerous methods by which to organize their societies, but the common link to all is the family unit—a father, a mother, and children living together in bonds of committed caring. It is the fundamental unit upon which societies are built.

By contrast, homosexuality is a disorganizing concept with regard to human relationships and ultimately disorganizing in building stable, enduring societies. Proponents wish to lift the status of homosexuality in society through its attainment of legitimacy, legal identity, and respect as a cultural tradition, a place at the table so to speak. These efforts involve court challenges to long-standing and culturally established norms, enactment of laws which favor the homosexual agenda and that diminish marriage, and promotion of homosexuality in the popular culture.

As marriage is the central organizing concept in society, it is critical for proponents of homosexuality to redefine what it means to be a family, and this has become the primary field of battle. There are two general conceptions of marriage in society. The first is that marriage is at its core about the children born of that marriage and by default is limited to heterosexual marriage relationships. The second concept held by the humanists is that marriage is essentially a private relationship.

This is from whence comes the attack by the proponents of the homosexual agenda. The legislative and legal efforts to redefine marriage to include homosexual couples of either gender, whether under the law or in culture, would weaken the idea of a mother and father for every child.

This is a seismic shift not only in how one views life but of culture itself. We have stated that culture is the central vision that binds, unifies, and gives direction to society, without which a society disintegrates. Individuals may think, feel, and act upon their personal and private liberties in any society as long as their actions fall *within the limits* of the laws that express the central vision of that society.

Heterosexual marriage is a universal, and the strength and unity provided by traditional marriage is the foundation of a strong and enduring society. Although traditional marriage is in broad disarray, as it is in most Western societies, that does not disprove the truth of the heterosexual marriage universal but rather speaks of the ravages caused by the ascending humanist worldview. Where traditional marriage declines, so do those societies decline that allow it to occur. America continues to invite cultural disintegration if we endorse homosexual marriage hidden within the Trojan horse of equality.[4]

Mr. Jones's Childish Things[1]

Part I (4-17-13)

Mike Jones, an associate editor of the *Tulsa World,* wrote the newspaper's April 14th Opinion section lead editorial titled, "Childish things – It's time to end the divide over gay marriage."[2] He is referring to 1 Corinthians 13:11 which says, "When I was a child, I spoke as a child, I understood as a child, I thought as a child, but when I became a man, I put away childish things."

Jones poses three general arguments in support of gay marriage. First, Jones attempts to label opposition to marriage between a same-sex couple a childish thing which results from prejudice and misunderstanding. Second, Jones believes that permitting gay marriage would be another step toward civil rights for all in the country. Third, Jones makes several biblical and religious arguments in support of gay marriage.

This article will demonstrate that Jones's statements and claims are untrue, misinterpretations, misleading, and are couched in assumptive language in which seemingly simple statements contain huge assumptions that are not true. In Part I we will discuss Jones's argument with regard to charges of prejudice and misunderstanding and the argument with regard to civil rights. In Part II we will address his arguments about presumed biblical/religious support of gay marriage.

> Argument #1 – Jones claims that opposition to gay marriage (and by inference, opposition to homosexuality in general) is a result of *prejudice and misunderstanding.*

There are two general conceptions of marriage in society. The first is that marriage can only be between a man and a woman which forms the basis for the ordered family structure. The strength and depth of spousal commitment and unity that derives from a marriage consummated by the reproductive act, whether intended for purposes of procreation or not, cannot be matched by any other relationship. The nature of the reproductive act in marriage is distinctly and intrinsically unitive. This ordered family structure is part of the human constitution, a universal truth, one of the permanent things, and is central in every known society. The family attains status within society—legitimacy, social identity, legal recognition, cultural tradition, and an estate. Humans have fashioned numerous methods by which to organize their societies, but the common link to all is the family unit—a father, a mother, and children living together in bonds of committed caring. It is the fundamental unit upon which societies are built.

By contrast, homosexuality is a disorganizing concept with regard to human relationships and ultimately disorganizing in building stable, enduring societies. However, proponents wish to lift the status of homosexuality in society through its attainment of legitimacy, legal identity, and respect as a cultural tradition, a place at the table so to speak. These efforts involve court challenges to long-standing and culturally established norms, enactment of laws which favor the homosexual agenda and that diminish marriage, and promotion of homosexuality in the popular culture. The basis for this opposing view is that marriage is essentially a private relationship, and because marriage is the central organizing concept in society, it is critical for proponents of homosexuality to redefine what it means to be a family. Success in the legislative and legal efforts to redefine marriage to include homosexual couples of either gender, whether under law or in culture, will cause a culture to decline and disintegrate as the ideal of a mother and father for every child is weakened. (See article: Thank you, Grace. You are worthy of your name.)

Therefore, the Christian's opposition to homosexuality is not about prejudice and misunderstanding as Mr. Jones would have us believe, but opposition is based on eternal truths and the commandments from the Bible. Mr. Jones and I will not agree as to who has the better argument because we have fundamentally different worldviews. The question is: which worldview is true? Undoubtedly, the weight of history supports the biblical worldview which is a reflection of truth received not only through biblical revelation to the ancient Hebrews and first century Christians but is also a reflection of those unchanging cultural universals built into God's creation and observed down through the ages.

> Argument #2 – Jones believes that permitting gay marriage would be another *step toward civil rights* for all in the country where "all men are created equal."

Jones argues that laws allowing civil union are not good enough, i.e., you are less than a citizen if you can't have a marriage ceremony and which means same-sex couples are "not worthy of rights held by the rest of us." It appears that Jones does not understand that people opposed to gay marriage are generally opposed to civil unions for the same reasons. Those reasons are based on a biblical worldview upon which the nation was founded (but that is another argument for another day which I am very willing to address).

Jones appeal is on the basis of equality, i.e., homosexuals have a civil right to marry as do heterosexuals. The usual defense of the pursuit of the humanist ideal of equality is that social harmony will be achieved because the nation is moving closer to the ideals upon which it was founded. However, such pursuit has the opposite effect. In America the pursuit of equality has resulted in the identification of an ever expanding array of social problems demanding governmental attention. Such attention is demanded because of the creation of "illusory rights" supposedly on par with the original Bill of Rights (in this case the right of homosexuals to marry).

But a culture that elevates these demands to the status of rights is doomed. In his book *Visions of Order*, Richard Weaver states that when a culture "... by ignorant popular attitudes or by social derangements" imposes a political concept that creates a different principle of ordering society contrary to universal truths, dissatisfactions arise because society has tampered with the "nature of things."[3]

The victim of this tampering is justice. The concept of justice is a universal truth, a thing of permanence that transcends the whole of man's time on this planet and pertains to all cultures. Ignoring corruptible man, the levelers of society admonish Justice to peek beneath her blindfold and act arbitrarily and capriciously to impose the latest standards dictated by the passions of the moment. Prescriptions of fairness, impartiality, and right action derived from an authority above the state and built up over the centuries are now considered quaint, failing to keep up with modern times, or just plain wrongheaded. In other words, the definition of justice has been changed by the humanists to fit their worldview. But no amount of humanist tinkering will change the heart of man with regard to a right understanding of right action in a civil society.

We will examine Mr. Jones's supposed biblical and religious support for gay marriage in Part II.

Part II (4-22-13)

Mike Jones, an associate editor of the *Tulsa World*, wrote the newspaper's April 14th Opinion section lead editorial titled, "Childish things – It's time to end the divide over gay marriage."[4] In Part I we discussed Jones's argument with regard to charges of prejudice and misunderstanding by those opposed to gay marriage and the argument with regard to civil rights. In Part II we will address his arguments about presumed biblical/religious support of gay marriage.

> Argument #3 – Jones's raises three *biblical/religious arguments* in support of gay marriage.

In his first religious argument, Jones cites the Apostle Paul who "believed that there is no need to get married because Jesus would return soon and the world would end... and that those on earth would better serve themselves if they remained celibate and directed their efforts to pleasing Jesus." However, Jones's statement contains both *factual and contextual errors*. These errors become evident without further comment when one looks at Paul's actual words and the context in which they were written.

> ...It is well for a man not to touch a woman. But because of the temptation to immorality, each man should have his own wife and each woman her own husband...I say this by way of concession, not of command. I wish that all were as I myself am. But each has his own special gift from God, one of one kind and one of another. To the unmarried and widows, it is well for them to remain single as I do. But if they cannot exercise self-control, they should marry. For it is better to marry than to be aflame with passion. [1 Corinthians 7: 1-2, 6-9. RSV]

Now if one takes Paul's statement as a license for homosexuals to marry, let's look at his words with regard to homosexuality.

> Therefore God gave them up in the lusts of their hearts to impurity, to the dishonoring of their bodies among themselves, because they exchanged the truth about God for a lie and worshiped and served the creature rather than the Creator, who is blessed forever! For this reason God gave them up to dishonorable passions. Their women exchanged natural relations for unnatural, and the men likewise gave up natural relations with women and were consumed with passion for one another, men committing shameless acts with men and receiving in their own persons the due penalty of their error." [Romans 1:24-27. RSV]

Jones's describes his second religious argument as simplistic but one which he says he cannot shake. Jones believes his simplistic arguments undermine biblical reasons for opposition to homosexuality. However, his arguments *contain huge assumptions which are false*. First, Jones asks if God made man in His own image where does that leave homosexuals. In other words, did He make a few mistakes when He made homosexuals? The assumptive language is that God made homosexuals the way they are. Therefore, God made a mistake *or* He created homosexuals that way as a reflection of His image. Neither is true.

Let's quickly dispose of the first question. God does not make mistakes. If he did, he wouldn't be all-knowing and all-powerful. In essence, he wouldn't be God. Second, to say that God made a mistake means that we recognized something He missed, and that is absurd. Third, we can't know the mind of God apart from His revelations to us about Himself. That revelation tells us that He does not make mistakes, "He is the rock, *his work is perfect*: for all his ways are judgment: a God of truth and without iniquity, just and right is he." [Deuteronomy 32:4. KJV]

If God didn't make a mistake, then that leaves us with Jones's assumption that God made homosexuals the way they are, i.e., they were born that way. Therefore, we are told we must accept them *and* their inborn inclinations as equals in society. In support of this assumption, proponents of homosexuality often cite various scientific studies that indicate sexual orientation is a matter of genetics, i.e., sexual orientation is involuntary, immutable, and rooted in nature. Thus, moral distinctions between homosexual and heterosexual behavior would be invalid.

The first response is to state that science has not proven that homosexuality is inborn. Many of the studies that purport to do so have proven to be flawed and brought into question by other studies showing the opposite is true. Time and space does not permit an extensive examination of this area, but what we can say at this point in time is that science has not proven that sexual orientation is a matter of genetics.

But for sake of argument let's assume that homosexuality in some cases was found to have a genetic basis (either causal or predisposition), then proponents of the homosexual agenda would argue that moral distinctions are invalid as it relates to differences between homosexuality and heterosexuality. But that is not a valid argument for neither causation nor predisposition *justifies* cultural acceptance. For example, some people are genetically prone to alcoholism. Another study established a genetic link to criminal behavior. But such genetic links do not justify immoral behavior whether it is alcoholism, criminal activity, or homosexual practices. People are not slaves to their passions, desires, and predispositions as humanists would have us believe. Some people will struggle with those forces more than others, but people have the ability to choose their behavior.

Jones also asks if homosexuality makes a person less human. Absolutely not—homosexuality does not make them less human. God created every human being, and He loved each one so much that He gave His Son on the cross for every person's sin (including the homosexual) to make it possible for them to be in right relationship with Him. But man has a free will, and many freely choose to reject that invitation and live a life of disobedience to His commands whether that disobedience is adultery, murder, theft, or being actively engaged in a homosexual lifestyle.

Jones's third religious argument is based on 1 Corinthians 13:13: "And now abideth faith, hope and charity, these three; but the greatest of these is charity." [KJV] Jones says, "That could go a long way in solving this difference of opinion." In other words, charity (love) trumps all. If we but love, all will be well.

It is one thing to disagree with the Bible's teaching on homosexuality or to reject biblical authority altogether in defending homosexual practices. However, it is blatantly disingenuous to revise or twist biblical teachings in order to excuse homosexual practices when the biblical record is unequivocally clear in its universal condemnation of homosexuality. Effectively, Jones is arguing that the basic thrust of Christ's teachings is that in the end we must place love above all other considerations. Implicit in this humanistic belief is that basic doctrines are inherently divisive and must be pushed aside in favor of the non-judgmental love and acceptance of people as they are. In other words such narrow and rigid doctrines as to how one must live are divisive and contrary to the inclusiveness which is demonstrated by the lives and teachings of Jesus and His disciples. However, this argument is clearly false and strikes at the foundation of the Christian worldview regarding mankind's Fall and man's need for redemption as chronicled from Genesis through Revelation.

Before we leave this argument, let's examine the sincerity of Jones's call for love that "...could go a long way in solving this difference of opinion." Apparently, Jones does believe that the same tolerance and love is needed when it comes to accepting the motives of Christians with regard to loving the sinner and hating the sin. "I don't believe the sincerity of that for a second. It's more often hate the sin, punish the sinner."

In summary, heterosexual marriage is a universal, and the strength and unity provided by it is the foundation of a strong and enduring society. Where traditional marriage is in broad disarray, as it is in most Western societies, it does not disprove the truth of the marriage universal but rather speaks of the ravages caused by the ascending humanist worldview. Where traditional marriage declines, so do those societies decline that allow it to occur.

Is God Out of Touch with Mainstream Views? (4-25-14)

For many in the media establishment, Easter is a great time to talk about religion, but for ABC News Easter was an opportunity to showcase the perceived decline of evangelical influence in America. One of the reasons given was Christianity's supposed intolerance with regard to homosexuality and same-sex marriage in America. Reverend Franklin Graham, president of the Billy Graham Evangelistic Association and son of its founder, and Cokie Roberts of ABC News were among guests on ABC's "This Week" panel whose topic was "Are Evangelicals Out of Touch with Mainstream Views?"[1]

In response to a question from panel moderator Martha Raddatz of ABC News, Graham reiterated his strong opposition to same-sex marriage. Graham assured the audience that any gay person can go to heaven if they will repent. However, he stated that gays, like others in adultery or some other type of sin, cannot stay in their sin and be accepted by God. He said, "Franklin Graham is a sinner, and I'm no better than a gay person. I'm a sinner, but I've been forgiven, and I've turned from my sins. For any person that's willing to repent in turn, God will forgive."

Ms. Raddatz responded that Graham's view appeared to be at odds with dramatic changes in the attitudes of many Americans as reflected by various polls. She pointed to a recent ABC poll that indicated 59 percent of Americans now approve of same-sex marriage and 61 percent approve of gay adoption. For those under age 30, 75 percent approve of same-sex marriage including 43 percent of evangelicals under 30.

ABC News' Cokie Roberts suggested reasons for this change in the attitudes of Americans regarding homosexuality and same-sex marriage.

> The reason the numbers have changed so fast and so dramatically on this question of gay marriage is because everybody in America now has experience with someone who is gay. People have come out of the closet and said, 'I am your brother. I am your sister. I am your cousin. I am your friend.' And then they have seen these families raising children and see these loving families.[2]

Ms. Roberts' comments and Ms. Raddatz's recitation of the results of recent polls imply that evangelicals are wasting political capital through their opposition to gay marriage because *they are out of touch with mainstream views*. Ms. Raddatz's poll numbers reflect the results of just one of the battles in the continuing secularization of America over the last 75 years. However, I strongly disagree with Ms. Roberts' assertion that Americans' change in attitude regarding homosexuality and same-sex marriage is because Americans have come to understand and respect homosexuals and the rightness of allowing same-sex marriage. To the contrary, the change of attitudes are the result of a three-generation slide into post-Christian and post-modern worldviews in which a large number of Americans have abandoned Christianity as the standard of truth and morality and have embraced a relativistic view of truth in which the barometer of right and wrong always points in the direction of popular opinion.

The assumptive language posed in "Are Evangelicals Out of Touch with the Mainstream Views" implies the highest importance to which ABC News attaches to being in touch with mainstream views and therefore being politically relevant. Of course ABC News is an entity that feeds on ratings and therefore must seek the mainstream and determine how to be in the middle of it.

It would be interesting to hear Raddatz' and Roberts' response to the following question. If evangelicals are deemed to be out of touch with mainstream views, by inference could they not also say that *God is out of touch with mainstream views*? Of course, this is a rhetorical question, and the answer must be found in either the opinions of man or God's word. To illustrate, we look to the biblical truth with regard to God's condemnation of homosexuality.

> For the wrath of God is revealed from heaven against all ungodliness and wickedness of men who by their wickedness suppress the *truth*...Therefore, God gave them up in the lusts of their hearts to impurity, to the dishonoring of their bodies among themselves, because they exchanged the *truth* about God for a lie and worshiped and served the creature rather than the Creator, who is blessed for ever! For this reason God gave them up to dishonorable passions. Their women exchanged natural relations for unnatural, and the men likewise gave up natural relations with women and were consumed with passion for one another, men committing shameless acts with men and receiving in

their own person the due penalty for their error. [Romans 1: 18, 24-27. RSV] [emphasis added]

Based on God's view of homosexuality, it would seem that Roberts and Raddatz must also label God as being out of touch with mainstream views. But God doesn't have a view. He is God, the great I AM, and Creator of the universe including the laws of nature and laws of human nature. God is truth, and how feeble are man's attempts to distort that truth revealed in His creation, the biblical revelation, and His image stamped on His special creation called man.

ABC News and much of secular media continue chipping away at the Christian principles upon which the nation was founded. Thirty-five years ago Malcolm Muggeridge identified the source of the attack on Western civilization (Christendom).

> Previous civilizations have been overthrown from without by the barbarian hordes. Christendom has dreamed up its own dissolution in the minds of its own intellectual elite. Our barbarians are home products, indoctrinated at the public expense, urged on by the *media* systematically stage by stage, diminishing Christendom, depreciating and deprecating all its values.[3] [emphasis added]

Rather than reinforcing Christian principles, morals, and manners upon which the nation was founded, the humanistic worldview of modern mass media molds public opinion by setting the agenda and influencing what people think about. From such manipulation has come a cultural shift as mass media's humanistic worldview has ascended while the Christian worldview is marginalized and demeaned through substantial and constant attack.[4]

So what should the evangelical do in the face of a rising tide of secular humanism in America? We take our instruction from the Apostle Paul's exhortations to Timothy.

> ...preach the word, be urgent *in season and out of season*, convince, rebuke, and exhort, be unfailing in patience and in teaching. For the time is coming when people will not endure sound teaching, but having itching ears they will accumulate for themselves teachers to suit their own and wander into myths. As for you, always be steady, endure suffering, do the

work of an evangelist, fulfill your ministry. [2 Timothy 4:2-5. RSV] [emphasis added]

In other words, evangelicals must evangelize whether they are in the mainstream or in the marginalized minority.

Does God lie? (5-16-14)

Recently, the U.S. Court of Appeals for the 10th Circuit heard arguments regarding the constitutionality of Oklahoma's ban on same-sex marriage. However, in a guest editorial in the Tulsa World,[1] the Reverends Justin Alan Lindstrom and Robin R. Meyers said that regardless of the outcome of the deliberations of the 10th Circuit, the case has already been settled by a different judge—meaning the God of the Bible. The Reverends said that, "...marriage equality is a fundamental right for all Oklahomans...The freedom to marry for all couples *fits squarely into the tenets of our faith, the teachings of our church* and reflects values of love and compassion that sustains our communities and congregations." In other words, same-sex couples have the right to marry and that right does not conflict with the tenets of the Christian faith as revealed in the Bible. However, the Apostle Paul's words are indisputable with regard to God's condemnation of homosexuality.

> For the wrath of God is revealed from heaven against all ungodliness and wickedness of men who by their wickedness suppress the *truth*...Therefore, God gave them up in the lusts of their hearts to impurity, to the dishonoring of their bodies among themselves, because they exchanged the *truth* about God for a lie and worshiped and served the creature rather than the Creator, who is blessed for ever! For this reason God gave them up to dishonorable passions. Their women exchanged natural relations for unnatural, and the men likewise gave up natural relations with women and were consumed with passion for one another, men committing shameless acts with men and receiving in their own person the due penalty for their error." [Romans 1:18, 24-27. RSV]

Therefore, we see that the Reverends' view of same-sex marriage *does not* fit squarely into the tenets of Christian faith. It is one thing to disagree with the Bible's teaching on homosexuality or to reject biblical authority altogether in defending homosexual practices. However, it is blatantly disingenuous to ignore, revise, or twist biblical teachings in order to excuse homosexual practices when the biblical record is unequivocally clear in its universal condemnation of homosexuality. However, the Reverends assume their beliefs supersede biblical commandments regarding homosexuality (and by inference same-sex marriage) on the grounds that those beliefs are "...*grounded in love and acceptance of everyone.*"

Love

The Reverends beliefs ultimately must place love above basic and clear biblical doctrines which are brushed aside in favor of non-judgmental love and acceptance of people *as they are*. God is willing to accept and save people as they are, but God was not willing to leave them that way. That is the reason He sent His son Jesus and allowed man to nail Him to a cross. God could not have fellowship with sinful man, and the crucifixion of sinless Christ for man's sin made a way for man to be restored to a right relationship with Him.

I am a sinner and my sin is no less sinful than that of a homosexual. We stand as equals before God and are given a choice. I am a sinner saved by Christ. I have repented of my sin and have been forgiven. Not only have I repented of past sins, I have turned from my sins. Homosexuals can repent, be saved, and fellowship with God for eternity. However, to do so, they cannot stay in their sin. God does not approve of homosexuality, and He will not contradict or overlook His own commandments regarding homosexuality by coating them with a liberal layer of "love and compassion." Man has a choice to accept or reject God's love. The creation of man with a free will meant the possibility of rejection of God and His love. In other words, free will and the potential for rejection of God was the penalty for the possibility of love.

Acceptance

Must Christians also unreservedly accept the homosexual as implied by the ministers? Christians must love the sinner, but it is not a blind love that overlooks sin. Although Christians should reach out in love to the homosexual, we cannot accept homosexuals into fellowship *as fellow believers* if they continue in their sin nor can we condone the sin of homosexuality by passing laws that allow same-sex marriage. We find our example in the Apostle Paul's chastisement of the Corinthians for allowing immorality to reside in the midst of their fellowship.

> It is actually reported that there is immorality among you, and of a kind that is not found even among pagans; for a man is living with his father's wife. And you are arrogant! Ought you not rather to mourn? Let him who has done this be removed from among you. [1 Corinthians 5:1-2. RSV]

Homosexuals must be welcomed into our churches if they are seeking truth and escape from their bondage to sin. But in his second letter to the Corinthians, Paul again warned against communion with unbelievers.

> Do not be mismated with unbelievers. For what partnership have righteousness and iniquity? Or what fellowship has light with darkness? [2 Corinthians 6:14. RSV]

Does God lie?

If the Reverends believe that God accepts everyone including partners in a same-sex marriage and persons engaged in homosexual conduct because of His boundless love, the ministers have effectively labeled God as a liar. But God cannot condemn homosexuality as He has throughout His word and at the same time embrace the homosexual that *persists* in rebelling against His commandments. If He does so as the Reverends imply, then God would be guilty of a lie. But Paul said that God never lies. [Titus 1:2. RSV]

God created heterosexual marriage as a cultural universal, and the strength and unity provided by it is the foundation of a strong and enduring society. Where traditional marriage is in broad disarray, as it is in most Western societies, it does not disprove the truth of the heterosexual marriage universal but rather speaks of the ravages caused by the ascending humanist worldview. Where traditional marriage declines, so do those societies decline that allow it to occur.

Humanism's equality handcuffs freedom and violates the Constitution (2-6-15)

Until recently most Americans had never heard of the highly respected Atlanta Fire Chief Kelvin Cochran. That changed dramatically when Atlanta Mayor Kasim Reed fired Cochran because of his religious beliefs. The facts behind the firing are straightforward. Cochran self-published a book in 2013 titled *Who Told You That You Were Naked?* One paragraph in the book labeled homosexuality as "a perversion." After the mayor learned of the book, he initially placed Cochran on a thirty-day suspension beginning November 24, 2014.[1] The mayor denied knowing that Cochran had written a book prior to his suspension. However, Cochran stated that he had given the mayor a copy of the book in January 2014, and that the mayor promised to read it on an upcoming trip. Cochran also said the director of Atlanta's ethics office had given him permission to write the book and to mention in his biography that he was the city's fire chief.[2]

Following the one-month suspension, the mayor fired Cochran just as he was preparing to return as head of the fire department. Defending his decision to fire Cochran the mayor stated, "This is not about religious freedom. This is not about free speech. Judgment is the basis of the problem." Prior to Cochran's firing, the mayor publicly condemned the fire chief on his official Facebook page. "I profoundly disagree with and am deeply disturbed by the sentiments expressed in the paperback regarding the LGBT community. I will not tolerate discrimination of any kind within my administration." Georgia Equality Executive Director Jeff Graham stated that Cochran's "anti-gay" views could result in a hostile work environment.[3]

Cochran said that the comments regarding homosexuality were contained in less than one-half page of a 160 page book he wrote for a men's Bible study group at his Baptist church. He stated that the reference to homosexuality was made in the larger context that sexual activity was designed to be between a man and a woman in holy matrimony. Outside of that, any other sexual activity including homosexuality is sin.[4] Further, Cochran defended his beliefs and his right to express himself.

> The LGBT members of our community have a right to be able to express their views and convictions about sexuality and deserve to be respected for their position

without hate or discrimination. But Christians also have a right to express our belief regarding our faith and be respected for our position without hate and without discrimination. In the United States, no one should be vilified, hated or discriminated against for expressing their beliefs.[5]

In an Opinion Page piece by *The New York Times*, it was not a surprise to find that the newspaper supported Cochran's firing. The *Times* Editorial Board stated that Cochran's claim of religious discrimination had it backwards.

> It is, as Mr. Reed said at a news conference, about 'making sure that we have an *environment* in government where everyone, no matter who they love, can come to work from 8 to 5:30 and do their job and then go home without fear of being discriminated against...It should not matter that the investigation found no evidence that Mr. Cochran had mistreated gays or lesbians. His position as a high-level public servant makes his remarks especially problematic, and requires that he be *held to a different standard*. The First Amendment already protects religious freedom...Nobody can tell Mr. Cochran what he can or cannot believe. If he wants to *work as a public official*, however, he may not foist his religious views on other city employees who have the right to a boss who does not speak of them as second-class citizens.[6] [emphasis added]

It appears that the *Times* Editorial Board subordinates religious freedom and the practice thereof to the whims of a hypersensitive workplace environment and totally extinguishes freedom of religion and speech for high-level public servants and governmental officials.

Should the *Times* Editorial Board have been present with the patriots at Valley Forge on March 10, 1778, their radical egalitarian sensibilities would have experienced great shock perhaps resulting in terminal apoplexy because of a high governmental official's supposed flagrant discrimination against one Lieutenant Enslin as a result of his attempt at homosexual actions.

> Lieutt. Enslin of Colo. Malcom's Regiment tried for attempting to commit sodomy, with John Monhort a

soldier; Secondly, For Perjury in swearing to false Accounts, found guilty of the charges exhibited against him, being breaches of 5th Article 18th Section of the Articles of War and do sentence him to be dismiss'd the service with Infamy. His Excellency the Commander in Chief [George Washington] approves the sentence and with Abhorrence and Detestation of such Infamous Crimes orders Lieutt. Enslin to be drummed out of Camp tomorrow morning by all the Drummers and Fifers in the Army never to return; The Drummers and Fifers to attend on the Grand parade at Guard mounting for that Purpose.[7]

Should the Editorial Board still be in doubt as to Washington's Christian beliefs, less than two months after Lieutenant Enslin's disgrace Washington issued these orders to his troops at Valley Forge.

While we are zealously performing the duties of good citizens and soldiers, we certainly ought not to be inattentive to the higher duties of religion. To the distinguished character of Patriot, it should be our highest Glory to laud the more distinguished Character of Christian.[8]

How did America arrive at such a state of affairs that the extreme egalitarian views of humanistic governmental officials equate one's Christian beliefs and the sharing of those beliefs with the creation of a hostile work environment? Even though the fire chief was not found guilty of mistreatment of homosexuals in or out of government, Cochran was deemed guilty because of his status as a public official who expressed religious beliefs that were contrary to the beliefs of the homosexual community. It is ludicrous for *The New York Times* to label Cochran's firing as anything other than a blatant violation of Cochran's First Amendment rights which apply to *every* American including public servants and officials of whatever rank or station.

Equality, rightly applied, is equality before God and the law. However, the humanist understanding of equality is synonymous with a rapacious egalitarianism that imposes regimentation and leveling. This twisted understanding of human equality places special emphasis on social, political, and economic rights and privileges and *focuses* on the removal of any imagined or invented inequalities among humankind. This focus results in a forced leveling of society which leads to socialism and ultimately loss of freedom.

Driving religious beliefs from the public square does not enhance but destroys religious freedom in order to attain the egalitarian ideal. Because of a growing humanistic worldview among the leadership of the institutions of American life, the nation's central cultural vision is under assault from humanists' surgically precise efforts to separate church and state and to sweep away all evidence of our Christian cultural heritage. Even our constitutionally guaranteed freedoms of religion and speech are no longer sacrosanct from such assaults. For humanists, religious freedom means only freedom to spread the humanist orthodoxy and worship their god of equality.

Part IV – Education

Education in America

Part I – America's *Original* Common Core Curriculum (7-26-13)

There has been considerable discussion in the press and halls of education with regard to The Common Core Curriculum Standards Initiative (CCSSI)[1], an attempt by the educational establishment to standardize and strengthen educational standards and expectations at the elementary and secondary levels. Quoting from the Initiative's English language arts standards, "As a natural outgrowth of meeting the charge to define college and career readiness, the Standards also lay out *a vision of what it means to be a literate person in the twenty-first century.*"[2] In developing core curriculum standards, it would be worthwhile for the curriculum designers to spend some time reviewing *what it meant to be a literate person in America from the arrival of the Pilgrims in 1620 to the beginning of the twentieth century.* A few excerpts from such a review will reveal the heart of America's *Original* Common Core Curriculum and its role in the creation of the greatest country in the history of the world.

- Harvard University was founded in 1636 under the following Rules and Precepts: "Let every student be plainly instructed, and earnestly pressed to consider well, the main end of his life and studies, is to know God and Jesus Christ which is eternal life (John 17:3) and therefore lay Christ at the bottom, as the only foundation of all sound knowledge and learning."[3]

- *The New England Primer* first published about 1690 was the only elementary textbook in America for a half century, retained its central role in primary education until 1800 and continued as a principal beginning textbook throughout the 19th century. The eighty-page Puritan primer contained lessons in the alphabet, spelling, short religious instruction, commands to piety and faith, and Bible questions.[4]

- Gouverneur Morris was a signor of the U.S. Constitution. Having been credited as the author of the preamble and having written large sections of the document, he was called the Penman of the Constitution. Morris was a gifted scholar and held a Master's degree from King's College (now Columbia College of Columbia University). Morris's views of education reflected those of his fellow Founding Fathers when he wrote, "Religion is the only solid basis of good morals; therefore education should teach the precepts of religion, and the duties of man towards God."[5]

- Thomas Jefferson called Samuel Adams "...truly the man of the Revolution...for depth of purpose, zeal, and sagacity, no man in Congress exceeded, if any equaled, Sam Adams." Samuel Adams was noted for his piety (professed and real) and had deep religious convictions. His views on education paralleled those of many other Founding Fathers. "Let divines and philosophers, statesmen and patriots, unite their endeavors to renovate the age, by impressing the minds of men with the importance of educating their little boys and girls, of inculcating in the minds of youth the fear and love of the Deity...in short of leading them to the study and practice of exalted virtues of the Christian System, which will happily tend to subdue the turbulent passions of Men..."[6]

- Thomas Jefferson designed of the first plan of education for the District of Columbia which used the Bible and a hymnal as its principal texts for teaching reading to students.[7]

- Noah Webster was a descendent of William Bradford of Plymouth Plantation. His 1828 *American Dictionary of the English Language* was produced when the American home, church, and school were established upon a biblical and a patriotic basis. The biblical worldview of Webster's dictionary produced during the first half of the 19th century stands as a testament to the continuing power and force of the Second Great Awakening. Webster held a belief in the importance of intertwining the Christian religion with a free government. "In my view, the Christian religion is the most important and one of the first things in which all children, under a free government, ought to be instructed…No truth is more evident to my mind than that the Christian religion must be the basis of any government intended to secure the rights and privileges of a free people."[8]

- Between 1836 and 1920, 120 million copies of the *McGuffey's Reader* textbooks were sold. The *Readers* hailed American exceptionalism, manifest destiny, and America as God's country although in more secularized terms beginning with the 1879 version. In a 1927 *Saturday Evening Post* article titled "That Guy McGuffey," Hugh Fullerton wrote that, "For seventy-five years his (McGuffey's) system and his books guided the minds of four-fifths of the school children of the nation in their taste for literature, in their morality, in their social development and next to the Bible in their religion."[9]

- As the nineteenth century neared its end, there was an extraordinary and dramatic struggle by the forces of humanistic progressive education to wrest power from conservative Protestantism in American education. The National Education Association responded to this struggle with a statement of protest in 1892: "…if the study of the Bible is to be excluded from all state schools; if the inculcation of the principles of Christianity is to have no place in the daily program; if the worship of God is to form no part of the general exercise of those public elementary schools; then the good of the state would be better served by restoring all schools to church control."[10]

This cursory review of American education between 1620 and 1900 conclusively illustrates that the Bible (along with supporting books with a biblical worldview such as *The New England Primer* and *McGuffey's Reader*) was the central text and provided the standards for the *original* common core curriculum in educating American children. But the influence of the Bible in education was merely a derivative of the pervasive biblical worldview that permeated every facet of American life including the law, politics, trade and business dealings, science, social relationships, and culture in general. So complete was this domination at the time of the American Revolution that 95% or more of the population held the biblical worldview, whether a professing Christian or not. So it is not surprising that the Bible and other books reflecting a biblical worldview were the standards for the original common core curriculum and formed the foundation of American education. In Part II, an examination will be made of the destruction of the original biblically-based common core curriculum in American education by the substitution of humanistic progressive education philosophies of John Dewey and others.

Part II – Secularization of America Education (8-2-13)

As we have seen in Part I, education at all levels in North America was an indisputably Christian enterprise from the arrival of the Pilgrims in 1620 to the early part of the 20th century. The Bible and other books reflecting a biblical worldview were the foundation of American education, that is, the original common core curriculum. In Part II, we will describe the destruction of the original biblically-based common core curriculum by the humanistic progressive education philosophies of John Dewey and others.

The churches were the principal founders of the first colleges and universities in the American colonies and whose purpose was for the training of pastors. During the eighteenth and nineteenth centuries, colleges and universities expanded their academic portfolios, and the cultural ties between the Church and higher education gradually weakened. However, the weakening ties generated little cultural controversy because the explicitly Christian and generally conservative ends of education were understood by the great majority of Americans. Nevertheless, as the end of the nineteenth century approached, "…the breach separating the universities and the churches widened suddenly and culminated in the extraordinarily rapid and dramatic 'disestablishment' of conservative Protestantism from North American academic life from about 1890 to 1930."[11]

John Dewey's admirers called him the greatest American philosopher and the philosopher of American democracy. His views and teachings during his exceptionally long career would influence many facets of American life—art, knowledge, education, morals, politics, science, and religion—and publication of his writings spanned seventy years. The breadth of change during Dewey's lifetime is astounding. Dewey was a grocer's son born in Burlington, Vermont, on October 20, 1859, while James Buchanan was president, a year and a half before Abraham Lincoln's inauguration. With remembrances of the Civil War, he would live to see two world wars and the atomic age by the time of his death in 1952, just five years before Sputnik would herald the beginning of the space age.[12]

Dewey's progressive educational agenda was framed by child-centeredness and psychology. Children were taught that an understanding of morality flowed from reason based on experience and that there was no one morality good for all societies. Reason through science became the determinant of what was good for society and replaced character education as modeled by Judeo-Christian morality. In other words, the standards of the new morality flowed from the dictates of science and reason. In Dewey's philosophy, there is no absolute, no transcendent being, no room for supernatural religion, and nothing beyond the possibilities of concrete human experience. Value and meaning in life exist in humanity and flow from individual and collective self-realization through civilization.

Psychology, published by Dewey in 1896, was the first American textbook on the "revised" subject of education. It became the most widely read, quoted, and used textbook in American schools of education. Beginning with his twenty-five-year affiliation with Columbia University's Teachers' College, Dewey's "...writings shaped the 20th Century U.S. curriculum..."[13] His ideas on education would extensively permeate American education, and the devastating results are still being felt today.

One measure of John Dewey's impact on American education can be judged by the level of criticism that was provoked by his teachings. In March 1959, President Eisenhower severely condemned Dewey's philosophy: "Educators, parents, and students must be continuously stirred up by the defects in our education system. They must be induced to abandon the educational path that, rather blindly, they have been following as a result of John Dewey's teachings."[14] For an individual deceased for seven years to have his work and philosophy receive the stinging rebuke of a sitting president, that individual's influence on American life, for good or ill, must be viewed as substantial.

Richard Weaver succinctly and superbly describes the disastrous consequences of progressive education's revolt against the traditional idea of education.

> Knowledge, which has been the traditional reason for instituting schools, does *not* exist in any absolute or binding sense. The mind, which has always been regarded as the distinguishing possession of the human race, is now viewed as a tyrant which has been denying the rights of the body as a whole. It is to be "democratized" or reduced to an equality with the rest. Discipline, that great shaper of mind and body, is to be discarded because it carries elements of fear and compulsion. The student is to be prepared *not* to save his soul, or to inherit the wisdom and usages of past civilizations, or even to get ahead in life, but to become a member of a utopia resting on a *false view of both nature and man*.[15] (emphasis added)

For almost one hundred years, a major conflict has grown between the dominant American culture including the beliefs and values upon which the nation was founded and the ascendant progressive theory of education and its proponents. This conflict arose because of a systematic and successful attempt by a radical minority of educators and their allies to undermine through the educational system American society's traditions and beliefs. Of all American institutions under assault, the subversion of American culture through the humanistic educational establishment's progressive movement represents the greatest single threat to the central cultural vision upon which the nation was founded.

Part III – Common Core State Standards – Educational excellence or secular cultural conformity? (8-9-13)

The Common Core State Standards Initiative (CCSSI) is a state-led effort that established a single set of educational standards for kindergarten through 12th grade in English language arts and mathematics that states voluntarily adopt to standardize and strengthen educational standards and expectations. The nation's governors and education commissioners, through their representative organizations, the National Governors Association (NGA) and the Council of Chief

State School Officers (CCSSO), led the development of the Common Core State Standards and continue to lead the Initiative. The mission of the Common Core State Standards Initiative (CCSSI) reads as follows:

> The Common Core State Standards provide a *consistent, clear understanding of what students are expected to learn*, so teachers and parents know what they need to do to help them. The standards are designed to be *robust and relevant to the real world*, reflecting the knowledge and skills that our young people need for success in *college and careers*. With American students fully prepared for the future, our communities will be best positioned to compete successfully in the global economy.[16] (emphasis added)

The Common Core Curriculum is divided into two main sections: mathematical standards and English language arts standards (ELA). Mathematical standards appear very straight forward and of little cause for concern. Standards set for the ELA are not as straight forward. Standards are set for the ELA but also for literacy in *history/social studies, science, and technical subjects*. Quoting from the ELA standards, "As a natural outgrowth of meeting the charge to define college and career readiness, the *Standards also lay out a vision of what it means to be a literate person in the twenty-first century.*"[17]

This all sounds very noble and progressive. But for many in and out of the educational realm, there is a general trepidation or uneasiness when it comes to embracing curriculum standards fabricated by a centralized quasi-governmental authority or coalition of authorities. A thoughtful examination of the mission statement of the Common Core State Standards Initiative reveals three significant concerns.

First, who decides *what students are expected to learn* in the areas of English language arts, history, social studies, and science? These subjects by their very nature deal with worldview and yield themselves to both political and cultural manipulation. To whom do we entrust to define the *standards that lay out the vision of what it means to be a literate person*? To defuse resistance in adopting the standards, the CCSSI states:

> It is important to note that the 6–12 literacy standards in history/social studies, science, and technical subjects are not meant to replace content standards in those

areas but rather to *supplement them*. States may incorporate these standards into their standards for those subjects *or adopt them* as content area literacy standards.[18]

But a close reading of the CCSSI statement does not diminish those concerns of political and cultural manipulation in spite of assurances otherwise (e.g., radical interpretation and application of the so-called separation of church and state directives). Effectively, participating states must add the core curriculum standards as a supplement *or* adopt core curriculum standards as a replacement. But what if core curriculum standards are contrary to the existing standards desired by the citizens of that state? There appears to be no choice for states but to introduce standards that are in *conflict* with existing ELA standards (including history/social studies, science, and technical subjects) chosen by the citizens of that state. How long will it be before "supplement" becomes "replace"? Certainly the states do not have to participate in the CCSSI, but as we have seen in many areas of disagreement between federal and state authority, the federal government has the power of the purse strings to enforce their demands on rebellious state governments even though a state's participation is supposedly voluntary with regard to participating in the Initiative. In addition to federal pressure, additional pressures will be applied to non-compliant and non-participating states from the educational and business organizations that substantially align themselves with the dominant progressive education juggernaut within those states.

Second, the standards are to be *robust (strong) and relevant to the real world*.[19] This assumptive language is loaded with meanings that may not be fully comprehended by or acceptable to most people. For most educational professionals the reference to the "real world" means the humanistic progressive philosophy of education in which children are taught that morality flows from reason (based on experience) and science and that there is no one morality good for all societies. John Dewey summarized the essence of this philosophy, "The religious is emancipated from religion by transferring the object of our 'idealizing imagination' from the supernatural to 'natural human relations' or the 'comprehensive community'." In Dewey's religious framework, value and meaning exist in humanity and does not flow from a transcendent God. Dewey's religion focuses on humanity rather than God, and the goal of that religion is not a relationship with God but individual and collective self-realization through civilization.[20] It will be the educational professionals indoctrinated with the humanistic progressive educational philosophy who will craft and implement the common core curriculum standards and not the governors or legislative bodies of the participating states. After a mere glance at the existing standards and policies of the educational hierarchy, it becomes a foregone conclusion that the new CCSSI standards will not include a biblical worldview.

Third, the entire scope and purpose of education is directed toward "the knowledge and skills that our young people need for success in *college and careers*".[21] But one must make a distinction between instruction and education. A body of knowledge may be known by simple instruction, that is, the transmission of facts and principles. But historically education encompasses a far broader mission. Education should not only contain instruction but training for a way of life. Training for life must involve recognition of the central authority—the central vision—the collective consciousness in which the world is viewed. In America up until the beginning of the twentieth century, this meant a central authority derived from a biblical worldview. Therefore, the goal of education should involve far more than preparation for college and careers. The common core curriculum standards will not only perpetuate exclusion of the biblical worldview from education but in the long term result in even greater if not open hostility to that worldview as a basis for training for a way of life.

As America moves toward adoption and implementation of the common core curriculum standards, we must realize what the future holds. Schools will be required to teach things that are in opposition to the worldview of our Founders and most Americans today. That is happening now to a great extent, but there is still some restraint exerted by the states and local school districts. As national core curriculum standards are implemented, those restraints will be gone and the humanistic worldview of society's "conditioners" (as C. S. Lewis called them) will reign supreme in bureaucratic halls of the state capitols and Washington, D.C. infested with these conditioners. The national core curriculum standards may appear innocent at their inception, but the standards will evolve into something far from what Americans believe and want with regard to the education of their children.

The loss of state and local autonomy in education was predicted long-ago by H. Thomas James of Stanford University:

> As the states have denied, first to the family and then to local communities, the right to make decisions on education contrary to staff defined policy, so the nation may be expected to deny the states the right to make

decisions on educational policy that are not in accord with the emerging national policy for education."²²

Common Core Curriculum Standards – The devil is in the details (11-3-13)

The Common Core Curriculum State Standards Initiative (CCSSI) was previously examined in "Education in America – Part III – Common Core State Standards – Educational excellence or secular cultural conformity?" [August 9, 2013] This article takes a more in-depth look at the concerns about Common Core and the nationalization of education.

Initially, the CCSSI was a state-led effort that established a single set of educational standards for kindergarten through 12th grade in English language arts and mathematics. In that initiative, states were to voluntarily adopt Common Core standards to unify and strengthen educational standards and expectations. However, the seemingly voluntary adoption of standards by the states has evolved through the power of the federal purse strings into mandated standards under various federal programs.

The nation's governors and education commissioners, through their representative organizations, the National Governors Association (NGA) and the Council of Chief State School Officers (CCSSO), led the development of the Common Core State Standards which were published in December 2008. However, the federal government under the Obama administration effectively hijacked the program in February 2009 through a $4.35 billion stimulus money "executive earmark" (meaning no-strings-attached) transfer to the Department of Education to create and fund a program that became known as the Race to the Top (RTT), a federal grant competition that allowed cash-strapped states to compete for federal stimulus money.[31]

Strings!

But the federal purse had strings attached. To receive stimulus money, the states had to "commit" to the adoption of common education standards. The state commitments had to be made within two months of publication of the standards. State consent came from gubernatorial and bureaucratic offices without any consent of the people or their elected representatives as most of the state legislatures were not in session. The short time frame did not allow for thoughtful review and deliberation of the federal standards by citizens and their representatives. Forty-two states made the commitment (under a federally-imposed definition of commitment) without a single state legislature approving the commitment to adopt common educational standards.[32]

And More Strings!

On May 22, 2012, the U.S. Department of Education (DOE) announced another "strings-attached" $400 million federal grant program whose funds would go *directly* to qualifying local school districts. The program effectively *bypasses state governments* and undermines state sovereignty. The program is called Race to the Top-District (RTT-D) and includes the following elements [and the author's commentary].[33]

> To qualify, a district *must* serve at least 2,500 students of whom 40% or more must qualify for a free or reduced-price lunch program.
>
> Each district *must* create plans for "individualized classroom instruction aimed at closing achievement gaps and preparing each student for college and career."[34] [One would think that the experts at the DOE would know the average child spends about six and one-half hours per day in the classroom. Using a typical elementary school classroom with twenty-five students as an example, each child would be allotted about sixteen minutes in which to receive "individualized classroom instruction." And from the allotted sixteen minutes we must subtract the time necessary for lunches and other activities, the time needed for general group classroom instruction by the teacher, and all of the other daily interruptions. One wonders if any of these so-called DOE experts have ever taught in a real-world classroom.]
>
> Districts *must* demonstrate commitment to RTT's four core reform areas which include *adopting standards acceptable to the DOE* and building massive student-data tracking systems.[35] [Standards are *not voluntary if the standards must be acceptable to the DOE*, and this

requirement debunks the supposed voluntary nature of Common Core Standards.]

Districts *must* show they can track students from pre-K though college and tie the outcomes back to individual teachers.[36] [One wonders how a local school district will obtain the outcomes of a student's college career. Perhaps the task of accumulating that information will be assigned to the National Security Agency due to its vast stores of information on the private lives of American citizens.]

Applying districts *must* promise to implement evaluation systems that consider student outcomes – not just for teacher and principal performance, but also for district superintendents and school boards.[37] [Does this mean that the DOE will have the power to fire school superintendents and locally-elected school boards? If the DOE's power is not direct, perhaps federal funds will be withheld should the local officials not comply with DOE suggestions as to needed personnel changes.]

Applicant school districts *must* form partnerships with public and private organizations to . . . offer services that help meet students' academic, social, and emotional needs . . . ."[38] [Thus, it appears that local school districts are answerable to the DOE as to whether students are socially and emotionally well-adjusted. In effect, school teachers will now be responsible for providing time and services for their students' social and emotional needs in addition to the individualized educational instruction as previously mentioned, all in a six-and-a-half-hour school day.]

RTT-D is a power-grab through which the federal government will skirt citizens' elected legislative bodies and negotiate directly with school districts in implementation of federal educational policies. RTT-D will also undermine the state governmental structure by grouping school districts together on policy decisions and thereby making it more difficult for the group to disengage from federal programming.

Dr. Allan Carlson is a noted author and lecturer and former Reagan appointee who served five years on the National Commission on Children. In a recent lecture he succinctly described the problems of the Common Core Standards program: more testing, more centralization, more experts, less creativity, and more money for a failing system.[39]

School systems attempting to withstand the assault on their autonomy by rejecting the Common Core Standards, a national curriculum, and national testing will be financially starved into submission. Even faith-based private schools will feel the pressure to conform to Common Core standards. Because Common Core standards are leading to a national curriculum and national testing, ACT, SAT, GED, and other testing programs are being aligned to the Common Core standards. Yet, private school students take those same tests. Inevitably private schools will be pressured to teach to the Common Core standards even if that which is taught is contrary to what they believe. Otherwise, their students will not do well on the Common Core aligned tests. Also, credit transfers from a faith-based school not in alignment with the Common Core may not be accepted by other Common Core aligned schools. And accreditation agencies that require accredited schools to be aligned with the Common Core may not accredit non-complying faith-based schools.[40]

The DOE website disingenuously states that, "Education is primarily a State and local responsibility in the United States. It is States and communities, as well as public and private organizations of all kinds, that establish schools and colleges, develop curricula, and determine requirements for enrollment and graduation."[41] But, the Obama administration and a rapacious federal bureaucracy have seized control over America's educational system which makes a mockery of the DOE assertion that education is primarily a state and local responsibility.

The federal government is developing a national curriculum under the guise of the Common Core Standards Initiative. Not only is a national curriculum being established but for the first time ever the participating local school must certify that its curriculum complies with federal standards. Federal bureaucrats will determine what children all across America will read and be taught and for how long. Local school administrators are becoming mere toadies answerable only to faceless bureaucrats in Washington. Locally elected school boards would be virtually powerless if not obsolete. And if parents have questions, objections, or concerns about their child's education, to whom would they turn? With local education in the grasp of a nationalized educational system, the local school board, their local state representative and state government, and even their national representatives will be powerless to address a parent's concerns. And this massive accumulation of power without accountability is occurring in the absence of any explicit Constitutional authority.

President Woodrow Wilson warned against the concentration of federal powers, and his warning is applicable one hundred years later with regard to the transfer of control of America's educational system to the federal government.

> The history of Liberty is a history of limitations of governmental power, not the increase of it. When we resist, therefore, the concentration of power, we are resisting the powers of death, because concentration of power is what always precedes the destruction of human liberties.[42]

Parents, local school officials, and state legislators should be extremely concerned about the destruction of local control of America's educational system and should strongly resist attempts to do so through the Common Core standards.

George Will summarized the progressive education establishment's defense of the voluntary nature of Common Core. "If you like your local curriculum, you can keep it. Period."[43] Hmmm. That has a familiar ring to it. I wonder where I've heard that before…

Train up a child in the way he should go

Part I (11-22-13)

My grandmother and I had a lot of conversations. They were usually one-sided with me asking questions but mostly listening to her stories. Of Cherokee ancestry, Sally Pearl (Downey) Hart was born in 1890 in Indian Territory and lived near present-day Ryan on the Red River. She came by wagon with her parents, brothers and sisters to the banks of the Arkansas River across the river from the tiny settlement of Tulsa in 1895. As there was no bridge over the river, the wagon had to be ferried across in order to get to where present-day Owasso is located a few miles north of Tulsa. She and my grandfather met and married in the newly minted state of Oklahoma, and they eventually operated a dairy farm near Owasso.

She told many stories of her early life and family. She was an avid reader and read many stories to me. One of the few books she actually owned was Martin and Osa Johnson's *Four Years in Paradise*. I was fascinated as she read to me of their exploration of Africa in the early twentieth century. I still have that book. When I was about seven years old, I recall sitting on the couch beside her as she made a doll out of empty thread spoons, some yarn, and a few bits of cloth. She called it Ezra Taft Benson. Of course today not one in a thousand people will know who Ezra Taft Benson was, but at that time he was the newly appointed Secretary of Agriculture under President Eisenhower. As the wife of a retired dairy-farmer, she wasn't too enamored with his agricultural policies. Apparently it made such an impression on me that I still vividly remember that time sitting on the couch beside her and listening.

She was an exceptionally loving, wise, and Godly woman, and much of what I later learned in life and believe today had their beginnings in those conversations with her when I was a small child.

Conversations are important and none more so than those between a parent or grandparent and a young child. It is in such conversations that our cultural inheritance is passed on unimpaired. In a larger sense, family is where "socialization" takes place, that is, the generational transfer of moral and cultural values. From primitive peoples huddled around communal campfires in the millennia of the past to the generations of the early twentieth century, children received most of their values and worldview from their parents, and the local church and community almost universally reflected those same values and worldview.[44]

However, the generational transmission of America's cultural inheritance was challenged by the rapid rise of the humanistic worldview during the Boomer generation's formative years (born late 1945 through 1964). This new moral order not only challenged but significantly damaged the generational transmission of the moral order upon which American society had flourished for over one hundred and fifty years. What made the Boomers different was the occurrence of a series of significant shared events and formative experiences that came together in a unique time and place—the perfect storm as it might be called. This series of significant shared events and formative experiences would ultimately result in dramatic changes in family life and child rearing, education, religion, politics, the arts, government, and culture in general.[45]

One of the most significant formative experiences of the young Boomer generation was the dramatic arrival of television. With the advent of television, there was a new member of the family seated at the communal campfire, and in all of history no intruder into the family circle would so quickly and thoroughly usurp the authority of parents and family in transmitting cultural values. The American child would be exposed to substantial external influences for long periods of time each day. In a series of exceptional essays published in 1981 about television as a social and cultural force, Richard Adler wrote:

> The TV set has become the primary source of news and entertainment for most Americans and a *major force in the acculturation of children*...Television is not simply a medium of transmission, it is an active, pervasive force...a mediator between our individual lives and the larger life of the nation and the world; between fantasy and fact; between old values and new ideas; between our desire to seek escape and our need to confront reality.[46] (emphasis added)

Television was the perfect tool for the transmission of a humanistic worldview to the Boomer generation. Michael Novak called television a "...molder of the soul's geography. It builds up incrementally a psychic structure of expectations. It does so in much the same way that school lessons slowly, over the years, tutor the unformed mind and teach it 'how to think'." To Novak, television is a "homogenizing medium" with an ideological tendency that is a "vague and misty liberalism" designed "however gently to undercut traditional institutions and to promote a restless, questioning attitude." Television served its masters, the state and the great corporations, even when exalting "...the individual at the expense of family, neighborhood, religious organizations, and cultural groups...that stand between the isolated individual and the massive institutions."[47] The "restless, questioning attitude" is an excellent description of what the Boomer children of the 1950s would exhibit in the 1960s. Many historians and sociologists believe that the greatest number of significant shared events and formative experiences that defined the Baby Boomers as a distinctive group was provided by television—more than the influence of parents and more than the massive numbers that form the Baby Boomer cohort.[48]

Television robbed families of time together for conversations necessary for the transmission of their cultural inheritance and replaced it with a humanistic worldview. But television was just the beginning of a new media culture in which technological advances dramatically changed how we live, work, and communicate. In the last twenty-five years we have become a screen culture, but in our rush to connectedness, we have become disconnected.[49] We are inundated with information from television, computers, cell phones, iPads, and monitors in businesses, churches, restaurants, airports, and any other location where there is a concentration of human traffic. We may have hundreds of friends on Facebook, LinkedIn, and Twitter but are starved for real face-to-face relationships in which there is time to listen. And we cannot effectively transmit our cultural inheritance to our children with a few keystrokes and recorded sound bites.

Richard Weaver captured the essence of this loss of time for listening in *Visions of Order*:

> The individual conservators of the past exist no more or they are no longer listened to: the grandmother preserving the history and traditions of the family by the fireside, the veteran relating the story of his battles in the shaded courthouse square, even the public orator recalling the spirit of 1776 on commemorative days. *There is no time to listen to them, and time is of the essence.*[50] (emphasis added)

There is another thief that has also robbed three generations of American children of their cultural heritage—American education under the humanistic philosophy of John Dewey. This will be addressed in Part II.

Part II (11-29-13)

Marriage, family, and home are necessary elements in the socialization of children. However, nurturing is the glue that must be added to this mix for socialization to occur. As we learned in Part I, conversations between parent or grandparent and child are a major part of nurturing. It is in such an environment that "socialization" takes place, that is, the generational transfer of moral and cultural values—our cultural inheritance.

But nurturing is very difficult in modern society as family members are rarely together for extended periods of time. The demands on families in a fast-paced, technologically driven, and rapidly changing society makes nurturing of children difficult at best. The difficulties expand considerably in households requiring two-incomes, particularly in a society dominated by a humanistic worldview focused on the individual as opposed to the biblical worldview which emphasizes relationships. For most Americans home has become merely a place to sleep and store stuff, and family members are reduced to tenant status where there is little mutual dependence, connection, or cohesiveness.[51] There is little if any time for conversations and other elements of nurturing, but time is the essence of nurturing.

The cultural and moral values of the colonists and America's Founders were rooted in the biblical worldview. Regarding the education of children in this biblical worldview, parents are admonished "Train up a child in the *way* he should go, and when he is old, he will not depart from it." [Proverbs 22:6. KJV] The implication is plain that the *primary* purpose of a child's training was transmission of cultural and moral values. This purpose is upheld by the words of Samuel Adams, known as the "Father of the American Revolution." Adams instigated the Boston Tea Party, signed the Declaration of Independence, and served in both the Continental Congress and the U.S. Congress. His views on education paralleled those of many other Founding Fathers.[52]

> Let divines and philosophers, statesmen and patriots, unite their endeavors to renovate the age, by impressing the minds of men with the importance of educating their little boys and girls, of inculcating in the minds of youth the fear and love of the Deity...in

short of leading them to the study and practice of exalted virtues of the Christian System.[53]

Until early in the twentieth century, transmission of parents' cultural and moral values to their children was supported by the educational system and other institutions of American society such as religion, government, and popular culture in general. Beginning principally in the 1960s and 70s, the *generational transfer of a family's moral and cultural values* to their children has been significantly hampered in two ways by the progressive education establishment.

Train children to have a humanistic worldview

First, the American educational system is totally immersed in the philosophy of John Dewey that purveys the humanistic worldview which stands in opposition to the Founders' central cultural vision based on a biblical worldview. John Dewey was a signor of *Humanist Manifesto I* in 1933, and his humanistic philosophy and worldview have saturated substantially all of American education.

Robert J. Roth describes Dewey's philosophy as one of naturalism in that…"man with his habits, institutions, desires, thoughts, aspirations, ideals, and struggles is within nature, an integral part of it…and insists…on man's continuity with nature and on the fact that man can achieve self-realization only in and through nature." Effectively, Dewey is saying that the human being survives and develops only in and through his *material* environment.[54] In summarizing Dewey's philosophy, Roth states:

> Nothing can be admitted which transcends the possibilities of concrete, human experience. There is *no absolute, no transcendent being*, no extra-mundane reality…there is *no room for a supernatural religion*…and that "supernatural" means that which transcends the possibilities of concrete human experience and involves an absolute being.[55] (emphasis added)

Thus, we have the dominant theme of John Dewey's philosophy—denial of God and human self-realization accomplished only through interaction with nature. Under such policies, the *primary* purpose of this "progressive" education is to prepare children for a *career and to be a contributor to the goals of the secular state*. The educational system is no longer an ally but an enemy of the generational transmission of the cultural and moral values of the parents.

Limit exposure of preschool children to the biblical worldview of parents

The second way the American educational system stands in opposition to the status of parents and family in the socialization of young children of preschool age is to remove them from the home at a younger age and further isolate them from parental influence in those formative preschool years. The cradle to career approach of education undermines the philosophy that parents have the primary responsibility, right, and privilege to provide the best education for their children. But such social engineering that relegates parents to secondary status in the socialization of their children is unnatural with regard to human nature and results in dire consequences for such a society.

The pressures for universal preschool began in the 1960s. In the Preface for the Twenty-fifth Anniversary Edition of *The Hurried Child*, Dr. David Elkind wrote of the 1971 enactment of the Comprehensive Child Development Act (CCDA) which mandated compulsory attendance of every preschool child in America at federally run centers. The bill was vetoed by President Nixon who stated that the effect of the bill would be "...to pledge the vast moral authority of the federal government to the side of *communal approaches* to childrearing [nurturing] as against a *family centered approach*..." and ultimately lead to destruction of the American family.[56]

Almost a half century later, the educational progressivists are once again peddling the communal approach to nurturing through a vast, federally controlled early childhood learning program. This time it is Race to the Top-Early Learning Challenge (RTT-ELC) which provides grants at the state level "...to improve the quality of early learning and development programs and close educational gaps for children with high needs." RTT-ELC includes the establishment of early childhood systems that "ambitiously" moves forward a state's early learning and development program. Like the first RTT initiative, RTT-ELC mandates include early learning and developmental outcomes, common standards within the state, assessments that measure child outcomes and address behavioral and health needs, and extensive accountability and data gathering programs to name just a few. Families are also to be engaged in the RTT-ELC process (and therefore effectively buy into the concept of federal control).[57] All of the flaws associated with federal control of education are enumerated in "Common Core Curriculum Standards – The devil is in the details" and need not be repeated in this article. [See "Common Core Curriculum Standards – The devil is in the details." November 8, 2013.]

Not only does RTT-ELC push federal control of education downward to the preschool level, more importantly it is also flawed in the same manner as is the decades-old Head Start program, and children are the unwilling victims. Dr. Elkind gives an insight into our Orwellian future under the current educational model.

> The concept of childhood, so vital to the traditional American way of life, is threatened with extinction in the society we have created. Today's child has become the unwilling, unintended victim of overwhelming stress—the stress borne of rapid, bewildering social change and constantly rising expectations.[58]

The homogenizing progressive education system is the force that maintains the factory model of education. Such a model allows the progressives to control the child and ultimately to instill a humanistic worldview. Parents have been shoved aside and the emotional damage to their children will last a lifetime. Elementary schools have become assembly lines where textbooks and curriculum are standardized on a national level, testing has become standardized and one-size-fits-all, teaching is driven by the curriculum content necessary to pass the tests, teachers and administrators are held accountable for educational failures with roots that go far beyond the classroom walls, and teacher creativity and innovation are smothered as they spend as many hours in non-teaching work activities as they do in teaching.[59] The value of many highly qualified and hard-working teachers as well as schools and school districts is measured by test scores significantly influenced by external circumstances and the realities of children's capabilities over which the teacher has little or no control.

Somewhere in the midst of all of these progressive educational reforms the child has been forgotten as the factory model of education relentlessly hurries children into adulthood. Individual differences in mental abilities as well as learning rates are ignored as children are pressed to meet uniform standards as measured by standardized tests. There is a progressive downward thrust of curriculum, i.e. the pressure to introduce curriculum material at an ever younger age.[60] Parents contribute to the problem by rushing children to a multitude of programmed extra-curricular activities which allow little down-time for un-structured play. Hovering over all of this haste is the omnipresent fear of retention if one doesn't measure up. Dr. Elkind believes that we have lost perspective about what childhood really means.

...it is important to see childhood as a stage of life, not just as the anteroom to life. Hurrying children into adulthood violates the sanctity of life by giving one period priority over another. But if we really value human life, we will value each period equally and give unto each stage of life what is appropriate to that stage...In the end, a childhood is the most basic human right of children.[61]

Shake and Bake History - Engineering the future while forgetting the past (8-1-14)

Two recent syndicated newspaper columns contained two views of history that frame the two worldviews contending for dominance in the nation's central cultural vision—humanism and Christianity. The first was written by David Turnoy, a retired elementary teacher and author.[1] Mr. Turnoy is a proponent of 'honest" history of the warts and all variety with a strong emphasis on the warts. Turnoy's article is peppered with numerous phrases descriptive of the humanistic worldview, and some of his quotes will help understand that worldview.

> For any *progressive* student or observer of history, it is well-known that the United States has a mixed record in its treatment of Native Americans, African Americans, women and other groups, including some especially cruel treatment...So what information should be taught? Should it be the *traditional bland summary* showing America as always in the right, led by truly admirable heroes who bring about change while leaving out any negative actions, which leads to *disinterested, unquestioning citizens* who allow government and other elites to do as they like? Or should it be a more balanced, honest approach?...If we want a better country with more *equality and justice*, this is where it starts.[2] [emphasis added]

To summarize, it appears that Turnoy believes that traditional history lessons will be bland summaries if not focused on the negatives and therefore produce disinterested and unquestioning citizens who are unconcerned about equality and justice. Turnoy assumes his approach is more balanced and honest. We will examine how Turnoy's "honest and balanced" approach really plays out in the American education system dominated by a humanistic worldview.

A contrary view is held by Daniel Burnett who believes that there has been a "...growing trend in historical illiteracy for years, and the culprit is our nation's education system...it fails to prepare students with the knowledge they'll need for informed citizenship." Quoting various research studies on knowledge of history in America, Burnett reported that only five percent of the top fifty public universities in the U.S. required even one survey course on American history. Most college and university curricula require only niche courses to take the place of American history courses. He cites several examples: "Foundations of Rock," "Human Sexuality," "History of Avant-Garde Film," and "America Through Baseball." Burnett believes that the American education system has produced a population of illiterates and amnesiacs as it relates to the nation's history.[3]

One must ask why there is such an aversion to teaching American history in primary and secondary schools and at colleges and universities. Turnoy argues that history teachers are not honest with regard to America's failures. Burnett cites the educational system's focus on niche courses and a failure to teach a comprehensive history of the nation. Both points of view are a result of the educational system's dominant humanistic worldview and its aversion to the lessons of the past.

American education's humanistic worldview

The American education system is extremely humanistic in its worldview, teaching, policies, practices, and course content. The great architect of engineering the future through education without a historical foundation was John Dewey. Dewey was "...recognized as the leader of the *'progressive movement' in education*."[4] [emphasis added] His educational philosophy, writings, and twenty-five years at Columbia University dramatically shaped the educational system in the U.S. from the early years of the twentieth century until the present day. His philosophy was centered on humanistic concepts of man with regard to his origins, purpose, and future. Dewey had a substantial disdain for historical influence, tradition, patrimony, and religion (particularly the Christian worldview), all of which were noticeably absent in his development of American education's modern paradigm.[5] The progressive movement in education resulted in faculty hostility to the courses and fields of study that examine the traditional roots of Western civilization and American institutions. Turnoy's sought after "honest and balanced" presentation of history has been cast aside in favor of indoctrinating American students with a humanistic worldview.

Humanism's aversion to history

In the humanist worldview history is excess baggage that must be tossed to make way for new, bold, and progressive ideas. Therefore, humanists subscribe to the Whig theory of history which states that the most advanced point in time is the point of its highest development. This fits nicely with humanists' progressivism whose foundation is the Enlightenment belief of the perfectibility of man, a "...belief that critical and autonomous human reason held the power to discover the truth about life and the world, and to progressively liberate humanity from the ignorance and injustices of the past."[6] Those holding the humanistic worldview eliminate the traditional historical narrative of America unless that narrative can be sifted and parsed to present *selected* evidence of America's *supposed* widespread historical inequality and injustice.

Rob Koons, a philosophy professor at the University of Texas, has called the modern American university's array of unconnected courses the Uncurriculum. Koons defines the Uncurriculum as a smorgasbord approach to curriculum offerings whose design usually exhibits a general lack of required courses, structure, and systematic order in meeting core course requirements for liberal arts studies.[7] From such comes a citizenry that is profoundly illiterate with regard to America's story and the reasons for its preeminence among the past and present nations of the world.

The story of America

America cannot be understood without a comprehensive historical narrative. Such a narrative reveals that America's founding originated from a biblical worldview that runs through the history of Western civilization since its inception. One cannot understand America by substituting a shake and bake curriculum that substitutes courses such as "America Through Baseball" or "History of Avant-Garde Film" for traditional comprehensive history courses that present the matchless story of America. Russell Kirk expressed the true ideal of education.

> True education is meant to develop the individual human being, the person, rather than to serve the state. In all our talk about "serving national goals" and "citizenship education"—phrases that originated with John Dewey and his disciples—we tend to ignore the fact that schooling was not originated by the modern nation-state. Formal schooling actually commenced as an endeavor to acquaint the rising generation with religious knowledge: with awareness of the

transcendent and with moral truths…to teach what it is to be a true human being.[8]

Writing of the humanistic view of education, Richard Weaver's words capture the goal of such education. "The student is to be prepared not to save his soul, or to inherit the wisdom and usages of past civilizations, or even to get ahead in life, but to become a member of a utopia resting on a false view of both nature and man."[9]

It is safe to say that the great majority of modern Americans do not understand the true story of America and its institutions. Turnoy and Barnett's prescriptions to achieve an informed citizenry with regard to America's history follow starkly different avenues. Turnoy's humanistic education model has ruled for the better part of a century and has utterly failed. Barnett offers hope that a return to telling the comprehensive though politically incorrect story of America will result in an informed and politically adept citizenry.

Progressive view of American history: The good old days were all bad. (10-31-14)

There seems to be few things that are exempt from the battlefields of the culture war. The latest casualty is history...you know, the stuff that is learned in high school or at least what people used to learn in high school. But the history lessons taught in American schools for 200 years following the founding has been dumped by the education establishment in recent years. American history is no longer the grand story of American culture since the arrival of the first Europeans but has become a tool to promote the liberal political/cultural agenda. The nation's history recorded by each generation's citizens and eye-witness historians is an accurate record of America's story. But now we have the latest two or three generations which claim the five hundred years of American history recorded by thousands of historians over the period is distorted and not reflective of the real story. Therefore, it must be trashed and replaced by a revised interpretation of history consistent with the *current enlightened understanding of what really happened.*

This approach to history is not new for it has been around since the early 1800s. It is called the Whig theory of history and is also known as the Progressive theory of history. This theory rests on the belief that the most advanced point in time represents the point of highest development. It assumes that "...history is an inevitable march upward into the light. In other words, step by step, the world always progresses, and this progress is inevitable."[1] Thus, the historical record must be judged only in light of current beliefs, assumptions, and politics, all devoid of timeless truths, wisdom accumulated through the ages, tradition, and heritage. The roots of the Whig theory reach back to the humanistic concept of human perfectibility of the French philosophers which arose during the Age of Enlightenment during the eighteenth century. Known as progressivism, the theory contradicts the Christian view of man as having a fallen nature.

The progressive theory of history is alive and well in the twenty-first century halls of academia and the organizations that serve its needs. One of those organizations is the College Board whose membership is comprised of 6,000 institutions of higher education. Its mission is to expand access to higher education by helping students to achieve college readiness and college success through such programs as the SAT and the Advanced Placement Program. The organization also acts in areas of research and advocacy for the education community.[2] It is in the College Board's new Advance Placement course in history that dramatically advances the progressive view of history and which has caused considerable concern to many including the Texas State Board of Education and the Republican National Committee as well as some of the more conservative members of the Golden, Colorado school board.

The school board wants to review the College Board's Advanced Placement U.S. history course which they believe contains significant anti-American content. The school board proposed to establish a committee to review texts and course plans to assure the course materials were balanced and "promote more citizenship, patriotism, essentials and benefits of the free-market system, respect for authority and respect for individual rights" and "don't encourage or condone civil disorder, social strife or disregard for the law."[3]

Now, who could argue with teaching that promotes a good citizenship and patriotism in a well-ordered and lawful society? Well, hundreds of students, parents, and teachers are bothered by such radical ideas and have been protesting the school board's planned review for weeks. The protesters claim the board is attempting to change the course content to suit their views (what about the views of the people that elected them?). The College Board's Advanced Placement history course content being taught for the first time this school year "gives greater attention to the history of North American and its native people before colonization and their clashes with Europeans, but critics say it downplays the settlers' success in establishing a new nation." The College Board stated that the course was built "around themes like 'politics and power' and 'environment and geography'." However, what is missing from the course framework is as significant as that which is included. For example, Martin Luther King isn't mentioned, but the Black Panthers are. The Board explained that the content was not to be considered exhaustive, but one New Jersey teacher cut to the heart of the College Board's unspoken agenda. He argues that the course "...has a global, revisionist view" and "depicts the U.S. as going from conquering Native Americans to becoming an imperial power, while downplaying examples of cooperation and unity."[4]

To a large extent, Americans are a people that are ignorant of their history. Because they don't know where they came from, they are unaware of the dangers into which the dominant humanistic worldview is leading America. This was not always so, and it has occurred by design and not by accident or neglect. The teaching of history falls within the sphere of education, and education has been in the hands of progressives for a hundred years. Of all of the institutions of life in

America, the educational establishment is the one that is most saturated in the humanistic worldview which stands in direct opposition to the biblical worldview upon which the nation was founded.

The founder and architect of America's progressive education was John Dewey who was bitterly hostile to Christianity and traditional Western thought. Dewey did not believe in the existence of God, supernatural religion, and life after death. Man was an evolutionary product and nature is all there is. The only thing that mattered was human self-realization through interaction with nature. On this foundation he built the progressive theory of education which emphasizes experience, observation, social responsibility, problem solving, and fitting in to society as opposed to centuries of traditional education by which is meant the acquisition of knowledge.[5] For progressives, the historical record holds little importance as a guide to the present and future unless it is used as the "horrible example" of America's past sins for the purpose of leading ignorant citizens to surrender their values and freedom. From this denigration of American history, we see the obvious disconnect between progressive education and the traditional understanding of that history. If one holds the progressive view of history, the views of the present generation *must* be superior to those of past generations and by default superior to their concepts of timeless truths, ancestral wisdom, tradition, and heritage. In this denigration of America's past, the progressive theories of education and history support and promote the larger all-encompassing philosophy of humanism which has been described in several earlier articles.

Ashley Maher is an eighteen year old Chatfield High School senior who helped organize the protests against the Golden school board's plan to review the content of the Advance Placement history course. She assures that, "We are going to fight until we see some results."[6] By "results," it must be assumed she means that the school board's desire to promote citizenship, patriotism, the free-market system, respect for authority, respect for individual rights, civil order, national unity, and respect for the law will be duly censored from any Advance Placement American history courses at Golden's high schools. It would be interesting to hear Ms. Maher's response to the question as to why her values and interpretation of American history are superior and should be taught while at the same time suppressing and/or misrepresenting the factual historical record about which she knows nothing. Following that moment of silence from Ms. Maher, it is also doubtful her parents or her Boomer grandparents peopling the picket lines could give a coherent, logical answer. Should they manage some sort of response, we counter with the words and actions of those eye-witnesses to American history: the Pilgrims and Puritans; colonial farmers and frontiersmen; Washington, Adams, Jefferson, Madison, Benjamin Franklin, Patrick Henry, and the rest of the founding generations; Alexis de Tocqueville's Democracy in America, the Abolitionists and Abraham Lincoln, the Doughboys of WWI and soldiers, sailors, and airmen of WWII, and millions of others who made America the greatest nation in the history of the world. For most modern-day Americans of the last three generations, it would be an answer they have not heard thanks to humanism's revisionist view of American history and suppression of the historical record of our ancestors.

FREEDOM ABUSED IS FREEDOM LOST

Part I – Government

Our Play-Doh® Constitution (5-7-13)

Pliable like Play-Doh®? Elasticized? Stretchable? No, liberals prefer to use the term, "Living Constitution." Irrespective of the singular success of the American Constitution in the history of the world and in spite of the intent of the Founders when writing the Constitution, the popular liberal mantra for most of the twentieth century and the beginning of the twenty-first century is that the Constitution is a "living document" that must be modified or bent to address the modern age and problems never foreseen by the Founders. By living document, the Constitutional liberals believe that its meaning and intent should be an instrument for enlightened social change to meet the needs of the hour.[1]

Now most liberals have difficulty understanding the difference between life and non-life. For the liberal, an unborn baby is merely a "fetus" or "potentiality for life." Yet, for the inanimate paper and ink document we call the Constitution, the liberals now wish to infuse it with life from which we are to infer that it must continually grow and change. What they mean is that it ought to be elastic or malleable but prefer the euphemistic "living Constitution" which sounds ever so much more dignified, even sacred.

In an April 23rd press conference, New York City mayor Michael Bloomberg wholeheartedly agreed with the concept of a living Constitution. Speaking of the loss of privacy through the use of an extensive surveillance camera system in New York City and the possible use of drones fitted with cameras, Bloomberg said:

> The people who are worried about privacy have a legitimate worry...But we live in a complex world where you're going to have to have a level of security greater than you did back in the olden days, if you will. *And our laws and our interpretation of the Constitution, I think, have to change."*[2] [emphasis added]

Now Mayor Bloomberg may have skipped his Constitutional government class the day when Article V was taught. If he had been there he would have learned that Article V outlines the procedures to amend the Constitution. Amendments may be proposed either by the Congress with a two-thirds majority vote in both the House of Representatives and the Senate or by a constitutional convention called for by two-thirds of the State legislatures. A proposed amendment becomes part of the Constitution as soon as it is ratified by three-fourths of the States (38 of 50 States). But Mayor Bloomberg doesn't want to mess with that long and laborious process. Let's just interpret the Constitution the way we want because times are "a changing" and problems are pressing. Furthermore, liberals know what's best even if the people don't. That's because "We live in a complex world where *you* are going to have to…"

We do agree that judicial interpretation of laws and the Constitution is the courts' proper role. However, because of decades of significant judicial activism by liberal judges usurping the role of the legislature, thoughtful judicial interpretation of the law is thrown aside in favor of passion and expediency that are employed to make law. Thus, human nature, through its passions, appetites, and desires of the moment, is released from the prescriptions of history, custom, convention, and tradition.

However, this was not the intent of the Founders. Sherwood Eddy wrote that Jefferson "…stood for a strict interpretation of the conservative Constitution to prevent ever-threatened encroachments upon the rights of the people, the legislature, and the states."[3] Russell Kirk confirms Eddy's view of Jefferson's opinion of the Constitution, "Thomas Jefferson, rationalist though he was, declared that in matters of political power, one must not trust the alleged goodness of man, but (in Jefferson's words) '*bind him down with the chains of the Constitution'*."[4]

We have established that the Founders preferred a strict interpretation of the Constitution and made it difficult to change based on the whims of the moment. Why did the Founders opt for a strict interpretation of the Constitution, and why do liberals so emphatically disagree?

Jefferson's remark regarding the Constitution gives us a hint. Ultimately, the disagreement stems from the differences in understanding of the fundamental nature of man. The Founders understood the truth of the fallen, corrupt nature of man and designed the Constitution with separation of powers and other devices to control or mitigate that corrupt nature. The liberals believe that man is inherently good, not fallen and in need of redemption. They also believe that man is perfectible, a process whereby he will become progressively better and better. Therefore, as man is perfected and society changes over time, we must update our Constitution accordingly.

As citizens turn from the Christian worldview as held by the Founders, they are unable to guide themselves internally with regard to ethical and moral issues and slide into moral relativism in which there is no right or wrong. Benjamin Franklin recognized the folly of this course when he said, "Only a virtuous people are capable of freedom. As nations become corrupt and vicious, they have more need of masters."[5] Perhaps Major Bloomberg sees Americans as no longer being virtuous and capable of guiding themselves internally and therefore are in need of more masters and more laws to address the failings of their human nature.

Mayor Bloomberg and the liberals of this world do not stop with diminishing your privacy. Ever the good liberal, Bloomberg is famous for a number of other restrictions of freedom we had back in the "olden days." Regarding the loss of freedom, his intent could not be clearer when he said, "I do think there are certain times we should infringe on your freedom."[6]

This statement was in response to a question about his fight to control sugary drink portion sizes in New York City and his intentions to go forth in spite of the court's rejection of his plan. In other words, when Joe Citizen can no longer make good decisions, the Mayor and his fellow elites will make them for him.

The modern humanist-liberal-progressive imbues (reads into or interprets) the Constitution with new rights, laws, and doctrines as well as restricting those old-fashioned rights the Founders thought important so that the modernists can conform man and society to the changes *required* by a modern world. Thereafter, modernists assure us that the greatest good for the greatest number will be dispensed, all under wisdom of the elites of a socialistic system and blessed by a Play-Doh® Constitution.

However, the modernists travel the same slippery path as those of the French Revolution when they base their societal changes on the ethereal, imaginary, or invented "rights of man" as well as imposing more and more laws to address the failings of human nature. In spite of the French Revolution's high-minded chorus of "Liberty! Equality! Fraternity!", the French reality was "monarchy, anarchy, dictatorship" all occurring in a little over a decade.

Death of the American Constitution[1] (5-24-13)

A constitution will die if it does not fulfill the purpose for which it was enacted. Not being a living thing, its death takes the form of being ignored, trivialized, or corrupted. The purpose of any constitution is to reflect a set of fundamental principles by which to govern rational and social beings, that is, people. A constitution in a free society is a blueprint for constructing a government fitted to the people's temper of mind, affections, or passions which I shall call the nation's central cultural vision or collective worldview. Thus, we have three elements: the people, their central cultural vision, and their constitutional blueprint.

If a constitution is not functioning as intended, one of three things has happened or is happening. First, the constitution as drawn did not reflect the fundamental principles of the people. Second, the fundamental principles of that people changed over a period of time and now stand in contradiction to the principles upon which the constitutional blueprint was originally drawn. Third, the leaders of a society through craftiness and corruption have undermined the intent of the constitution in a manner contrary to the central cultural vision of the people.

The power of the American Constitution to provide prescriptive rules, principles, and ordinances for the American people is waning. Something is amiss, and to determine which of the above reasons are the source of the decline we must examine our history.

The central cultural vision held by the colonists down through the Founding era was the basis for the set of blueprints for building the American form and practice of government, our national house so to speak. Those blueprints had been drawn largely from the Judeo-Christian tradition and its reliance on a transcendent God, His eternal truths, and His revelation to the Hebrews and first century Christians. To these central elements were added the prescriptions of history, custom, convention, and tradition—in essence, our patrimony. After a number of years certain wings of the house were demolished (e.g., slavery) and rebuilt to better adhere to those original blueprints.

Most of the governance of the house in the intervening years since its construction dealt with routine maintenance, interior decorations, and arrangement of furniture within. But the house was of sound construction, and apart from occasional errors in modification which were readily corrected, the structure served its inhabitants well.

The house was large and had many rooms, and many were welcomed to live therein, even those that did not like the architecture and the central vision of its culture—the over-arching banner of the Judeo-Christian worldview.

However, the Founders knew of the fallen nature of man and foresaw a time when men would attempt to change that which they had built on timeless truths. In their great wisdom, the Founders believed they should insure what they had built would not be changed capriciously by its inhabitants. So they drew the Constitutional blueprint to limit those changes so the house would continue to function within the time-tested guidelines, or as Thomas Jefferson said, to "…bind him down with the chains of the Constitution."

True to the Founders' prediction, several groups believed that the house should not be just maintained or periodically redecorated but be reconstructed in its entirety. They wished to tear down the structure and build a new house using a set of old blueprints based on the tenets of humanism (which the Founders had judged to be fundamentally flawed and structurally unsound).

For the humanists, the center of the cultural vision would have to be shifted, and the old overarching banner of the Judeo-Christian worldview would have to go. Their demolition efforts began in earnest in the nineteenth century and progressed rapidly throughout the twentieth century. The structural supports of the old house were identified as the first to be demolished—belief in a transcendent God, hierarchy, moral truths, right and wrong, the fallen nature of man, and the sanctity of life to name just a few.

However, the chains of the Founders' Constitution slowed the humanists' progress. So they took the Founders' words and invented new definitions and meanings to attach to those words. Once the new meanings were defined, taught in our schools, and embedded in our media-saturated consciousness, the humanists insisted that the old Constitution was outdated and must be modified and modernized to fit the new progressive understanding of the world and its problems. The old structure still stands, but for how long we do not know. Its future depends on its inhabitants. In spite of humanist assaults, the great majority of the inhabitants still like the original plans but seem to not know how (or care enough to rise from their lethargy) to stop the demolition and rebuild the house as it once was.

Our analysis leads us to conclude that the decline of the American Constitution is primarily due to the third reason listed above—the leaders of the institutions of American life through craftiness or corruption over several decades have undermined the Constitution's original intent which they now deem to be contrary to the central cultural vision of the people. But, there is also collateral damage from the humanist assault. Because of the unrelenting assault on the biblical worldview for three generations and a lack of truthful teaching in our schools about our Founding, America is seeing a shift by a growing segment of its citizens to a humanistic worldview devoid of belief in a transcendent God, objective truth, and the fallen nature of man. The consequences of such a shift in the American vision were foreseen by our Founding fathers.

> "The only foundation for...a republic is to be laid in religion. Without this there can be no virtue, and without virtue there can be no liberty, and liberty is the object and life of all republican governments."[2] [Benjamin Rush – Signor of the Declaration of Independence, attendee at the Continental Congress, physician and first Surgeon General]

> "Without morals, a republic cannot subsist any length of time; they therefore who are decrying the Christian religion...are undermining the solid foundation of morals, the best security for the duration of free governments."[3] [Charles Carroll – Signor of the Declaration of Independence, lawyer, member of the Continental Congress and first U.S. Senate]

> "We have no government armed in power capable of contending in human passions unbridled by morality and religion...Our Constitution was made only for a moral and religious people. It is wholly inadequate to the government of any other."[4] [John Adams – One of the drafters and a signor of the Declaration of Independence, 2nd President of the United States]

We have only to read the words of the Founders to understand why the power of the American Constitution to provide prescriptive rules, principles, and ordinances for the American people is waning. In summary, our Constitution won't save America if its citizens abandon virtue, morality, and religion. Such abandonment leaves the Constitution powerless to guide the nation as it enters the turbulent waters of humanistic moral relativism. And the ultimate consequence is a loss of liberty.

Government is not the problem, however... (6-7-13)

Recently, President Obama addressed the graduating class of Ohio State University. During his address he said:

> Unfortunately, you've grown up hearing voices that incessantly warn of government as nothing more than some separate, sinister entity that's at the root of all our problems; some of these same voices also doing their best to gum up the works. They'll warn that tyranny is always lurking just around the corner. You should reject these voices. Because what they suggest is that our brave and creative and unique experiment in self-rule is somehow just a sham with which we can't be trusted.[5]

In this politically-charged national debate, we have President Obama and much of the left arguing for a greater role of government in the lives of people, and on the right the Tea Party and others are arguing for a smaller government. But, government is merely a framework for governing and not the actual science of government which determines its size and reach. We call the science of government *politics*.

Look in any modern dictionary and you will find the definition of politics given in a half-dozen or more explanations, many with unfavorable connotations. One pushes the dictionary aside with the thought that the soup contains the ingredients but not the flavor. To find the flavor, particularly to understand what the founding Americans thought of politics, we need to go back to Noah Webster's *American Dictionary of the English Language* of 1828:

> The science of government; that part of *ethics* which consists in the regulation and government of a nation or state, for the preservation of its safety, peace, and prosperity; comprehending the defense of its existence and rights against foreign control or conquest ... and the protection of its citizens in their rights, *with the preservation and improvement of their morals.*[6] (emphasis added)

We see that the early Americans believed that politics dealt with *ethics* (the moral code) and was to be concerned with *the preservation and improvement of the morals* of the citizenry. So politics is not the "heavy" as it is so often portrayed in modern times. Politics are necessary to govern a people, but that governance can range between being very good and very bad. And bad politics can result in a bloated, socialistic government or an austere, aloof, uncaring government. This distinction between government and politics is important and not just an exercise in academic hair-splitting.

With this understanding, two observations are necessary: government is ordained by God and man has a fallen nature. The problem is not bad government but bad politics caused by corruptible man who is *not* guided by the North Star of a biblical worldview resting on objective truth. Therefore, it is not government that is the issue as portrayed by President Obama. Rather, it is bad politics that is the separate, sinister entity that is the root of our problems. Bad politics is the tyranny that constantly lurks around the corner.

Once again, bad politics comes from ignoring the corruptible nature of man in the governance of a people. The Founders held a biblical worldview. They understood the truth of the fallen, corrupt nature of man, and designed the Constitution with separation of powers and other devices to control or mitigate that corrupt nature. But the modern liberals believe that man is inherently good, not fallen and in need of redemption.

The contrast between the beliefs of the Founders and those of President Obama and the humanist-liberal-progressive establishment could not be clearer. James Wilson, a signor of the Declaration of Independence and the Constitution and an original Justice on the U.S. Supreme Court, said, "Human law must rest its authority ultimately upon the authority of that law which is divine… Far from being rivals or enemies, religion and law are twin sisters, friends, and mutual assistants. Indeed, these two sciences run into each other."[7] However, President Obama disagreed in a speech titled "Our Future and Vision for America."

> At some fundamental level, religion does not allow for compromise. It's the art of the impossible. If God has spoken, then followers are expected to live up to God's edicts, regardless of the consequences. To base one's life on such uncompromising commitments may be sublime, but to base our policy making on such commitments would be a dangerous thing.[8]

For President Obama, it appears that human law must exclude divine law in the nation's policy making. President Obama also says that we should reject those voices who say that "...our brave and creative and unique experiment in self-rule is somehow just a sham with which we can't be trusted." I would submit that self-rule without the restraints of God's law is the truly dangerous thing which can't be trusted. Ultimately, self-rule without God is the source of bad politics.

Although the state has a proper role in God's design of social systems, bad politics have allowed the state to dramatically usurp the authority of other spheres within God's social system: family, church, labor and economics, education, man, and God Himself. In America, God and Christianity are being driven from the public square. As the social order is swept clean of God's presence and influence, the lines between the spheres have blurred and opened the way for the state to appropriate to itself a presumed authority over all aspects of life. Such state authority ends in the tyranny of socialism or one of its various mutations which have been responsible for the greatest death, destruction, and misery in the history of the world. This is the sinister tyranny that Americans fear and which President Obama so blithely dismisses.

The Christian's Role in Politics and Government (6-7-13)

In the last article (Government is not the problem...however) we discussed the Founders' beliefs with regard to politics and government which are radically different from what most people believe today. Noah Webster's 1828 dictionary defined politics as:

> The science of government; that part of *ethics* which consists in the regulation and government of a nation or state, for the preservation of its safety, peace, and prosperity; comprehending the defense of its existence and rights against foreign control or conquest ... and the protection of its citizens in their rights, with the *preservation and improvement of their morals*.[9] [emphasis added]

Politics in the founding era included a belief that regulation and government of a nation had a moral component and that its responsibilities included the preservation and improvement of the morals of the citizenry. Contrast the Founders' beliefs with modern antiseptic attitudes and resultant cleansing of any hint of religion or moral absolutes not only from politics and government but from all institutions of American life.

This attitude is prevalent throughout America including a large segment of Christianity. The attitude has grown from decades of misapplication of the First Amendment and an erroneous understanding of Thomas Jefferson's wall of separation between church and state. The First Amendment is an "establishment" clause, not a "separation" clause. It was meant to prohibit the government from establishing one specific sect as the official church of the nation. The Establishment clause was not meant to banish religion and its influence from the public arena, politics, government, and the institutions of American life.

Jefferson's words with regard to a wall of separation between church and state were merely to assure the Danbury Baptists of Connecticut that no one church would be established as the official church of the United States. Effectively, it was meant to protect the church from the state, not the state's protection of the people from religion. Who better to explain the Founders' intent than a Supreme

Court Justice of the era? Joseph Story was appointed to the Supreme Court by James Madison, regarded as the father of the Constitution. Story wrote of the Establishment clause:

> The real object of the [First A]mendment was not to countenance, much less advance Mohometanism, or Judaism, or infidelity by prostrating Christianity; but to exclude all rivalry among Christian sects and to prevent any national ecclesiastical establishment which should give to a hierarchy (a denominational council) the exclusive patronage of the national government.[10]

This meaning was clearly understood by the vast majority of Americans and the courts until Jefferson's words were taken out of context by the Supreme Court in 1947. In the Everson case the Supreme Court extracted eight words ("a wall of separation between church and state") from Jefferson's speech with total disregard for its original meaning and context. This was the beginning of the systematic removal of religion from the public square and the nation's various institutions.

From this misunderstanding of religion's rightful place in government, many Christians have generally shied away from any significant involvement in politics and government over the last three decades. To dispel this notion, Wayne Gruden published a pamphlet titled, "Why Christians should seek to influence the government for good." Gruden presents a strong biblical basis for Christian involvement to *significantly* influence law, politics, and government ...according to God's moral standards and God's purposes for government as revealed in the Bible."[11] At the same time Gruden cautions that Christians "...must simultaneously insist on maintaining freedom of religion for all citizens." How is this balance achieved?

> ...the overarching moral suasion (influence or persuasion) of Christian principles under which our nation was founded made possible religious freedom for all faiths. Such moral suasion of Christian principles is not coercive as humanists would have us believe. The moral suasion of Christian principles provided the nation with a central vision and resulted in stability and unity by working through the individual as he voluntarily chooses the manner in which he orders his soul.[12]

As a result of the over-arching Christian worldview, the nation exhibited an exceptionally strong religious sanction at its founding. This religious sanction was the power of Christian teaching over private conscience that made possible American democratic society. The religious sanction resulted because colonial and founding-era Americans held the biblical worldview *and* were significantly involved in government and politics. To confirm the existence of this strong religious sanction that still held sway over the nation forty years after the Constitutional Convention, we look to the words of Alexis De Tocqueville's 1831 *Democracy in America*, one of the most influential political texts ever written about America.

> Americans so completely identify the spirit of Christianity with freedom in their minds that it is almost impossible to get them to conceive the one without the other...
>
> On my arrival in the United States, it was the religious atmosphere which first struck me. As I extended my stay, I could observe the political consequences which flowed from this novel situation.
>
> In France I had seen the spirit of religion moving in the opposite direction to that of the spirit of freedom. In America, I found them intimately linked together in joint reign over the same land.[13]

Tocqueville went on to say that the peaceful influence exercised by religion over the nation was due to separation of church and state. Unlike the modernists' separation of church and state, Tocqueville's separation was a separation of the spheres of power and *not* a separation of government from ethics and moral guidance supplied by the moral suasion of Christianity.[14]

In twenty-first century America, the Christians' role in politics and government should be the same as the role played by Christians in the founding of America. They were significantly involved in government, politics, and law such that the power of Christian teaching over private conscience made possible American democratic society. To restore the biblical worldview as the basis for governing the nation, Christians must become significantly more involved in government and politics, and it must happen now before it is too late.

Would Jefferson label the modern Judiciary as the "Despotic Branch"? (5-22-15)

George Will is one of the brightest and most articulate columnists on the national scene (*Washington Post* Writers Group). I normally savor every one of his appearances on the opinion page. This is why I am disturbed by Will's false and malicious criticism of presidential candidate Mike Huckabee ("Huckabee's 'appalling' crusade for nullification").[15] Will is a huge fan and student of baseball and occasionally writes a column on the subject. Using a baseball analogy, Will must know that his column's pitches at Huckabee were not only far outside the strike zone but that they were intended as bean balls meant to injure and harm Huckabee. This disappoints because Will has not lowered himself to such levels in past columns that I have read.

Will claims to be "appalled" by Huckabee's recent remarks that deal with the question of judicial error and overreach with regard to the Constitution, an issue that also concerns a great number of Americans. Will takes Huckabee to task for rejecting "judicial supremacy" and suggesting that a ruling by the Supreme Court does not make its ruling the "law of the land." In doing so, Will incorrectly links Huckabee's remarks with the pre-Civil War doctrine of nullification which arose in 1830 during Andrew Jackson's presidency.

The doctrine of nullification evolved from resolutions initially adopted by the South Carolina legislature in December 1828 and which opposed certain tariffs imposed by the federal government. In opposition to President Jackson with regard to the tariffs, Vice President John Calhoun authored a lengthy essay on state government which supported the Southern position of state sovereignty and minority rights. According to the doctrine of nullification, individual states did not have to follow a federal law and in effect could "nullify" the law. By 1830, the nullification debate had evolved to the larger questions of origin and nature of the Constitution. Massachusetts senator Daniel Webster defended the federal position by "…attempting to show that the Constitution was not the result of a compact, but was established as a popular government with a distribution of powers binding upon the national government and the states."[16]

It is misleading for Will to accuse Huckabee of crusading for nullification of federal laws at will because the Constitution was merely the product of a compact. Huckabee's concern is with modern judicial efforts to create legislation as opposed to interpreting the law. What is interesting and lends authority to Huckabee's position on interpreting the Constitution is Andrew Jackson's response to the U.S. Supreme Court's view of the constitutionality of a re-charter of the 2nd Bank of the U.S. Although the Supreme Court viewed the legislation passed by Congress as constitutional, Jackson did not and vetoed the legislation. The bank charter debate became the major issue of the 1832 presidential campaign.[17] In defending his veto, Jackson made a noteworthy description of the duties of the three branches of government with regard to interpreting the Constitution.

> The Congress, the Executive, and the Court must each for itself be guided by its own opinion of the Constitution. Each public officer who takes an oath to support the Constitution swears that he will support it as he understands it, and not as it is understood by others...The opinion of the judges has no more authority over Congress than the opinion of Congress has over the judges, and on that point the President is independent of both.[18]

In the first seven decades following the writing of the Constitution in 1787, the Supreme Court ruled only twice that a law created by Congress was unconstitutional, and *both times the ruling was ignored by Congress and the President.*

Marbury v. Madison

In the last hours of the presidency of John Adams, he made several Federalist judicial appointments in the District of Columbia in an attempt to further load the bench with Federalist appointees. Under President Adams, John Marshall was both Adams' Secretary of State and the Chief Justice of the Supreme Court. As Secretary of State, it was Marshall's duty to deliver President Adams' legally executed appointments, but he failed to do so. When James Madison became Secretary of State under newly elected President Thomas Jefferson, the president refused to have the appointments delivered. The disappointed appointees sued, and in *Marbury v. Madison* (1803), Chief Justice Marshall and the Supreme Court at first ruled that the Court had no judicial authority over the case. Then with a surprisingly contradictory action, the Chief Justice ruled that President Jefferson should deliver the appointments. Jefferson and Madison ignored the ruling and received virtually no condemnation voiced by Congress, the Supreme

Court, or the public. Jefferson called the Court's attempt to interfere with the business of the Executive decision a "perversion of the law" by attempting to strike down the Judiciary Act of 1789 in which on two occasions the Supreme Court had found no objection or fault.[19]

Nineteen years later, Jefferson affirmed the general view of the Founders that *any* of the three branches could interpret the Constitution.

> [E]ach of the three departments has equally the right to decide for itself what is its duty under the Constitution without any regard to what the others may have decided for themselves under a similar question.[20]

Jefferson specifically rejected the belief that the Judiciary was the final voice and described the damage to the Constitution of a contrary opinion.

> [O]ur Constitution...has given – according to this opinion – to one of them alone the right to prescribe rules for the government of the others; and to that one, too, which is *unelected by and independent of the nation*...The Constitution, on this hypothesis, is *a mere thing of wax in the hands of the Judiciary* which they may twist and shape into any form they please.[21] [emphasis added]

Jefferson and the other Founders would be greatly alarmed with the modern view of the Judiciary that it may prescribe rules for the other branches of Government.

Dred Scott v. Sanford

Dred Scott was a Negro slave, a household servant for Dr. John Emerson who had taken Scott to various areas in the North where slavery was prohibited. Scott eventually sued for his liberty in Missouri courts and maintained that he was free because of his stays in a free state and a free territory. In March 1857, the Supreme Court ruled (*Dred Scott v. Sanford*) that Scott (and all other slaves) was not a citizen of the U.S. or the state of Missouri and therefore not entitled to sue in the federal courts. For Scott and all other slaves, the effect of the ruling reinforced the status quo of slavery and made it impossible for slaves to gain their freedom through the courts or legislation.[22] Effectively, the Supreme Court had declared that Congress could not outlaw slavery and that slaves were not citizens but property.

Several of Abraham Lincoln's remarks in his first Inaugural Address were prompted by the Dred Scott decision.

> I do not forget the position assumed by some that constitutional questions are to be decided by the Supreme Court...At the same time, the candid citizen must confess that if the policy of the government upon vital questions affecting the whole people is to be irrevocably fixed by decisions of the Supreme Court, the instant they are made...the people will have *ceased to be their own rulers*, having...resigned their government into the hands of that eminent tribunal.[23] [emphasis added]

Like Jefferson's response to the Supreme Court's ruling in *Marbury v. Madison* sixty two years earlier, both Lincoln and the Congress ignored the ruling of the Supreme Court in the Dred Scott case. Not only was the ruling ignored but directly disobeyed. On June 9, 1862, Congress prohibited the extension of slavery into free territories and in 1863 Lincoln issued the Emancipation Proclamation ending slavery.[24]

Jefferson, writing to Abigail Adams in 1804, said of the Supreme Court, "[T]he opinion which gives to the judges the right to decide what laws are constitutional and what not, not only for themselves in their own sphere of action, but for the Legislature and executive also in their spheres, would make the Judiciary a *despotic branch*."[25] [emphasis added] But this is what the Supreme Court has become in 2015 America. Thoughtful judicial interpretation of laws in light of the Constitution is the courts' proper role. But through judicial activism by liberal judges usurping the role of the legislature in making laws, the courts have appropriated unto themselves a law-making role never intended by the Founders and breaches the coveted separation of powers.

Will is not only incorrect in his spurious charge that Huckabee was crusading for nullification, he crudely disparages Huckabee's Christian faith because of his call for prayer for the Supreme Court justices considering the fate of same-sex marriage (see 1 Timothy 2:1-2). He also belittles Huckabee's well-founded concern that the nation is moving toward the criminalization of Christianity which is amply demonstrated by the growing trend of the judiciary and bureaucracy to punish Christians for practicing their faith.

In the age of the "living" Constitution, the Judiciary has made it pliable in order to accommodate the whims of a humanistic society unhooked from mores, norms, traditions, and voices of the past. In Jefferson's words such a Constitution becomes, "...a mere thing of wax in the hands of the Judiciary which they may twist and shape into any form they please." Combining the words of Jefferson and Lincoln, such a Judiciary would become a "despotic branch" and "the people will have ceased to be their own rulers."

Helicopter government

Part I – A Nation of Wimps (5-29-15)

Back in the late 1980s the term *helicopter parenting* came into vogue to describe a style of parenting in which overprotective parents discourage a child's independence by being too involved with the child's life. In other words, a helicopter parent hovers over a child like a helicopter, ready to swoop in at the first sign that their child may face a challenge or discomfort.[26] According to Dr. Robert Hudson, a clinical professor of pediatrics and co-director of the Center for Resilience at the University of Oklahoma College of Medicine, there are four ways helicopter parenting manifests itself: overprotecting, overpraising, overindulging, and overprogramming. Each of these types of parenting has serious consequences for the child.[27]

A nation of wimps

Bad things happen to everyone in life, and children must learn through experience including bad experiences while growing up. *Psychology Today's* Editor-at-Large Hara Estroff Marano described the consequences resulting from parents who overprotect their children from experiencing failure and discomfort: inability to adapt to the difficulties of life, psychologically fragile (depression and anxiety), risk-averse, loss of identity, loss of meaning and a sense of accomplishment, lack of self-control, and lack of perseverance. These consequences can last into adulthood. Quoting one child psychologist, "Kids need to feel badly sometimes. We learn through experience, and we learn through bad experiences. Through failure we learn to cope." According to Marano, "Whether we want to or not, we are on our way to creating a nation of wimps."[28] As these overprotected children move into adulthood, American government and its bureaucracies have willingly assumed the role of surrogate parents of this nation of wimps.

It appears that unhealthy consequences of helicopter parenting for children are strikingly similar to the pathologies resulting from a nanny-state government increasingly involved in its citizens' lives and which we might also label *helicopter governing* by a *helicopter government*. Government involvement with the details and intricacies of the lives of American citizens has grown dramatically commencing with Roosevelt's New Deal and the Judiciary's exceptionally expansive re-interpretation of the Constitution's general welfare clause in the 1930s. This involvement was greatly exacerbated by the Great Society programs of the 1960s and continues under the socialistic policies of the current Obama administration.

Under modern judicial, legislative, and executive branch interpretations, the general welfare of American citizens has come to mean far more than those fiercely independent and self-reliant Founders ever imagined. In twenty-first century, America's helicopter government stands ready to swoop down and fix, mend, change, smooth-out, correct, adjust, or repair any problem, difficulty, or perceived injustice that may arise. No aspect of its citizens' general welfare is too large or too small to escape our helicopter government's attention and involvement, be it the size of our sugary soft drinks or the kind of cars we are permitted to drive.

Before we examine the consequences of a helicopter government, we must understand the driving forces behind it and how these forces have changed America over the last 75 years. America has changed because the worldview of much of the leadership of the institutions of American life and the organizations they represent have changed. A worldview is a person's belief about things, an overall perspective or perception of reality or truth from which one sees, understands, and interprets the universe and humanity's relation to it and that directs his or her decisions and actions.

The collective worldviews of a nation's citizens becomes its central cultural vision, and in America there are two worldviews contending for dominance in its central cultural vision. One is the Christian worldview which reflects the central cultural vision of the colonial Americans, the Founders, and the nation for 150 years following its founding. The Christian worldview rests on the universals reflected in God's creation and the biblical revelation to the ancient Hebrews and first century Christians. Humanism is the competing worldview that contends that Nature is all there is and that man is a product of a long, developmentally progressive period of evolution. For humanists, there is no God or life after death, and all truth is negotiable and determined by the current needs of society.

The best way to contrast the two worldviews is to look at two fundamental differences that stand at the heart of the conflict. The first centers on the *purpose* for which man was created. For Christians, the fundamental purposes of life center on an eternal relationship with God and earthly relationships with his fellowman. For the humanist, the ultimate purpose is happiness through the exaltation of self. From these basic differences flow a whole myriad of conflicts which we call the culture wars.

The second major point of divergence relates to the *nature* of man. Christians view man as having been created by God but subsequently having a fallen nature because of his disobedience that resulted in a broken relationship with God. Consequently, man is in need of redemption. Humanists believe that man is basically good and therefore not fallen nor in need of redemption. Hence, humans are masters of their own destiny, and reason and science alone point the way to an ever-progressive improvement of mankind.

Because the humanistic worldview does not present a true picture of reality (truth) as it relates to the purpose and nature of man, the tenets of its faith are flawed and from this flawed perception of truth we see pathologies develop as humanism fails to adequately address the basic questions of life.

America's helicopter government is the product of a humanistic worldview that has gained ascendency in America during the last seventy-five years. The required method of organizing society under a humanistic worldview is socialism. As the humanistic worldview has advanced, so has America's tendency toward socialism of which a helicopter government is its heart and soul.

In this series of articles we shall examine the four types of helicopter governing (overprotecting, overpraising, overindulging, and overprogramming), the pathologies associated with each, and the impact on American culture.

Part II – Helicopter government – Overprotecting (6-5-15)

This series of articles describes helicopter governing and its similarities with helicopter parenting, the pathologies associated with each, and the impact on American culture. A helicopter government is one that exhibits characteristics similar to those of helicopter parenting which are expressed in four types of behavior: overprotection, overpraising, overindulging, and overprogramming. In Part I we observed that a helicopter government is rooted in socialism which is the required and eventual end of government under a humanistic worldview. A humanistic worldview is flawed because if fails to reflect truth as to the purpose and nature of man and therefore cannot give answers to the basic questions of life for which man continually seeks in developing his worldview. In Part II we shall examine the origins of our helicopter government's propensity to overprotect and the pathologies and consequences thereof to individuals and culture at large.

Overprotecting

First we must ask why helicopter parents are overprotective of their children. A short, vague, and somewhat unsatisfying answer is that parents are a product of their overprotective culture. And much of that culture has been shaped and defined by the radical element (about 25%) of the Boomer generation (born between the end of World War II and the end of 1964) which has ascended to positions of leadership in the institutions of American life. That leadership has embraced the humanistic worldview and imposed and implemented laws, regulations, policies, and practices consistent with the tenets of humanism. In essence, we can say that over time the rise of helicopter parents are a derivative of an overprotective government. And from the overprotectiveness of parents and government arose both individual and cultural pathologies. In support of this view we again contrast the perceptions of the two worldviews regarding the *purpose and nature of man*.

Purpose of Man

For the Christian, the ultimate purpose of man is to know God and dwell with Him as His child for eternity. Therefore, relationship is the focus and end purpose of man and implies a right relationship not only with God but one's fellowman. According to renowned humanist Paul Kurtz, the ultimate purpose of man is happiness and is further refined as "...the greatest-happiness-for-the-greatest-number..."[29] In other words, the focus is on the individual but only in the larger context of the common good. Under the humanistic worldview, government has become the judge and guarantor of happiness for the individual. However, humanism judges economic systems by whether or not they "...increase economic well-being for *all* individuals and groups, minimize poverty and hardship, increase the *sum* of human satisfaction, and enhance the quality of life...and judge it by its responsiveness to human needs, testing results in terms of the *common good* ."[30]

In his influential book *The Philosophy of Humanism*, Corliss Lamont agrees with Kurtz.

> On the whole, however, a society in which most individuals, regardless of the personal sacrifices that may be entailed, are devoted to the *collective* well-being, will attain greater happiness and make more progress than one in which private self-interest and

advancement are the prime motivators.[31] [emphasis added]

Again, we see the humanists' supremacy of the common good over the individual. But how is the humanist's "common good" different from the Christian's emphasis on relationship? It is different because the Christian's concern for his fellow man is based on the eternal and unchangeable laws of God through an act of his or her *freewill* as opposed to the humanist's *required group adherence* to state-defined interpretations of an ephemeral "common good" which is susceptible to revision with each change of leadership.

And it is here we see humanism's overprotective government collide with man's freewill and consequent desire for freedom. *The tenets and assumptions of the humanistic worldview are inherently collectivist* and are a direct contradiction to the independence, self-reliance, and pioneer spirit demonstrated by Americans in the colonial era and first 150 years of the nation's history. And with this brief understanding of the humanist worldview with regard to the purpose of man, we begin to see the rise of a helicopter government that breeds dependency of the populace on a government that will be the provider and guarantor of happiness as opposed to merely making possible the pursuit thereof.

It is not that the Christian worldview is opposed to the happiness of the individual. Rather, it is the source of a Christian's happiness that is different. A recent op-ed piece by Arthur Brooks, president of the American Enterprise Institute, made some very shrewd observations which hit at the heart of what it means to be happy. He pointed out that personal moral transformation was the most important factor in social justice. Using information from the 2010 General Social Survey, the nation's best sociological database, he made the following observations as to what makes people happy.

> Take the example of two men, identical in age, education, race, and income. The first is religious. He's married with two kids. He also works more and participates in his community more than 90 percent of the rest of the country. The other man meets none of these qualifications. The first man is nearly 400 percent more likely to be happy…real social justice must encourage people to participate in faith, family, and community. Their chances of happiness—and success—are inextricably linked with these moral institutions.[32]

In other words the true happiness is a collateral result of focusing on right relationships with God, spouse, family, and community.

Nature of Man

Contrary to humanist belief that man is basically good, the Founders held a biblical understanding of the corruptible nature of man and a belief that government was untrustworthy due to man's corruptibility and therefore should be limited. Traditional ideas of limited government prevailed until the Great Depression and World War II in the first half of the twentieth century. Americans still distrusted government, but as a result of the growing influence of the humanistic worldview, they saw government as a mechanism for dealing with a multitude of societal problems. Politicians happily acquiesced and more and more "problems" were discovered that required governmental answers or intervention. Because man was basically good according to the humanists, social problems arose not because man was fallen but because of corrupt social systems. Thus, a growing number of social and political solutions by government social engineers in the name of the general welfare of its citizenry became the catalyst for a monolithic and overprotective government.[33]

However, funding government and the growing list of wants, wishes, and synthetic rights of the populous has become difficult if not impossible because government cannot do everything for everybody. Samuelson calls this "the politics of overpromise…the systematic and routine tendency of government to make more commitments than can reasonably be fulfilled. First, government resources are not adequate and never can be. People (and institutions) must do some things for themselves. A second problem arises when a helicopter government can't fix the problems of the day; it is perceived as a failure and leads to less trust in government and growing disunity.[34]

The falseness and failures of the humanistic worldview become evident when one examines the pathologies of an overprotective helicopter government that is based on a wrong understanding of the purpose and nature of man. These pathologies are evident in much of America's citizenry and include self-centeredness, disunity, petulance, lack of discipline, inability to function well in organized endeavors, aimlessness or lack of purpose, inability to cope (addictions), codependency, poor problem-solving skills, and a false sense of entitlement. These labels apply in varying degrees to both children who have experienced helicopter parenting and adults conditioned by a helicopter government.

The application of the overprotective policies and practices of the humanistic worldview in all institutions of American life (particularly in government and education) has resulted in a pervasive *victim mentality*. The consequences of this mindset have led to cultural carnage including institutionalization of poverty through multiple generations of welfare recipients; broken families without the presence of a father to be the role model of a responsible provider in lieu of various welfare agencies and social workers; and an obsession with "rights" as opposed to fulfilling one's responsibilities, duties, and obligations to family, clan, community, and country.

Part III – Helicopter government – Overpraising (6-12-15)

This series of articles describes helicopter parenting and helicopter governing, the pathologies associated with each, and the impact on American culture. A helicopter government is one that exhibits characteristics similar to those of helicopter parenting which are expressed in four types of behavior: overprotection, overpraising, overindulging, and overprogramming. In Part III we shall examine the consequences of a culture of overpraising encouraged by the indirect but pervasive influence of our helicopter government and the American educational system. The obsessive, destructive, and faulty efforts of the educational establishment to build child self-esteem at any cost has enabled a culture of overpraising resulting in pathologies and consequences harmful to children, adults, and the culture at large.

Overpraising

To understand the emphasis on self-esteem we must look at the development of a new view of self in America following World War II. Alan Petigny summarized the seismic change in the view of self as, "...a rejection of the belief in the innate depravity of mankind, the celebration of spontaneity, and a pronounced turn toward self-awareness...[This] gave rise—on an unprecedented scale—to a more secularized notion of the individual." From this humanistic view of self came a belief in the basic goodness of man and a rejection of Original Sin; loosened behavioral codes that allowed one to get in touch with one's true self rather than discover truth as defined by tradition, scripture, natural law, and other authoritarian sources; and a preference for self-expression as opposed to self-discipline. Rejecting the external, there was a decided inward turn to discover one's guiding principles and the meaning of life. In the 1950s this process of getting in touch with one's self was called self-actualization in which answers to the big questions of life come from within and can only be found by trusting one's own reactions and doing "what feels right."[35]

However, the self must not only be actualized but must be made to feel good about it. Dr. Robert Hudson believes that the whole "overprotection racket" with regard to children began with a popular fad of the 1980s in which a child's self-esteem was built through giving them a multitude of choices.[36] Through the efforts of the American educational system and complicit parents, this process of self-actualization or getting in touch with one's true self, co-joined with building self-esteem, begins in the earliest preschool years and continues through all primary and secondary levels and into adulthood at the university level. So many hours are spent by educators on building self-esteem that teaching skills and knowledge are neglected which is one of the major reasons for the dismal condition of American education, the most humanistically-indoctrinated institution in American life.

The problem of overpraising children and efforts to build high self-esteem are fundamentally linked to humanism's false assumption of the basic goodness of man. The root of the problem of overpraising children lies in the mistaken belief that achievement follows self-esteem rather than self-esteem as a result of achievement.[37] Here we must distinguish between overpraising children and that of expressions of love and affirmation that all children need. Although we must not put love, affirmation, and encouragement of a child on a praise-as-you-achieve basis, we must be careful to not persistently build up within a child a false understanding of the source and value of his or her self-worth and abilities through overpraising. Overpraised children are being setup for disappointment and failure in their adult years because they were never taught how to cope with failure and disappointment in their formative years. And the consequences of those lessons denied in the childhood years are far more painful, longer-term, and costly in the adult years and radiate outward to family, friends, and society in general.

So what does all this overpraising of children have to do with a helicopter government? The emphasis on high self-esteem for children has effectively robbed them of those learning and coping experiences (especially bad experiences) in their growing up years. The effect for many is to extend childhood forever.[38] These adults living in perpetual childhood often become *wards of the state.* And our helicopter government is always ready to swoop in and minister to the wounded self-esteem of those individuals or groups who feel themselves slighted, offended, insulted, or snubbed. In other words, the feelings of these pseudo-adults have been hurt, and the government must punish the perpetrators.

Professor John Portmann, professor of religious studies at the University of Virginia, believes that the quest for high esteem in children is *damaging the whole fabric of society*. Marano quotes Portmann who

> ...sees young people becoming weaker right before his eyes, more responsive to the herd, too eager to fit in— not just less assertive in the classroom, but unwilling to disagree with their peers, afraid to question authority, more willing to conform to the expectations of those on the next rung of power above them.[39]

Children raised on the pacifier of high self-esteem disconnected from reality become weakened adults living in an extended childhood. These overpraised, self-actualized adults continually in need of a self-esteem fix attempt to find their value and worth from within but are constantly demoralized by the external world's failure to affirm their inner vision of themselves. Their dismay and distress is a result of the humanistic worldview's false understanding of the source of a person's value and leads to an attack on the biblical view of man which is really an attack on his *true* dignity and worth.

Richard M. Weaver has identified the steps in the progressive demotion of man in modern society while he unsuccessfully attempts at the same time to elevate himself through humanism's false measures of self-worth.[40] The author has previously written of Weaver's analysis of modern man's confusion as he struggles to understand why humanistic concepts of his worth do not bring satisfaction.

> First, astronomers in the last half millennium have discovered that the earth is but a mere speck on the fringes of a vast universe. Because the earth is physically "insignificant" in relation to the totality, it is implied that man is also *insignificant*. As reasoning goes, the creator must have little concern for insignificant man...
>
> Darwin's theory of the descent of man was the second means of depreciating the worth of man. No

longer the center of creation, he was robbed of his *special origins*, the divine spark snuffed out, and was now counted among the animal kingdom sharing a common ancestry with other creatures that struggled out of the primeval ooze and late of the anthropoid clan...

The third assault on biblical individualism occurred when man was robbed of his *freewill*, and his actions are now explained by material causality. He is now brute beast, a slave to animal passions, and those actions can be predicted and explained (or will be at some future point after enough study) by materialistic determinism... [41]

Humanists speak eloquently of the individual, his dignity, his worth, and his freedom to choose. They promise a freedom from the mores, norms, tradition, and distant voices of the past by which humanity has achieved a measure of civilization. However, it is a false freedom that gives unbridled control to the self and senses and ultimately leads to bondage. For all of man's time on this earth this personal license has been the path toward disaster. To believe that such personal freedom will lead to the greater good of mankind is folly for man is a fallen creature, and he cannot lift himself by pulling at his own bootstraps.[42] And no amount of societal or self-generated esteem will fix fallen and unregenerate man.

In the humanistic worldview, the praise of self is a relentless chorus and signals the retreat from relationship and unity. This humanistic emphases on self and its consequent conceits and egotism are systemic poisons leading to fragmentation of culture through redefinition and radicalization of various concepts such as egalitarianism, multiculturalism, tolerance, feminism, and diversity. Such fragmentation of culture leads to cultural decline and disintegration because of the loss of a unifying central cultural vision.

In the Christian worldview, value or worth of a person is not dependent on what that person or someone else thinks of him. Man's worth has been pre-determined by our Creator, and that worth is inestimably great. God did not create man out of need. Rather, it was a will to love, an expression of the very character of God, to share the inner life of the Trinity. Being God, He knew the course and cost of His creation. Rejection was not a surprise to an omniscient God. Before creation, God knew the cost of the regeneration of man would be the death of His Son, and this is hinted at in Revelation 13:8, "...Lamb slain from the foundation of the world." God's infinite love exceeded the cost of that love at Calvary.[43] To compare the value humanism places on self-actualized and highly self-esteemed man with the value God places on His special creation is to compare ashes with gold dust.

Part IV – Helicopter government – Overindulging (6-19-15)

This series of articles describes helicopter parenting and helicopter governing, the pathologies associated with each, and the impact on American culture. A helicopter government is one that exhibits characteristics similar to those of helicopter parenting which are expressed in four types of behavior: overprotection, overpraising, overindulging, and overprogramming. In Part IV we shall examine our helicopter government's ruinous overindulgence and the pathologies and consequences thereof to individuals and culture at large.

Overindulging

Life is one of limitations. In every facet of life we face restrictions, either natural (e.g., gravity) or man-made (e.g., laws, codes of conduct, regulations, rules). Children must learn at an early age that those limitations include both actions and material things. A child who is always given whatever they want or allowed to do anything they want will have difficulty relating actions with consequences, developing a work ethic, understanding the relationship between effort and reward, and appreciating the concept of delayed gratification. Many parents have ignored these lessons when training their children, and their overindulged children have grown up to be overindulged adults with a sense of entitlement. Richard Weaver compared those with an entitlement mentality to a spoiled child. He wrote, "The spoiled child has not been made to see the relationship between effort and reward. He wants things, but regards payment as an imposition or as an expression of malice by those who withhold for it. His solution…is to abuse those who do not gratify him."[44]

The Boomer generation (born between the end of World War II and the end of 1964) was the first to wear the badge of entitlement. Boomers grew up in an era of unbridled economic optimism, abundance, and prosperity which they assumed would last forever. In 1965, the first year after the Boomer generation officially ended, Charles Reich wrote, "Society today is built around entitlement." In other words, there was a firm popular expectation that some specific or general outcome will occur, whether or not it is formally embodied in law. These expectations include professional licenses, executive contracts, stock options, social security pensions, and education, and most of the more important entitlements flow in some form or fashion from government. But, whether private or from government, "...to the recipients they (entitlements) are essentials, fully deserved, and in no sense a form of charity."[45]

The growth of the Boomers' embryonic entitlement mentality would be dramatically boosted during the last birth year of their generational cohort. In his 1964 State of the Union address, President Johnson proposed a massive legislative assault that would move an already "...rich society...upward to the Great Society." This was the beginning of the war on poverty built on a massive array of new federal programs designed to aid the poor. However, over the next two decades, federal legislation and social policy engineers and architects would "...re-enslave many poor and minorities into a web of government dependency." One of the most damaging programs was the Aid for Dependent Children whose qualifying requirements were changed to include any household with no male family head present, that is, it became more lucrative to not be married than to be married. The effects of these policies were devastating to the family and traditional marriage. In 1950, families comprising a husband and wife in a traditional marriage were represented by 88 percent of white families and 78 percent of black families. With the modification of AFDC guidelines by Johnson and Congress, the black family structure began a rapid decline in 1967. By the late 1970s, intact black families had declined to 59 percent compared to 85 percent for white families.[46]

The entitlement society is a derivative of humanism as can be seen in the Humanist Manifesto. If an individual cannot contribute to their own betterment, "...then society should provide means to satisfy their basic economic, health, and cultural needs, including whatever resources make possible, a minimum guaranteed annual income."[47]

As the humanistic worldview has ascended in America, the nation has moved toward economic bondage in both government and private sectors as socialism and its entitlement mentality have become ingrained in the American consciousness.[48] An entitlement society ultimately fails because it is based on a false understanding of human nature. The fatal flaw of an entitlement society is utopianism, "...its presumption that we are inexorably on our way toward a perfect society."[49] This is humanism's faith in the utopian concept of human perfectibility known as progressivism which denies the fallen, corruptible nature of man.

It is right and proper to distinguish between what is government's responsibility and what is private (individual or institution) responsibility. However in this division of responsibility, Americans have forgotten that they are the government and that the government has and always will have limited resources. The political system now dances to the music of the entitled who have the loudest and/or largest band. With an entitlement mentality, we attempt to fix unlimited numbers of problems with limited resources rather than reasonably allocate available resources to the most pressing problems while providing a safety net for the poor but not a chaise lounge.

In 2006 Leonard Steinhorn published *The Greater Generation-In Defense of the Baby Boom Legacy.* He makes an exceptionally revealing statement about the general mindset and attitude of the Boomers—that of entitlement—which had become pervasive by the end of the twentieth century. He wrote, "The problem is that the reality of Greatest Generation America fell far short of the ideal—the America that Boomers beheld wasn't even close to the America they were *promised."* [50] [emphasis added] What generation was ever *promised* anything? Each generation receives the cultural heritage of all that have gone before. Each generation is given the opportunity to do great and good things, and they should do better for they stand on the shoulders of their ancestors. Each generation is given an opportunity, *not a promise nor an entitlement.*[51]

America has become the land of entitlements whose national anthem is now "We deserve", and for three generations there has been little memory of the historical relationship between actions and consequences, effort and reward, a work ethic, and delayed gratification. Americans' concept of the role of government has changed dramatically in the last eighty-five years. To illustrate the transition from an independent, self-reliant people to an overindulged entitlement generation, I retell the story of an incident my long-deceased grandmother told to me many years ago and about which I've written before.

> My father's family was considered poor even by the standards of the Great Depression. During that time, my father's mother, my grandmother, cared for a sick husband and five children, cleaned people's houses, and did laundry and sewing for others. When she was in her eighties, she told me of an incident that she experienced during the Depression. There was no food to feed her family. So she went to the back door of a little restaurant at closing time in the small rural town of Collinsville, Oklahoma, where they lived. She asked for any leftover soup. It was some fifty years later, but

she still called it the worst day of her life. Her attitude may seem strange to a twenty-first century citizen with a typical entitlement mentality prevalent in United States today, but such were the people of the Greatest Generation and their ancestors.[52]

Part V – Helicopter government – Overprogramming (6-26-15)

This series of articles describes helicopter parenting and helicopter governing, the pathologies associated with each, and the impact on American culture. A helicopter government is one that exhibits characteristics similar to those of helicopter parenting which are expressed in four types of behavior: overprotection, overpraising, overindulging, and overprogramming. In Part V we shall examine our helicopter government's overprogramming of the lives of its citizens through excessive and burdensome rules and regulations on individuals and culture at large and the pathologies and consequences thereof.

Overprogramming

One of the great tragedies of modern life over the last several decades is the loss of childhood in America. Perhaps a better word is "condensation" of childhood. Dr. David Elkind described this phenomenon in his 1981 book *The Hurried Child*.

> ...it is important to see childhood as a stage of life, not just as the anteroom to life. Hurrying children into adulthood violates the sanctity of life by giving one period priority over another. But if we really value human life, we will value each period equally and give unto each stage of life what is appropriate to that stage...In the end, a childhood is the most basic human right of children.[53]

Helicopter parents overprogram the lives of their children through obsessive scheduling, micromanaging, and monitoring. In such a regimented world the child becomes a pawn of the clock and calendar rather than a child of the moment or season. We see well-meaning parents over schedule their children's lives with play-dates, organized sports, extra-curricular school activities, and the like with virtually no down time for just being a kid. The cell phone has become a child's wireless umbilical cord by which parents micromanage and monitor the minutest actions and decisions of their children. One of the signs of an overprogrammed child is a frequent complaint of boredom (which means they have found themselves with an unfilled gap in their schedule). But whatever happened to good old-fashioned play? By "old-fashioned" play is meant unstructured, voluntary, no goals, curiosity unplugged, and fun. In other words, when does a child have his own personal and private downtime?

For many serious psychologists, sociologists, and education professionals, old-fashioned unstructured, purposeless play is as outmoded as yesterday's bell-bottoms, a waste of time and energy, and non-productive. Yet, researchers have discovered the enormous benefits of unstructured play. It stimulates the brain; thrives on complexity, uncertainty, and possibility; makes us mentally quick; teaches social and survival skills; and stretches us as we grow toward adulthood. Effectively, play is practice for adulthood.[54] But in our children's overprogrammed lives, play is now work and its activities (sports, music, camp, and other such activities) are now competitive and professionalized.[55] Children are now treated as miniature adults.

The governmental equivalent to parental overprogramming is a pervasive governmental interference in the lives of its citizens. Socialism is the practical application of the tenets of humanism which are being infused into society. The essence of a life overprogrammed by a humanistic helicopter government is a loss of freedom, a freedom by which is meant the absence of coercion as opposed to humanism's new freedom which is not freedom at all. The new freedom is merely another name for leveling society through an equal distribution of wealth and circumstance. Rather than expanding the range of choice, leveling results in greater limitations on choice, and those limitations, which by definition is a loss of freedom, are the ultimate outcome of all socialistic systems.[56]

Leveling society requires omnipresent rules—petty, complicated, convoluted, uniform, voluminous, tedious, wearisome rules which dulls the mind, weakens the spirit, saps energy, crushes creativity, and opposes initiative. To give an inkling of the size of the overprogrammization of American life, Title 27 of the U.S. Code of Federal Regulations is the U.S. Tax Code which contains 16,845 pages including the part written by Congress. It is available for purchase from the U.S. Government Printing office for $1,153. However, the U.S. Tax Code is just one of 50 titles found in the U.S. Code of Federal Regulations, each of which contains one or more individual volumes, which are updated once each calendar year, on a staggered basis.[57] To these we add a multitude of state, county, city, and other regulatory entities' rules and regulations. These have become the official handbook for living life. Who needs freedom when the government has all the answers?

Overprogramming life, whether the catalyst is a helicopter parent or a helicopter government, robs child and adult alike of perspective as to the important things in life. As we travel through various seasons of life, perspectives change but the things of importance never do. As we enter adulthood, the appointment book fills and the "to do" list lengthens. That is a normal part of life, but such things are temporal and appear much less important in life's rear view mirror. It is the moments and seasons we savor, store in our memory banks, and protect for they cannot be recreated or rescheduled.

Who hasn't smiled at the joy and wonder of a four-year-old boy focusing on the fascinating complexities of a dandelion or gazing at the playful wanderings of a butterfly on a sunny spring afternoon all the while oblivious to yells from parents and coaches as the soccer ball rolls past him?

How many of us adults are secret Walter Mitty types who have on occasion snatched a moment from our childhood to ride with the Commander as he pilots the Navy hydroplane through the worst storm in twenty years of Navy flying...or stand beside Captain Mitty as we strap on our Webley-Vickers 50.80 automatics and prepare to fly forty miles through hell while the cannonading shells from the box barrage crash around the dugout...[58] We all deserve a childhood, and if we are fortunate, a little bit of our childhood's innocence, wonder, and adventure will survive in us and act as a respite if not a reprieve from our helicopter government's overprogrammed world.

This was done by ordinary people

Part I (5-30-14)

The end-product of the Holocaust lay in the gas chambers and ashes of the crematoria within the German death camps spread across Europe in 1945. But the beginning of the Holocaust was much more subtle and seemingly innocuous except to the Jew and others on the wrong side of the German cultural and political wars of the 1930s. In his biography of Dietrich Bonhoeffer, the German theologian and spy, Eric Metaxas described the events that led to the Holocaust.

On January 30, 1933, Adolf Hitler became the democratically elected chancellor of Germany. On February 27, the Nazis set afire the building that housed the democratically elected Reichstag and blamed it on the Communists. That same day Hitler pressured the highly respected Field Marshall Hindenburg to sign the Reichstag Fire Edict which suspended certain sections of the German constitution and allowed restrictions on personal liberty, free expressions of opinion, rights of assembly and association; violations of privacy of communications (postal, telegraphic, and telephonic); warrants for searches of homes; and confiscations of and restrictions on private property.[59]

Following the Reichstag Fire Edict, Nazi storm troopers began immediately to arrest, imprison, torture, and kill their opponents. On March 23rd the Reichstag bowed to Nazi pressure and approved the Enabling Act which placed the whole power of the government under Hitler's control.

> With the tools of democracy, democracy was murdered and lawlessness made "legal." Raw power ruled, and its only real goal was to destroy all other powers besides itself...In the First months of Nazi rule, the speed and scope of what the Nazis intended and had begun executing throughout German society were staggering. Under what was called the *Gleichschaltung* (synchronization), the country would be thoroughly *reordered along National Socialist lines*. No one dreamed how quickly and dramatically things would change.[60] [emphasis added]

Hermann Goring described this reordering of society as mainly an "administrative" change. An understanding of what this "reordering" meant for the Jews would come swiftly.

- April 1 – Boycott of Jewish stores across Germany. The reason given was to stop the international press supposedly controlled by the Jews from printing lies about the Nazis.
- April 7 – Removal and prohibition of anyone of Jewish descent from holding civil service jobs. Government employees must be of Aryan stock. (Enabling Act – Aryan Paragraph.)
- April 22 – Jews were not allowed to serve as patent lawyers. Jewish doctors were prohibited from working in hospitals with state-run insurance.
- April 25 – Strict limits on the number of Jewish children that could attend public schools.
- May 6 – Laws expanded to include all honorary university professors, lecturers, and notaries.
- June – Jewish dentists and dental technicians were prohibited from working with state-run insurance institutions.
- Fall – Laws restricting non-Aryans expanded to include spouses of non-Aryans.
- September 29 – Jews banned from all entertainment and cultural activities including literature, the arts, theater, and film.
- October – Jews expelled from journalism when all newspapers were placed under Nazi control.[61]

It was another spring twelve years later that World War II ended in Europe and the gates of the death camps would swing open to reveal to the world the real meaning of Goring's "administrative" change. The pogroms of medieval Europe and Tsarist Russia had been reincarnated and perfected in one of the most advanced societies of the early twentieth century. Germany's organized destruction of helpless people has few equals in the history of mankind. With scientific precision coupled with administrative order, the Nazis murdered eleven million people including between five and six million Jews in the gas-chambers and crematoria of the death camps, through shootings in other parts of Europe, and by overwork and starvation. In 1901, 75% of the world's Jews lived in Eastern Europe. A century later one-half of all Jews live in English speaking countries and 30% live in Israel.

Germany's "final solution" to the Jewish problem changed forever the map of Jewish life in Europe.[62]

The momentary euphoria, goodwill, and hopes for a more cooperative order at the end of World War II quickly melted away as the realities of the war exposed the heart of mankind and his capacity for evil. J. N. Roberts summarized the post-war search for answers as to the "why" of Nazi Germany.

> In many ways, Germany had been one of the most progressive countries in Europe; the embodiment of much that was best in its civilization. That Germany should fall prey to *collective derangement* on this scale suggested that *something* had been wrong at the root of that civilization itself. The crimes of the Nazis had been carried out not in a fit of barbaric intoxication with conquest, but in a systematic, scientific controlled, bureaucratic (though often inefficient) way, about which there was little that was irrational except the appalling end which it sought.[63] [emphasis added]

The post-war world remained puzzled at Germany's "collective derangement" given its veneer of rationality and scientific and cultural progress. But along with Germany, much of the world also worshiped the same gods of rationalism, science, materialism, secularism, and progress. Man was assumed to be basically good, but the realities of the war removed humanism's mask of goodness to reveal the face of evil. The answer to the "why" of Nazi Germany was evil—that *something* that had been wrong at the root of civilization itself and which Roberts sought to identify. It was the source of Germany's collective derangement, but it also resides in the heart of every man.

With few exceptions, the Nazis and their collaborators were not mere madmen as one would suppose. Rather, the whole story of the Holocaust can be summed up in one sentence, "*This was done by ordinary people.*"[64] Those words by Ravi Zacharias cut to the heart of the source of evil for it reveals the inescapable conclusion that there is an indelible stain upon the soul of man. In his Gospel account, Mark described the diseased heart of man.

> For from within, out of the heart of man, come evil thoughts, fornication, theft, murder, adultery, coveting, wickedness, deceit, licentiousness, envy, slander, pride, foolishness. All these evil things come from within, and they defile a man. [Mark 7:21-23. RSV]

Christians call the root of this evil *original sin*. It is the evil that is found within the soul of every human being that ever lived. But in the great meta-narrative of the Bible, we learn of the way for fallen man to be cleansed of that evil and mend his broken relationship with God. We find the answer in John's Gospel: "For God so loved the world that he gave His only Son, that whoever believes in him should not perish but have eternal life." [John 3:16. RSV]

Part II (6-6-14)

Many years ago I read a book about Adolf Hitler and the rise of Nazism in Germany during the early 1930s. Although I don't remember the details of what I read, the book contained a photograph that disturbed me to such an extent that I still vividly remember it after all these years. It was a picture of a beautiful, well-dressed young woman perhaps in her thirties. She was attending a rally at which Hitler spoke during the time he was gaining political power over the German people. As she gazed at the Fuhrer, there was a smile on the young woman's face which glowed with admiration if not absolute idolization. Her rapt attention made her appear as though hypnotized by Hitler and his words. The reason I was so disturbed was because I knew the end of the story. How could this young woman and the crowd around her be so naïve and susceptible to the Nazi message? She and the others were just ordinary people! But these ordinary people, in their gullibility and rejection of their Christian heritage, allowed themselves to be deceived and as a result made possible the greatest conflagration of death and destruction in the history of mankind.

The Germans had lost the First World War in 1918, and the fierce German pride was dealt a succession of body blows. The 50-year-old monarchy ended with Kaiser Wilhelm's forced abdication. Communists and Social Democrats warred for control as the nation was near anarchy. The Weimer Republic was the victor but a deeply flawed democratic regime. Germany was forced to eviscerate its armed forces, give up much of its European territories, abandon Asian and African colonies, and pay huge reparations to the Allied nations.[65] Germany sank into years of hyperinflation and depression (both economically and psychologically).

Because of the consequences of the First World War, the German people and especially the younger Germans were disillusioned and lost all confidence in the traditional authority of the monarchy and the church. They wanted a fuhrer, and for the German people salvation would come from Adolf Hitler who promised that he would restore order, resurrect the economy, and return the nation to its rightful place on the world's stage.[66] But their desire for a fuhrer required a loss of rights and freedom which led to totalitarianism and eventual destruction of Germany.

Hitler's message was not a new one. Eve succumbed to its seductions in the third chapter of Genesis...Ye shall be as gods. In the eleventh century BC, King David wrote, "The fool hath said in his heart: there is no god." [Psalms 14:1. KJV] Humanism is man's second oldest faith—the great alternative faith of mankind—man without God. But it was the Greeks of the fourth through sixth centuries BC that gave form and body to the man-made philosophy of humanism that would impact the world second only to Jesus Christ.[67] Seventeenth century Enlightenment thought gave new life to Greek humanism and the doctrines of progress, rationality, secularism, and political reform. Values did not arise from fixed notions of right and wrong prescribed by a non-existent transcendent God but were a product of moral relativism in which man is merely a bundle of instincts and urges.[68]

Dietrich Bonhoeffer called "...'the Greek spirit' or 'humanism' as 'the most severe enemy' that Christianity ever had."[69] And in twenty-first century America, Christianity is once again at war with humanism. From this battle we can see alarming parallels between the political and cultural changes that occurred in Germany during the early 1930s and those of the United States since 2009.

- April 1, 1933 – Boycott of Jewish stores across Germany. The reason given was to stop the international press supposedly controlled by the Jews from printing lies about the Nazis.[70]

  July 26, 2012 – The Christian owner of Chic-Fil-A was urged to back out of his expansion plans in Boston and Chicago because his company gave money to nonprofits that support limiting marriage to unions between a man and a woman. Because of his biblical beliefs, he had run afoul of Chicago mayor Rohm Emanuel, former White House Chief of Staff for President Obama. Emanuel said, "Chick-Fil-A's values are not Chicago values. They're not respectful of our residents, our neighbors and our family members. And if you're gonna be part of the Chicago community, you should reflect Chicago values..." Chicago

Alderman Joe Moreno said he will seek to block a permit for Chick-Fil-A to expand into a Chicago neighborhood. "To have those discriminatory policies from the top down is just not something that we're open to," Moreno said.[71]

- April 22, 1933 – Jews were not allowed to serve as patent lawyers. Jewish doctors were prohibited from working in hospitals with state-run insurance.[72]

March, 2009 – An Eastern Michigan University student was expelled because she would not counsel clients regarding sexual relationships outside of marriage which she viewed as immoral because of her Christian beliefs. Julea Ward was in her last year of her completing work for her master's degree in counseling at EMU. While in a practicum in which she counseled clients, she asked that a prospective client wanting advice on a homosexual relationship be referred to another counselor. A faculty panel of three professors and one student ruled that Ward had violated the American Counseling Association's code of ethics. However, the Association's code of ethics "...broadly allows for referrals anytime a counselor determines an 'inability to be of professional assistance'."[73] The university and Ms. Ward settled the matter out of court in December 2012.

- May 6, 1933 – Anti-Jewish laws expanded to include all honorary university professors, lecturers, and notaries.[74]

April, 2007 – Dr. Mike Adams, a criminology professor at the University of North Carolina–Wilmington was denied promotions because of his religious beliefs following his conversion from atheism to Christianity in 2000. "Subsequently, the university subjected Adams to a campaign of academic persecution that culminated in his denial of promotion to full professor, despite an award-winning record of teaching, research, and service." In April 2014, almost seven years after Adams filed suit, a federal court found in his favor and ordered the university to promote Dr. Adams with back pay.[75]

- June, 1933 – Jewish dentists and dental technicians were prohibited from working with state-run insurance institutions.[76]

    May 15, 2014 – Pasadena City Health Director Dr. Eric Walsh resigned after being suspended for two weeks pending investigation by city officials after their discovery of videos of sermons by Lay Pastor Walsh "...criticizing homosexuality, calling the founder of Islam a Satanist, and calling evolution a 'religion of Satan'." There was no evidence of bias or misconduct while serving in his capacity as the city's health director, but the city's Human Relations Commission Chairman Nat Nehdar strongly criticized Walsh for his beliefs. "We don't tolerate this type of behavior, *this type of thought*." Following his resignation in Pasadena, the Georgia Department of Public Health announced Walsh would be hired to manage a six-county health district. Strong pressure from the gay-activist community in Georgia resulted in an investigation of Walsh's background including the video sermons and led the department to withdraw its offer.[77] [emphasis added]

- September 29, 1933 – Jews banned from all entertainment and cultural activities including literature, the arts, theater, and film.[78]

    May 7, 2014 – Home and Garden TV canceled a home-flipping program planned for October by former major league baseball brothers David and Jason Bentham because of their Christian beliefs regarding homosexuality and abortion. Background reports from a left-wing organization given to HGTV labeled the brothers as "anti-gay, anti-choice extremists."[79]

- October, 1933 – Jews expelled from journalism when all newspapers were placed under Nazi control.[80]

September 6, 2013 – A college football commentator was fired by Fox Sports Southwest because of his Christian beliefs regarding same-sex marriage. A committed Christian, Craig James said, "…gay civil unions are wrong, homosexuality is 'a choice,' and gays will 'have to answer to the Lord for their actions'." He made the statements during his 2012 campaign for the Texas GOP nomination for the U.S. Senate. Fox Sports Southwest fired him one week after being hired. A spokesman said, "We just asked ourselves how Craig's statements would play in our human resources department. *He couldn't say those things here.*"[81] [emphasis added]

Change was the banner under which the Nazis marched. It would be accomplished by *Gleichschaltung* (synchronization) in which the country would be reordered along National Socialist lines "…which meant that everything must fall in line with the Nazi worldview."[82]

The American *Gleichschaltung* of 2009 would also be a reordering of the nation to reflect the humanistic worldview whose default setting for organizing society is socialism. A Barak Obama campaign speech on February 5, 2008 captured both the message of change and the worldview behind it. "Change will not come if we wait for some other person or some other time. We are the ones we've been waiting for. We are the change that we seek."[83] President Obama's words resonate with the clarion call of the humanists whose God is self as opposed to He who created the universe.

Part III (6-13-14)

Adolf Hitler believed that "…Christianity preached 'meekness and flabbiness,' and this was simply not useful to the National Socialist ideology…" Hitler hated Christianity, but as a practical man, he was a pretend Christian and found the German Christian church temporarily useful in consolidating Nazi power. In time he subverted much of the church and changed its basic ideology.[84]

At the beginning of 1933, the German church stood at a crossroads. The great majority of German Lutheran churches chose the path of Hitler and the Nazis instead of the teachings of Jesus Christ.[85] All of German life was to be synchronized under Hitler's leadership, and "...the church would lead the way." The majority of churches called themselves "German Christians" and advocated a strong unified church seamlessly wedded to the state that would restore Germany to her former glory. The union of the state church with the Nazi regime required churches to conform to Nazi racial laws and ultimately swear allegiance to Hitler as the supreme leader of the church and by doing so "...blithely tossed two millennia of Christian orthodoxy overboard."[86]

There was a minority of Christians and churches in Germany that opposed Hitler and the German Christians. The resistance centered within the new "Confessing Church" led by Dietrich Bonhoeffer, Martin Niemöller, and a few others. When Hitler heard of a potential church split because of objections to his policies, he summoned several dissenting church leaders including Niemöller to the Reich Chancellery. He lectured the assembled churchmen and said all he wanted was peace between Church and state and blamed them for obstructing his plans. Hitler warned them "...to confine yourself to the Church. I'll take care of the German people." Niemöller responded that the Church also had a responsibility toward the German people that was entrusted to them by God and that neither Hitler nor anyone else in the world had power to remove that responsibility. Hitler turned away without comment, but that same evening the Gestapo ransacked Niemöller's rectory while searching for incriminating material. Within days a homemade bomb exploded in the hall of the rectory.[87]

As Nazi pressure was ratcheted up against the dissenting churchmen, Bonhoeffer and Niemöller were criticized by their fellow churchmen for opposing Hitler and his policies. Eventually over two thousand would choose the route of appeasement and safety and abandoned support of Bonhoeffer and Niemöller's efforts in resisting the Nazis. "They believed that appeasement was the best strategy; they thought that if they remained silent they could live with Hitler's intrusion into church affairs and his political policies."[88]

However, not all Confessing Church pastors and lay leaders bowed to Hitler's demands, but they would pay a price for their courage. In 1937, a remnant of more than eight hundred were arrested and imprisoned including Niemöller who spent the next eight years in prison, seven of which were in Dachau, one the Nazis' most infamous concentration camps.[89]

We have identified three groups of churches in Nazi Germany of the 1930s: the apostate German Christian church, the Confessing church which became the silent church of appeasement, and a faithful remnant that became the suffering church.

In the twenty-first century, the enemy of the American church is still the one that Bonhoeffer identified as the "...the most severe enemy" that Christianity ever had—humanism.[90] We are seeing the same patterns and methods used by Hitler to marginalized and make powerless much of the American Christian church through its seduction by the humanistic spirit of the age. The god of Hitler has been replaced by the god of humanism and its lesser god of equality in all of its destructive humanistic definition and interpretation.

In America there is an apostate church that has abandoned any pretense of adherence to the gospel message. Biblical truths are twisted, mocked, or dismissed altogether. Others champion a social gospel or preach a gospel of health, wealth, happiness, harmony, and cheap grace in place of the cross and death to self. Eighty years ago, Bonhoeffer described "cheap grace."

> Cheap grace is the deadly enemy of our Church...In such a Church the world finds a cheap covering for its sins; no contrition is required, still less any real desire to be delivered from sin...Cheap grace means the justification of sin without the justification of the sinner...Cheap grace is grace without discipleship, grace without the cross, grace without Jesus Christ, living and incarnate.[91]

Apart from the apostate church, there is also a faithful but mostly silent church in America that is content to preach the gospel and ignore the culture. Erwin Lutzer wrote, "Whether in Nazi Germany or America, believers cannot choose to remain silent under the guise of preaching the Gospel...we must live out the implications of the cross in every area of our lives. We must be prepared to submit to the Lordship of Christ in all 'spheres'."[92] Yet, as we live out the implications of the cross in every area of our lives, we must understand that the culture wars in which we soldier for Christ are *not* about maintaining the American dream however one may define it. Rather, the culture wars are about restoring the biblical understanding of truth in all spheres of our national life. To do so one must speak the truth in the face of lies, stand on biblical principles when others compromise, and take right actions in spite of consequences. A hostile culture and an adversarial government and culpable legal system will extract a price from those that dare to oppose them. What is accomplished by such opposition when it seemingly brings only hardship, suffering, and defeat?

"Suffering communicates the gospel in a new language; it authenticates the syllables that flow from our lips...It is not how loud we can shout but how well we can suffer that will convince the world of the integrity of our message."[93]

In recent years the forces of humanism have gained sustained power and critical mass in all spheres of American life and have become openly hostile and threatening to the true church of Jesus Christ. However, there is a bold remnant of the faithful church that is listening to the voices of modern Bonhoeffers and Niemöllers who are speaking out in those spheres of American life against the evils that have spread over America and much of the church. Such boldness follows the path of costly grace, and very soon that remnant may be able to claim the cloak of the suffering church.

Most in the American church cannot comprehend the meaning of the suffering church. It is something that happens "over there," something that is foreign to their thinking. They believe the American church somehow has been exempt from the consequences of costly grace. To suggest otherwise is almost heresy. But the Apostle Paul would disagree.

> ...it is the Spirit himself bearing witness with our spirit that we are the children of God, and if children, then heirs, heirs of God and fellow heirs with Christ, *provided we suffer with him in order that we may be glorified with him.* [Romans 8:16-17. RSV] [emphasis added]

In the dark days of World War II, Bonhoeffer wrote, "When God calls a man, he bids him come and die." On April 9, 1945, Dietrich Bonhoeffer answered Christ's final call. After two years in prison, he was hanged on the direct order of Adolph Hitler who ended his own life three weeks later in an underground bunker in Berlin.

Part IV (6-20-14)

The role of government and the role of the church as it relates to government

Dietrich Bonhoeffer went to his death on a Nazi gallows in 1945 with a very definite understanding of the role of the church in society, and his death was the eventual outcome of his living that understanding. God ordained the establishment of government for the preservation of order and the establishment of laws that define that order. The church has no right to interfere with the actions of the state in purely political matters. That said, Bonhoeffer also firmly believed the church plays a vital role in helping the state be the state by continually asking if the state's actions can be justified as a legitimate fulfillment of its role. In other words, do the actions of the state lead to law and order and not to lawlessness and disorder? Where the state fails, it is the role of the church to draw the state's attention to its failures. Likewise, if the state creates an atmosphere of "excessive law and order," the church must also remind the state of its proper role. Excessive law and order becomes evident when the state's power develops "...to such an extent that it deprives Christian preaching and Christian faith...of their rights."[94]

Bonhoeffer demonstrated his belief of limits on state authority in his arguments to the German Lutheran church (effectively the state church) against its acceptance of the Nazi Aryan paragraph in the synchronization of all German life in accordance with Nazi dictates. The Aryan paragraph served as the basis for many laws that denied Jews their rights as German citizens.

But Bonhoeffer's arguments regarding the German government's treatment of the Jews really framed the larger question of "what is the church?" In other words, from where does the church receive its authority? Is it an instrument of the state and therefore subject to the state or is it apart from the state? If it is apart from the state, then what does the church do when the state oversteps the boundaries of its *legitimate* authority?[95]

Actions of the church with regard to government

Bonhoeffer listed three actions the church should take regarding the state. The first has been described—the church must question the state with regard to its actions and whether its actions can be justified as a legitimate concern of the state. Second, the church must "...aid victims of state action in its ordering of society...even if they (the victims) do not belong to the Christian community." Bonhoeffer did not stop there but said a third step may be necessary. The church must "...not just bandage the victims under the wheel...but a stick must be jammed into the spokes of the wheel to stop the vehicle. It is sometimes not enough to help those crushed by the evil actions of a state; at some point the church must directly take action against the state to stop it from perpetrating evil." But Bonhoeffer's stick in the spokes of the wheel of state is justified *only* if the church's very existence is threatened by the state *and* the state is no longer a state as designed by God.[96]

In Part III we identified three groups of churches in Nazi Germany of the 1930s: the apostate German Christian church, the Confessing church which became the silent church of appeasement, and a faithful remnant that became the suffering church. The great majority of German churches during the Nazi era subordinated themselves to the Nazi state, did not speak out against Nazi tyranny, and did not aid the victims crushed by the wheel of state.

We also drew disturbing parallels between the German church of the 1930s and the American church of the twenty-first century. Christianity and its values are under full-scale attack in America. The church must decide what it will or will not do in response to that attack. Some will choose to do nothing and as justification point to Paul's letter to the Romans with regard to a Christian's conduct in relation to the state.

> Let every person be subject to the governing authorities. For there is no authority except from God, and those that exist have been instituted by God. Therefore he who resists the authorities resists what God has appointed, and those who resist will incur judgment. For rulers are not a terror to good conduct, but to bad. Would you have no fear of him who is in authority? Then do what is good, and you will receive his approval, for he is God's servant for your good. But if you do wrong, be afraid, for he does not bear the sword in vain; he is the servant of God to execute his wrath on the wrongdoer. Therefore one must be subject, not only to avoid God's wrath but also for the sake of conscience. [Romans 13:1-5. RSV]

But to do nothing is a misinterpretation of Paul's message. Paul is not saying that we should be obedient to government regardless of what it does. It is nonsensical to claim that *all* rulers are legitimate authorities who must be mindlessly obeyed because of a misunderstanding of the meaning of Romans 13:1-5.

So how do we resolve the dilemma of whether we are to obey a specific ruler (government) or not? The issue revolves around whether or not a government is one that receives its authority from God. Christians must be subject to governing authorities if the authority is instituted by God, but Christians are not required to submit to those rulers whose authority is *not* instituted by God and therefore is illegitimate. The distinction becomes apparent from Paul's words when he says that rulers are not a terror to good conduct, but to bad conduct.

But we know that many rulers in this world *are a terror to good conduct* and therefore do not fall within Paul's description of a government that receives its authority from God.

The church and bad government

Even where there is a bad government, Christians must be subject to governing authorities *to a point*. Christians are required to be subject to government laws and regulations even when they disagree with them. However, when those laws and regulations require Christians to compromise or disobey biblical commands with regard to one's personal life or the lives over which they have been given charge, the Christian must be obedient to God's word and not government authority.

Two current examples come to mind which give meaning to this distinction. The Christian owners of Hobby Lobby have refused to provide health insurance to their employees under the Affordable Care Act because of the requirement for the inclusion of abortion services. A Christian Colorado baker refused to make a cake for a homosexual couple's wedding. Both are laws which conflict with what it means to be a Christian who is obedient to the word of God. Christians must still be subject to the governing authorities except when their obedience conflicts with the higher laws of God.

The church and illegitimate government

There is a step beyond bad government when a government's authority becomes illegitimate because it no longer fulfills its role in providing order and has become lawless and disorderly. Therefore, Christians must be careful to distinguish between bad government and illegitimate authorities not ordained by God. We must also realize that bad governments, through a succession of actions upon which evil is piled upon evil, will at some point forfeit their legitimacy as God withdraws His authority. At that point the ignored *warnings and admonishments* of the church to a state rushing head-long into lawlessness and disorder must be exchanged for *sticks to be thrust into the spokes of the wheel* of that illegitimate government. However, Bonhoeffer cautioned that casting sticks into the spokes of the wheel of state is justified *only* if the church's very existence is threatened *and* the state is no longer a state upon which God's authority rests.

The very existence of the American church is being threatened by excessive laws and the heavy hand of the government as it attempts to drive Christianity from the cultural and institutional landscape of

America. The church and Christians must continue to admonish the state as to its over-reach and a possible loss of legitimacy. As the American government deprives its citizenry of their rights regarding Christian preaching and Christian faith, society will continue to slide into a cultural swamp devoid of any hint of morality. There may come a point at which God will lift His authority as the government fails to fulfill its proper role. At such a time the church must be ready with sticks to thrust into the spokes of the wheel of a lawless and chaotic government.

Part II - Socialism

The New Despotism

Part I (4-2-13)

Equality is a good thing. Right? Your first reaction may be, "Of course it is. It's even in the Declaration of Independence...'All men are created equal'." But let's give a little more thought and consideration to this topic. Do you really want your doctor to be equal to all other doctors? Do you want the airline pilot on whose plane you are a passenger to be equal with all other airline pilots? Of course not! You want your doctor to be the best doctor available when dealing with your health and that of your family. The same goes for the airline pilot on whose plane you are a passenger. So, we can't just worship at the shrine of equality and say that equality in everything is good as so much of society seems to be doing these days. In the culture wars, both sides support equality but have fundamentally different notions about what equality means and how it should be implemented and administered in all institutions of American life. One understanding of the meaning of equality has contributed to the United States becoming the most exceptional nation in the history of the world. The other meaning is contributing significantly to the disintegration of American culture as envisioned by the Founders.

Now, I don't want your eyes to glaze over as you think about the concept of equality. This is not an academic exercise because a correct understanding of equality will help you determine on which side of the culture war you stand and allow you to recognize and defend the meaning of equality as understood by the Founders in establishing this nation and designing our Constitution.

We begin with an abbreviated summation of the meaning of equality. Here we speak of equality in light of the individual within the Founders' meaning on the one hand versus the meaning as defined by the humanist levelers of the twenty-first century.

The founding Americans held a biblical worldview and relied on order that rested upon a respect for prescriptive rights and customs as opposed to the egalitarian notions of the French philosophers during the French Revolution. This difference was made clear by John Adams' definition of equality which strikes at the heart of what it really means—"a moral and political equality only"—by which is meant equality before God and before the law.[97] This definition does not teach that all men are born to equal powers, mental abilities, influence in society, property, and other advantages. Rather, all men are born to equal rights before God and the law and by implication to enjoy equal opportunity.

The humanistic definition of equality is clearly stated in *Humanist Manifesto II's* eleventh common principle, "The principle of moral equality must be furthered...This means equality of opportunity..."[98] But, the humanists' meaning of "equal opportunity" is immediately and drastically corrupted to mean an equality of outcome as measured by humanist requirements. To further clarify the intent of the signors of the *Manifesto,* the document states that, "If unable [by means of equal opportunity], society should provide means to satisfy their basic economic, health, and cultural needs, including whatever resources make possible, a minimum guaranteed annual income."[99]

This concept of human equality flows from the flawed humanistic assumption of the perfectibility of man. Under this concept, what men are comes from experience. Therefore, men are equal at birth, and differences and inequalities arise due to environment. The goal of humanists was to achieve an egalitarian society (and eliminate inequalities due to environment) through political means in which man, achieving perfect equality in their political rights, would at the same time be perfectly equalized and assimilated in their possessions, their opinions, and their passions. When humanists failed to achieve equality of outcome through political equality, the levelers demanded economic democracy, a new and expanded humanist definition of equality. However, economic democracy still means an equality of *condition* as opposed to equality of *opportunity* and is to be achieved through recognition of invented or synthetic rights coupled with broad but non-specific egalitarian ideals. As society is leveled with guarantees of certain outcomes to its citizens, political equality suffers, that is, imposed equality of outcome will destroy equality before the law.

We see evidence of the humanistic definition of equality being imposed on every institution of American life and the ensuing erosion of equality before the law. On an almost 24/7 basis we see and hear media reports from the battle fronts of the culture wars with regard to issues of perceived inequality including gay marriage, universal health care, women in combat roles, immigration, race, and employment. Some are issues dealing with equality before the law (excluding laws based on synthetic or invented rights), and the nation has and is promoting equality in those areas (e.g., race and employment discrimination). But even in those legitimate areas of concern, humanist organizations, politicians, and bureaucrats push the envelope beyond equality of opportunity.

Democracies are under grave and severe attack by a new despotism. Humanistic definitions of equality have played a central role in the ascendance of this despotism. In Part II we shall name this despotism and diagnose its operation and impact on the nation.

Part II (4-9-13)

In Part I we learned that humanistic definitions of equality have played a central role in the ascendance of a new despotism in America. About 175 years ago, Tocqueville gave a vivid picture of this new type of oppression that would threaten democracies and "...which will not be like anything there has been in the world before..." He admitted that he was having trouble naming this new despotism but "wished to imagine under what new features this despotism might appear in the world":

> I see an innumerable crowd of men, *all alike and equal*, turned in upon themselves in a restless search for those petty, vulgar pleasures with which they fill their souls…Above these men stands an immense and protective power which alone is responsible for looking after their enjoyments and watching over their destiny. It is absolute, meticulous, ordered, provident, and kindly disposed. It would be like a fatherly authority, if, father-like, its aim were to prepare men for manhood, but it seeks only to keep them in perpetual childhood; it prefers its citizens to enjoy themselves provided they have only enjoyment in mind. It works readily for their happiness but it wishes to be the only provider and judge of it. It provides their security, anticipates and guarantees their needs, supplies their pleasures, directs their principal concerns, manages their industry, regulates their estates, divides their inheritances. Why can it not remove from them entirely the bother of thinking and the troubles of life? (emphasis added)

> Thus, it reduces daily the value and frequency of the exercise of free choice; it restricts the activity of free

will within a narrower range and gradually removes autonomy itself from each citizen. Equality has prepared men for all this, inclining them *to tolerate all these things and often see them as a blessing.* (emphasis added)

Thus, the ruling power, having taken each citizen one by one into its powerful grasp and having molded him to its own liking, spreads it arms over the whole of society, covering the surface of social life with a networked of petty, complicated, detailed, and uniform rules through which even the most original minds and the most energetic of spirits cannot reach the light in order to rise above the crowd. It does not break men's wills but it does soften, bend, and control them; rarely does it force man to act but it constantly opposes what actions they perform; it does not destroy the start of anything but it stands in its way; it does not tyrannize but it inhibits, represses, drains, snuffs out, dulls so much effort that finally it reduces each nation to nothing more than a flock of timid and hardworking animals with the government as shepherd.[100]

The word Tocqueville was searching for in describing this new despotism was *socialism*, and his words have painted a prophetic and hauntingly real picture of the United States in the twenty-first century under the humanists' leadership in the institutions of American life: government, education, economics, the sciences (physical, biological, and social), popular culture, and the family. Socialism is the end result of a society that pushes towards the humanist worldview of which the humanists' definition of equality is central.

Why does humanism require a society organized under socialistic principles? First, socialism is a prerequisite for a humanist society. It is a cardinal tenet of the *Humanist Manifesto I* of 1933 which says: "A socialized and cooperative economic order *must* be established to the end that the equitable distribution of the means of life be possible."[101] For the humanist, equitable distribution means redistribution and redistribution means socialism. Second, if one examines humanism and its goals, those goals can only be achieved through the imposition of a socialistic system of controls because the fundamental nature of man conflicts with the humanistic worldview. Being created in the image of God and given a free will, humans have an innate thirst for freedom which socialism suppresses.

The restrictions of the humanist society are decided by the social engineers of that society, the elites or "conditioners" as C. S. Lewis called them. Thus, humanism is a top down affair. Its leaders determine what is best for the masses based on man's laws, not God's laws. Socialism is humanism's default setting for organizing society and is inherently domineering, restrictive, and restraining in the details of life and ultimately leads to loss of freedom in every aspect of life.

In a society built upon the biblical worldview, men join together and voluntarily limit their freedom. But the imposition of limits comes from a group of like-minded individuals whose central cultural vision reflects the same biblical worldview of freedom and the nature of man.

In concluding his description of the new despotism, Tocqueville stated that, "The vices of those who govern and the ineptitude of those governed would soon bring it (the nation) to ruin and the people, tired of its representatives and of itself, would create freer institutions or would soon revert to its abasement to one single master."[102] Given the apparent abdication by Congress of its designated role in the separation of powers and the proclivity of the Executive Branch in disabusing the judiciary, ignoring enforcement of the laws passed by Congress, and governing through illegitimate executive orders and presidential whim, it appears that America, through the ineptitude of the electorate, has chosen its abasement through one single master.

It's time for pushback.

March Madness: Nanny State 1 – Freedom 0 (3-28-14)

Jeanne Mandeville is the School of St. Mary's health-room director for kindergarten-through-eighth-grade. Loved by parents and children alike, Ms. Mandeville has been known as the school's Tooth-Fairy for many years because she helped students in the final stages of a tooth falling out. For the children, going to the school's Tooth Fairy was a rite-of-passage; a badge of honor in a child's growing up years. But not all liked Ms. Mandeville's role as Tooth Fairy. A complaint was emailed to Susan Rogers, Executive Director of the State Board of Dentistry.[103] In response to the complaint, Ms. Rogers warned that,

> Maybe a kid avoids a dentist because they know she'll (Mandeville) do it and it will be cheaper. She may not be able to evaluate things that need to be evaluated...There are so many diseases in your mouth that can happen...There's biological waste there. Someone needs to ask where it's going...A general citizen is not allowed to go pull several kids' teeth in a row; that is illegal practice of dentistry. It's technically a felony.[104]

Ms. Rogers stated that the complaint will be investigated because "...the dentistry board has authority over anyone determined to be practicing dentistry, whether they know they are technically 'practicing dentistry' or not."[105]

The State of Oklahoma has approximately 175 agencies, boards, commissions, and offices charged with varying degrees of oversight ranging from abstracts and boll weevils to wheat, wildlife, and women. Although not all have the authority to have someone charged with a felony for violating its rules, many have the ability to interject their regulatory noses into the lives of citizens and their businesses.[106] Most have worthy and important roles to play in governing and providing for the wishes of the people, but nevertheless something has gone wrong with the regulatory process.

As government involves itself with an ever expanding array of concerns for its citizens' welfare, various occupations and professions are swept into the net of regulation. Few complaints are heard from these regulated professions and occupations whose prestige and bank balances are elevated as competition is restricted by limiting ease of entry and prohibition of competing services.

Government intrusion and over-regulation in the lives of its citizens have grown exponentially since the New Deal and beginning in 1936 with the court's exceptionally expansive interpretation of the Constitution's general welfare clause. Laws and regulations have become repressive tools of a nanny-state government interfering in the lives of a free people capable of making rational decisions without government interference.

But in the larger picture of government interference in the lives of a free people, over-regulation of businesses, occupations, and professions is only one facet of the general trend toward organizing a socialistic society. This trend is the direct result of the rapid abandonment over the last three-quarters of a century of the Christian worldview upon which the nation was founded. In its place has risen the humanistic worldview which has been embraced by the institutions of American life and most of its leadership. Christianity leads to truth and freedom. Humanism leads to relativism and socialism whose ultimate end is totalitarianism.

Writing about America 180 years ago, Alexis de Tocqueville described this new type of despotism that would eventually threaten democracies.

> I see an innumerable crowd of men, *all alike and equal*, turned in upon themselves in a restless search for those petty, vulgar pleasures with which they fill their souls…Above these men stands an immense and protective power which alone is responsible for looking after their enjoyments and watching over their destiny. It is absolute, meticulous, ordered, provident, and kindly disposed. It would be like a fatherly authority, if, father-like, its aim were to prepare men for manhood, but it seeks only to keep them in perpetual childhood; it prefers its citizens to enjoy themselves provided they have only enjoyment in mind. It works readily for their happiness but it wishes to be the only provider and judge of it. It provides their security, anticipates and guarantees their needs, supplies their pleasures, directs their principal concerns, manages their industry, regulates their estates, divides their inheritances. Why can it not remove from them entirely the bother of thinking and the troubles of life?…

> Thus, the ruling power, having taken each citizen one by one into its powerful grasp and having molded him to its own liking, spreads it arms over the whole of society, covering the surface of social life with a network of petty, complicated, detailed, and uniform rules through which even the most original minds and the most energetic of spirits cannot reach the light in order to rise above the crowd.[107]

Tocqueville did not have a name for this new despotism, but today we know it as socialism. Socialism is humanism's template for organizing society and is inherently domineering, restrictive, and restraining in the details of life and ultimately leads to loss of freedom.

The political/intellectual/bureaucratic class will deny they are socialists or that their actions are socialistic by nature. However, their denials appear similar to those of the small boy who denies he ate the chocolate chip cookies even though his face and hands are smeared with chocolate and cookie crumbs. Hmmm. Children, teeth, chocolate…cavities? I'm sure the Oklahoma Board of Dentistry will have something to say about this.

Work (2-12-14)

A few years ago before my mother passed away at age 79, we were talking about life on the family dairy farm when my brothers and I were kids. For those that don't know, a dairy farm is a seven-day-a-week job with long hours, and as kids we thought everyone worked like that. Teasingly, I told my mother that if I knew then what I know now, I would have reported her and my father for child abuse! We both had a good laugh. While my brothers and I may not have appreciated it when we were children and teenagers, the instilled work ethic molded us, shaped our characters, and contributed to the joys and blessings we've had in our lives.

However, as our nation staggers toward the looming welfare state, work has become just another profane four-letter word. The denigration of work has been around for thousands of years and flourished in the classical civilizations of Greece and Rome in which physical work was considered demeaning to all except slaves and the lower classes. In ancient Athens, one-third of freemen sat daily discussing the affairs of state in the court of Comitia. Slaves, who outnumbered citizens five-to-one, performed all manual labor. In the "bread and circuses" pleasure-seeking Roman culture, it was again slaves who did all of the manual labor.[108]

But during the first century, at the eastern edge of the Mediterranean, a child was born that would give voice to God's view of the dignity of labor. His name was Jesus, the promised Messiah. His early disciples were mostly callus-handed fishermen, tradesmen, and even a local IRS agent. And the arch-persecutor-turned-apostle of this tiny Christian sect was a brilliant theologian and evangelist but also a tent-maker by trade. And the Apostle Paul admonished the Thessalonian Christians that, "If any one will not work, let him not eat." [2 Thessalonians 3:10. RSV] It was in the first century that Christians were driven from their homeland and made their first appearances in the Greco-Roman world. Because Christians believed in the dignity and honor of work, they were held with contempt by their Roman masters. Persecution arose, in part, because those strange Christian beliefs about work conflicted with the Romans' view of the world and also because of suspicions and jealousies of the Christians' prosperity due to their strong work ethic.[109]

But the first century Christian view of work was not a new philosophy but a reflection of the image of the Creator stamped on man, the pinnacle of His creation. Biblical instruction and admonitions regarding work are abundant. The first chapter of Genesis records God's labors in creating the universe. Not only does God work, He charged man with responsibilities and duties of being fruitful, replenishing and subduing the earth, and having dominion over all living creatures. When Adam and Eve were driven from the Garden of Eden because of their sin, God told Adam that "...cursed is the ground because of you; in toil you shall eat of it all the days of your life...In the sweat of your face you shall eat bread till you return to the ground..." [Genesis 3: 17, 19. RSV] Notice that God did not impose work as a punishment for their sin. Rather, the curse was on the ground upon which they would toil. In other words, the curse was upon the conditions under which the work would be performed, not on work itself. But God loved man and would make possible a way for man to re-enter right relationship with Him by sending His Son Jesus in human form as a babe. Perhaps this gives us another insight into God's view of work in that the earthly father of God's Son was a carpenter.

With the decline and fall of the western half of the Roman Empire by the end of the fifth century, a remnant of the Christian heritage of the western portion of the Roman Empire was pushed northward into the sparse and hostile forests of France and western Germany. The inhabitants were Gauls whom the Romans had conquered and brought civilization at the beginning of the Christian era. To this group was added a smaller number of Teutonic invaders that had come from the East and hindered for a time the building of an organized social life and assimilation of the Mediterranean culture. Life was harsh in the pioneer wilds of northern Europe at the beginning of the Middle Ages around A.D. 500. However, out of this difficult and meager existence was built a cohesive and somewhat refined civilization, and the broad and general characteristics of their medieval society remained for centuries. Those characteristics and viewpoint, worldview if you will, became the ideas and ideals of Christendom which were the foundations of the American experience from the earliest colonial days to the middle of the twentieth century.[110]

Christendom's creedal reverence for work and the practical necessity of work amidst primitive conditions in the forests and clearings of early Europe produced the phenomenon of the middle class, unknown before the advent of Christianity and now present in all of Western civilization. With the birth of the middle class came the reduction of poverty and its attendant disease. And from the middle class arose political and economic freedom of a magnitude unknown in the history of the world to that time.[111]

In the very earliest years of Europeans on the American continent, socialistic answers were sought to replace the Christian work ethic as the North Star for organizing society. Because of their isolation from the civilized world, Jamestown and the Plymouth Colony stand as great laboratory experiments regarding questions as to the validity and worthiness of socialistic principles. Communism of an almost pure variety, in the isolated and controlled environment of the New World, failed miserably in its initial years as laziness and inefficiency trumped thrift and industry. As the colonists abandoned their experiment in socialism, the colonies flourished.[112] Karl Marx's ideas regarding socialism presented in *The Communist Manifesto* became the twentieth century's grand socialist experiment which led to the enslavement of a third of humanity behind the iron and bamboo curtains. For three quarters of a century, the consequences of these socialistic systems were death and misery unparalleled in the history of mankind.

But our collective memory is short and socialism's propaganda machine is strong. Christianity and its values are being rapidly abandoned in Western societies in favor of a humanistic worldview requiring socialistic solutions to society's problems. As a result, socialism is destroying the middle class and its indispensable Christian work ethic, and America is becoming a bread and circuses culture.

The displacement of the work ethic by the actions of the American government's social engineers since the 1960s has had a multitude of far-reaching consequences. Just one example is the humanistic welfare solutions that have fractured the concept of family by substituting governmental assistance to unwed pregnant teenage girls. Fathers are not required to work and provide for the mother and child for whom they are responsible. This welfare system perpetuates itself through ensuing generations that repeat the cycle. The direct consequences of institutionalization of illegitimacy in American life are a rise in the illegitimacy rate (6% in 1963 to 41% in 2014) and consequent increases in drug use rate, dropout rate, crime rate, and incarceration rate.[113]

In the mid-1990s Congressional welfare reforms required those seeking welfare to work. However, this requirement was removed by an executive order by President Obama in 2012. Additionally, governmental subsidies provided by the Affordable Care Act have now been determined to be a *disincentive to work* by those receiving subsidies with a consequent loss of 2.5 million jobs over the next three years according to a Congressional Budget Office Report.[114]

The operation of man's fallen human nature exposes the soft and rotten underbelly of the tenets of the socialism and humanistic faith in mankind and their commitment to the principle of the greatest-happiness-for-the-greatest-number which humanists consider to be the highest moral obligation for humanity as a whole.[115] The operation of human nature conflicts with man-made socialistic solutions to the problems of life, and the end result is failure. People fail, families fail, and cultures ultimately fail. The socialists' false view of man's nature leads to poverty, starvation, and loss of freedom. The antidote is a rejection of socialism and a return to the Christian work ethic.

Newspeak 2014: The Language of Socialism (3-14-14)

Truth is the foundation of all morals, and the meaning of truth is obscured in direct proportion to the elasticity allowed in defining the meaning of words within a language. For 1,500 years the source of truth for much of Western civilization has been the Bible. The meaning of words such as truth, freedom, good and evil were relatively *inelastic* within the Christian worldview. Their meanings were based on absolutes called by various names: permanent things, universals, first principles, eternal truths, and norms.[116] These absolutes were revealed to man by God through His creation and His revelation to the ancient Hebrews and first century Christians.

Socialism requires an *elastic* language. For humanists, truth is defined in terms of cultural relativism which requires a suspension of judgment since all belief systems contain some truth within while no one belief system has all the truth. Therefore, all social constructions are culturally relative as they are shaped by class, gender, and ethnicity. Thus, there can be no universal truths because all viewpoints, lifestyles, and beliefs are equally valid. As a result, no man or group can claim to be infallible with regard to truth and virtue. Rather, truth is produced by the free give and take of competing claims and opinions—i.e., truth can be manufactured.[117]

Words are the means by which order is achieved in society. The dominant worldview of the members of a society determines the elasticity allowed in defining the meaning of words within the language and ultimately the meaning of truth and the freedom of the individual. The principal worldviews contending for dominance in Western civilization are Christianity and humanism. Christianity leads to truth and freedom. Humanism leads to relativism and socialism whose ultimate end is totalitarianism. Three modern prophets from the mid-twentieth century foresaw the effects of an elastic language with regard to the meaning of words.

George Orwell (1903-1950)

Orwell's prophetic novel *1984* paints a graphic and unsettling picture of life under a vast, insidious socialistic regime called Ingsoc (acronym for English Socialism) that covers a large part of the globe (See "The New Ministry of Truth 2014"). Control of the population is guided by Ingsoc's Inner Party and its leader, Big Brother, and the

Ministry of Truth. The ministry of Truth controls the news media, entertainment, the arts, and publishing and is responsible for propaganda and revision of the historical record to conform them to the government-approved version of events.

The regime invented *Newspeak* in which speech and writing use words in a way that changes their meaning, especially to persuade people to think a certain way or diminish the range of thought.[118]

> The purpose of Newspeak was not only to provide a medium of expression for the worldview and mental habits proper to Ingsoc, but to make all other modes of thought impossible. It was intended that when Newspeak had been adopted once and for all and Oldspeak forgotten, a heretical thought—that is, a thought diverging from the principles of Ingsoc—should be literally unthinkable, at least so far as thought is dependent on words...This was done partly by the invention of new words, but chiefly by eliminating undesirable words and by stripping such words as remained of unorthodox meanings, and so far as possible of all secondary meanings whatever. To give an example, the word *free* still existed in Newspeak, but it could only be used in such statements as "This dog is free from lice" or "This field is free from weeds. It could not be used in its old sense of "politically free" or intellectually free" since political freedom and intellectual freedom no longer existed even as concepts...[119]

Once immersed in Newspeak, it becomes relatively easy to doublethink which is the acceptance of two contradictory ideas or beliefs at the same time.

F. A. Hayek (1899-1992)

In his *Road to Serfdom*, Hayek has much to say about the language of socialism which he considers synonymous with totalitarianism. Whether it is the socialism of extensive redistribution of incomes through taxation and the institutions of the welfare state or socialism through the nationalization of the means of production and central planning, Hayek rightly believed that the outcome is essentially the same for both systems—totalitarianism.[120] And it is socialism's perversion of the language (words and their meaning) that is of particular concern. Once the sources of all information are under the control of a totalitarian regime, it has the power to mold the minds of the people. The minds of the people will then be indoctrinated with the precepts of the regime and no others will be tolerated. The moral consequences of totalitarian propaganda are destructive to the one of the essential foundation of all morals, that is, "...the sense of and respect for truth."[121]

Hayek described the means whereby language is perverted by socialism's propaganda.

> The most effective way of making people accept the validity of the values they are to serve is to persuade them that they are really the same as those which they, or at least the best among them, have always held, but which were not properly understood or recognized before...And the most efficient technique to the end is to use the old words but change their meaning. Few traits of totalitarian regimes are at the same time so confusing to the superficial observer and yet so characteristic of the whole intellectual climate as the complete perversion of language, the change of meaning of the words by which the ideals of the new regimes are expressed. The worst sufferer in this respect is, of course, the word "liberty." It is a world used as freely in totalitarian states as elsewhere.[122]

The quest for equality in socialistic society becomes an officially enforced inequality. Enforced inequality is labeled the new freedom or "collective freedom" which is not the freedom of the individual "...but the unlimited freedom of the planner to do with society what he pleases."[123]

Richard M. Weaver (1910-1963)

Weaver wrote of the power of the word in *Ideas Have Consequences*. Weaver accepted the ancient belief that there was "...a divine element present in language. The feeling that to have power of language is to have control over things is deeply imbedded in the human mind." Weaver believed that the heightened interest in semantics is the most notable development of our time with regard to the study of language. Semanticists question how the fixities of language can account for a changing reality through time. They desire that words not represent truth but a range of perceptions and reflect the circumstances of the user.[124]

In our world of progressive education, scientism, and mass media, the semanticists have captured the linguistic high ground through redefinition of key concepts. Regarding the consequences thereof, Weaver cut to the heart of the matter in a 1952 essay.

> Just as soon as men begin to point out that the word is one entity and the object it represents is another, there set in a temptation to do one thing with the word and another different thing with the object it is supposed to represent; and here begins that relativism which by now is visibly affecting those institutions which depend for their very existence upon our ability to use language as a permanent binder.[125]

The prophecies of Orwell, Hayek, and Weaver were published between 1944 and 1950. The fulfillment of their prophecies with regard to the perversion of the meaning of words is abundantly evident in twenty-first century America. The ascending humanistic worldview requires that society be organized upon socialistic principles. During the last half of the twentieth century, the redefinition of the meanings of certain words has become the feedstock of socialism's propaganda machine: multiculturalism, diversity, freedom, tolerance, good, evil, right, wrong, justice, freedom, and equality to name just a few. The new meanings are being used to mold the thinking of society in support of a humanistic worldview and its socialistic agenda.

The enemy of truth and morality is relativism. Relativism is the child of the false and destructive worldview of humanism that is tied to time and therefore temporal. Humanism and other false religions may ascend and dominate for a time, but the seeds of destruction lie in their own falseness. Truth is eternal and therefore a permanent binder that transcends time. Truth rests in the unadulterated word. "In the beginning was the Word, and the Word was with God, and the Word was God…And the Word became flesh and dwelt among us…For the law was given through Moses; grace and truth came through Jesus Christ." [John 1:1, 14a, 17. RSV] In response to Pontius Pilate's question regarding Jesus' kingship, Jesus answered, "You say that I am a King. For this I was born, and for this I have come into the world, to bear witness to the truth. Everyone who is of the truth hears my voice." [John 18:37. RSV]

Truth is reality, and it is the nature of man to seek and know truth. To know God is to know truth.

Part III – America

Disunited States of America (3-17-13)

George Washington's farewell address to the nation was published on September 17, 1796 near the end of his eight years as the first president of the newly minted United States. He spoke of his concern for the nation's welfare as expressed his "sentiments which are the result of much reflection, of no inconsiderable observation, and which appear to me all important to the permanency of your felicity as a people..."[126] His advice, warnings, and prescriptions have influenced generations of Americans but have been largely forgotten or ignored in modern times. Upon the occasion of his recent February birthday, it is well that we review some of the salient points from his farewell address that are particularly pointed and appropriate in twenty-first century America. I will quote liberally from his address and then revisit those quotes in light of the disunity caused by the culture wars and the resultant American angst.

Washington expressed his greatest concern with regard to maintaining the unity of the nation, both geographically and culturally. Unity and the prescriptions for its preservation were the central themes of his address. Speaking of the importance and source of the nation's unity, Washington said:

> The unity of government which constitutes you one people is also now dear to you. It is justly so, for it is a main pillar in the edifice of your real independence, the support of your tranquility at home, your peace abroad, of your safety, of your prosperity, of that very liberty which you so highly prize. But it is easy to foresee that from different causes and from different quarters much pains will be taken, many artifices employed, to weaken in your minds the conviction of this truth...[127]

In other words, unity of government is the main pillar of America's independence, tranquility at home, peace abroad, safety, prosperity, and liberty.

> For this [unity of government] you have every inducement of sympathy and interest. Citizens by birth or choice of a common country, *that country has a right to concentrate your affections*. The name of American, which belongs to you in your national capacity, must always exalt the just pride of patriotism more than any appellation derived from local discriminations. With slight shades of difference, you have the same religion, manners, habits, and political principles....[128]

Whether a person was native or foreign born, Washington believed that America has a right to concentrate its citizens' affections such that local or tribal differences would be subservient to the quest for national unity. As the eighteenth century was near its end, Washington was most concerned with the geographical differences that might damage the national unity. Those things which gave him hope that unity would be preserved and the nation would survive were the similarities of its citizens' religion, manners, habits, and political principles. Effectively, Washington was saying that Americans to whom he addressed his farewell had a central cultural vision, a common worldview if you will, that would sustain them in a quest for unity. Furthermore, Washington said that America had a right to concentrate its citizens' affections in the preservation of national unity.

Let's fast forward to the twenty-first century and examine our national unity or, more accurately, our national disunity. First, we must recognize that the rapidity of modern communication and transportation generally have erased the boundaries imposed by geographical self-interests as was the case in Washington's time. If that is the case, why is America not all the more unified than it was in the 1790s? The answer is evident when we look at America's failure to concentrate the affections of its citizens as Washington believed it should. In other words we have lost a common central cultural vision (worldview) held by the Founders and the great majority of America's citizens up until the mid-twentieth century.

This common cultural vision was biblical Christianity. Of course those imbued with modern sensibilities dominated by a humanistic worldview will scoff at this suggestion and point to the First Amendment's guarantee of freedom of religion. However, it is important to understand that the United States is not a nation that attempts to impose Christianity on all of its citizens but rather it is a nation founded upon Judeo-Christian principles that form the nation's central cultural vision. Americans can worship anyway they please or choose to not believe in a divine creator altogether. This is what the Founders meant by "...the free exercise of religion," but freedom of religion does not mean we abandon the central cultural vision upon which the nation was founded.

To understand why American culture is in decline, one must understand the larger picture as to why cultures in general decline and ultimately fail over time. First, a culture declines and ultimately fails as it loses it cohesiveness or unity. Washington recognized this and made it the central theme of his farewell address. Second, even if a culture maintains unity and cohesiveness, its worldview must over the long term be based on truth. Again, Washington's words point to the importance of truth in a nation's central cultural vision.

> Of all the dispositions and habits which lead to political prosperity, religion and morality are indispensable supports. In vain would that man claim the tribute of patriotism who should labor to subvert these great pillars of human happiness—these firmest props of the duties of men and citizens...And let us with caution indulge the supposition that morality can be maintained without religion. Whatever may be conceded to the influence of refined education on minds of a particular structure, *reason, and experience both forbid us to expect that national morality can prevail in exclusion of religious principle.*[129]

Now, who is this God in whom the Founders believed? Is He some "generic, one-size-fits-all, and all religions lead to the same God" variety? No! The Founders' God is the God of the ancient Hebrews and first century Christians as revealed in the Bible. From these beliefs arose the power of Christian teaching over private conscience that made possible an American democratic society that is unrivaled in the history of the world.

In twenty-first century America, a majority of its citizens still hold the biblical worldview, but most of the leadership of American institutions have abandoned it for the humanistic worldview. For America to survive, we must once again "concentrate our affections" and restore unity under the central cultural vision of the Founders.

American Exceptionalism

Part I – Myth or God's Blessing? (7-5-13)

What is this thing called "American exceptionalism" that surfaces periodically in political speeches, esoteric articles and books in the academic world, and an occasional mention on talk radio? The term "American exceptionalism" is of recent origin (less than 100 years) but the concept of the unique and exceptional nature of the United States has been recognized and accepted for more than 200 years.

The unique and exceptional nature of the United States was noted by numerous Founders during and after the American Revolution. However, widespread recognition of the unrivaled and exceptional nature of the United States in comparison to the rest of the world began with Alexis de Tocqueville's *Democracy in America*, a monumental study of America. The visiting Frenchman described what he saw during his nine-month journey across America in 1831.[130] But for America and the concept of American exceptionalism, there are many detractors in the twenty-first century, both here and abroad, many of whom are of the "hate America" variety and which are especially found in academia.

Tocqueville's *Democracy in America* has been called one of the most influential political texts ever written on America. Yet, Terrence McCoy in an article written for *The Atlantic* dismissively calls Tocqueville's *Democracy in America* a "travelogue." The title of McCoy's article claims that Soviet leader "Joseph Stalin invented American exceptionalism." McCoy states, "There's only one problem with that (American exceptionalism): It's not strictly true. Although a superiority complex has long pervaded the national psyche, the expression 'American exceptionalism' only became big a few years ago." McCoy is referring to the first use of the term "American exceptionalism" in the 1920s. The phrase came from an English translation of a condemnation made in Stalin's 1929 criticism of the Communist supporters of Jay Lovestone for their heretical belief that America was independent of the Marxist laws of history "thanks to its natural resources, industrial capacity, and absence of rigid class distinctions."[131] Marxist laws flow from the humanistic worldview which says there is no creator, man is basically good, and man can establish his own laws devoid of any independent supernatural authority.

It appears that McCoy believes that the non-existence of the *label* of "American exceptionalism" prior to the 1920s proves that the *concept and reali*ty of American exceptionalism since the nation's inception did not exist. To agree with McCoy's shallow analysis and conclusions with regard to the existence of and belief in American exceptionalism is only possible when one ignores *Democracy in America* and other considerable evidence of wide recognition and acceptance of the concept following publication of Tocqueville's book in 1835.

The theme of American exceptionalism became common in the nineteenth century, especially in textbooks. From the 1840s to the late twentieth century, 120 million copies of the *McGuffey's Reader* textbooks were sold. Most American students studied the *Readers* which hailed American exceptionalism, manifest destiny, and America as God's country even in the more secularized versions beginning in 1879.

For others who believe that America may have once been the greatest nation in the world, they now say that is no longer true. In an article by Tyler Gobin in the *Technician Online*, he states that America is no longer at the top of the heap. Our competiveness has fallen and Americans are perceived as lazy and culturally unaware. Mr. Gobin believes that, "...we ought to stop believing we are unique...and stop ignoring that we are only one part of a larger whole." Gobin believes that, "Obama correctly recognized that exceptionalism stands for uniqueness and not superiority."[132]

Following Stalin's use of "American exceptionalism," the phrase fell into obscurity for half a century, until it was popularized by American newspapers in the 1980s to describe America's cultural and political uniqueness. The phrase became an issue of contention between presidential candidates Barack Obama and John McCain in the 2008 presidential campaign.

President Obama again landed in hot water during the 2012 campaign against Mitt Romney for saying that while he (Obama) "believed in 'American exceptionalism,' it was *no different* from 'British exceptionalism,' 'Greek exceptionalism,' or any other country's brand of patriotic chest-thumping."[133] Joseph Stalin denied American exceptionalism. Barak Obama effectively does the same by equating American exceptionalism to that of many other nations. But if everyone is exceptional, then no one is exceptional...thus the denial of American exceptionalism and its denigration as mere "patriotic chest thumping." President Obama's position is understandable given a thing such as American exceptionalism would offend his radical egalitarian sensibilities.

With unequivocal certainty, the Founders would *not* have agreed with President Obama. Rather, they would agree with James Madison. Speaking of the American Revolution and the crafting of the Constitution, Madison said, "It is impossible for the man of pious reflection not to perceive in it a finger of that Almighty hand which has been so frequently and signally extended to our relief in the critical stages of revolution."[134] Madison's words echo the beliefs of many other Founders that America was an exceptional nation and the product of God's providence.

We have examined the origins and spread of the concept of American exceptionalism as well as the claims of the deniers and detractors. In Part II we will search for that one element that made possible American exceptionalism and *why* its deniers and detractors are so adverse to any consideration of its reality in the history of the nation.

Part II – The Essential Ingredient of America's Greatness (7-12-13)

In Part I we looked at the origins and spread of the concept of American exceptionalism as well as the claims of its deniers and detractors. In Part II we will discuss the one essential ingredient that led to America's exceptionalism and *why* exceptionalism's deniers and detractors are so adverse to any consideration of its reality in the history of the nation.

To be exceptional is a condition of being different from the norm; *also*: a theory expounding the exceptionalism especially of a nation or region. In their book titled *Understanding America – The Anatomy of an Exceptional Nation,* James Q. Wilson and Peter H. Schuck assembled a collection of essays which examined Alexis de Tocqueville's declaration that America was "exceptional." In their summation, the authors wholeheartedly agree with Tocqueville's assessment and strongly refute the popular assertion, especially in Europe, that although the United States is the sole global superpower, America is no longer any more distinctive that other democratic societies.[135]

Schuck identified seven overarching themes that connect the essays that point to America's exceptionalism.

- American culture is different than all other nations due to its patriotism, individualism, religiosity, and spirit of enterprise.

- The American Constitution is unique due to its emphasis on individual rights, decentralization, and suspicion of government authority.
- Although generating greater inequality, the American economy has produced a high standard of living due to its competitiveness, flexibility, and decentralization.
- America has had a diverse population throughout its history. In spite of booms or busts, people all over the world want to come to America.
- A strong civil society has made America qualitatively different. This is evidence by the large share of responsibility for social policy borne by the nonprofit sector.
- America has historically relied on certain entities and institutions to provide benefits and minimize dependence on being a welfare-state.
- America has been exceptional demographically due to its population's relatively high fertility rate.[136]

As we read through this list, we begin to realize that none of the elements are exclusive to America and its founding but are found to varying degrees in other democratic societies. Also, there is no hint as to a special combination or mixture of these elements that made America exceptional. Wilson and Schuck's book does a commendable job of analyzing the possible sources of America's exceptionalism, but we still do not have a definitive answer as to that one ingredient that allowed America to become the greatest and most unique nation in the history of the world. Perhaps we can find a clue in the words of two of the nation's Founders.

> The highest glory of the American Revolution was this; it connected in one indissoluble bond the principles of civil government with the principles of Christianity...From the day of the Declaration...they (the American people), were bound by the laws of God, which they all, and by the laws of their Gospel, which they nearly all, acknowledge as the rules of conduct.[137] [John Quincy Adams, Sixth President of the United States]

> To the kindly influence of Christianity we owe that degree of civil freedom, and political and social happiness, which mankind now enjoys...Whenever the pillars of Christianity shall be overthrown, our present republican forms of government—and all blessings which flow from them—must fall with them.[138] [John Jay, Co-Author of the *Federalist Papers*, First Chief-Justice of the US Supreme Court]

From these words we see the influence of Christianity and Christian principles that permeate and bond with the principles of civil government. It is this influence that is the defining element necessary in creating and maintaining America's exceptionalism, and it remained strong after more than four decades following the end of the Revolution and adoption of the Constitution and its Amendments. Tocqueville's first-hand account also provides ample evidence of the centrality of religion and Christianity in particular in America of the early 1830s:

> The Americans so completely identify the spirit of Christianity with freedom in their minds that it is almost impossible to get them to conceive the one without the other...
>
> On my arrival in the United States, it was the religious atmosphere which first struck me. As I extended my stay, I could observe the political consequences which flowed from this novel situation. In France I had seen the spirit of religion moving in the opposite direction to that of the spirit of freedom. In America I found them intimately linked together in joint reign over the same land.
>
> ...America is still the country in the world where the Christian religion has retained the greatest real power over people's souls and nothing shows better how useful and natural religion is to man, since the country where it exerts the greatest sway is also the most enlightened and free.[139]

Therefore, from the words of the Founders and Tocqueville, we see the defining element that distinguishes America as the most exceptional of any nation in history. That element was not just religiosity but the influence of Christianity and its principles upon the new nation, its civil government, and citizens.

Among most of the institutions of American life and their leaders in the twenty-first century, the God of the Founders is no longer welcome. The Founders, if alive today, would not recognize America. Look at the seven themes Wilson and Schuck identified as important to America's exceptionalism. Patriotism has been replaced by the "hate America first" crowd. Individualism and spirit of enterprise have been replaced by a drive toward a nanny-state government, entitlements, and invented and illusory rights. Individual rights and decentralization of government have been replaced by a "greatest good for the greatest number" mentality enforced by a monstrous bureaucracy. The American economy is losing its competitiveness due to confiscatory taxes, onerous regulatory burdens, and erosion of and loss of individual property rights as the country marches toward socialism. American culture has become a moral sewer as Christian morality is replaced by moral relativism in which there are no standards of right and wrong. Humanistic definitions of multiculturalism, tolerance, and equality are undermining the nation's central cultural vision resulting in a loss of unity necessary for it to survive.

Those that deny American exceptionalism do so from the perspective of a humanistic worldview. Those holding that worldview have no trouble embracing various aspects contributing toward exceptionalism such as abundance of natural resources, isolation from the problems of Europe and other parts of the world, America's cultural diversity, and the absence of class distinctions apart from the stain of long-ago slavery. However, the central, defining, and dominating presence of one element in birthing American exceptionalism is an embarrassment to them: America's Christian religion. Therefore, American exceptionalism is judged guilty by association and like Christianity must be denied and driven from the public square. However, such denial is nothing more than historical revisionism.

Part III – R.I.P. or Revival? (7-19-13)

John Adams said, "We have no government armed with power capable of contending with human passions unbridled by morality and religion...Our Constitution was made only for a moral and religious people. It is wholly inadequate to the government of any other."[140] In other words, the America of the Founders was based upon the assumption that people who accept the biblical worldview are capable of governing themselves *internally* where ethical and moral issues are concerned. Thus, the architects of America's early government structure envisioned the Republic supported by a foundation of common morality, and that morality rested on the bedrock of the Christian faith.

As we noted in Part II, Christianity and Christian principles that permeated and bonded with the principles of civil government formed the basis for America's exceptionalism. The recognition of the truth of Adam's words that our Constitution was made *only for a moral and religious people* has monumental implications for America in the twenty-first century as Christianity and Christian principles are being driven from the public square. If America rejects Christianity and Christian principles in guiding and informing American civil government and culture, we will cease to be great and America will no longer be exceptional. As a consequence we will lose our freedoms.

Daily we are seeing the loss of freedom in America. As citizens turn from a Christian worldview, they are unable to guide themselves internally with regard to ethical and moral issues. Benjamin Franklin recognized the folly of this course when he said, "Only a virtuous people are capable of freedom. As nations become corrupt and vicious, they have more need of masters."[141] This is a picture of America in the twenty-first century as we see the power and reach of the state expanding rapidly before our eyes.

The Bible outlines the course of events for nations and points to ancient Israel as the prime example. The cycle begins with a nation being blessed by God. From blessing comes satisfaction which begets pride, but as pride increases people forget God. God brings judgment so that they may remember, repent, and return to God. Without remembrance, repentance, and return, destruction follows. Today, the institutions of American life, its leaders, and a large percentage of the population have mostly forgotten God and deny the validity of the nation's biblically-based Christian roots in the governance of America and its various institutions. And, the sad fact is that people are ignorant, apathetic, uncaring, or just too busy with life to make a difference.

Much of American society in the twenty-first century cannot be called by His name for we are chiseling that name from our public buildings and monuments and silencing His mention in public discourse. Humility is no longer an American trait for God has been pronounced dead, and man is now the measure. Prayer is not only lacking but banned from our schools and the public square. The ways of the wicked are embraced wholeheartedly by a popular culture in which deference to maximum autonomy of the individual and abdication of the will to the senses reign supreme.

America's founding makes sense *only* when understood as the work of Christians who operated on the basis of a biblical worldview. Just as America was *founded* by believers, so it must be *sustained* by believers if it is to survive—believers who care deeply and passionately about their country. We must face the fact that the America as designed by the Founders is likely to disappear altogether if we do not take swift, deliberate, and resolute steps to salvage it.

American exceptionalism is not dead, but it may be on life support. The prescription for reversing America's cultural decline is a spiritual renewal within the individual which can subsequently transform a nation. Only then can America's central cultural vision be restored. Spiritual renewals have restored America during several times of crisis in the nation's history. How do such revivals come? Throughout all of history, *the remarkable and unfailing thread running through all of Western civilization's spiritual awakenings is concerted prayer*. That prescription is found in 2 Chronicles 7:14: "If my people who are called by my name humble themselves, and pray and seek my face, and turn from their wicked ways, then I will hear from heaven and will forgive their sin and heal their land." [KJV]

Freedom (7-4-14)

Fifty-six traitors to the crown signed their own death sentences and then fought to escape the hangman's noose. So began the first steps in forming a new nation. It was a typically hot summer in Philadelphia in 1776. Day after day a group of men met to argue, pray, sweat, and wonder what would be the outcome of their deliberations. Eventually, the product of their labors was the Declaration of Independence from Great Britain. The wording of the revered document was approved on July 2nd by the Continental Congress, and on July 4th the delegates voted to accept it. What was so valuable that these men would risk their lives for it? It was freedom.

The word "freedom" is misused much as is the word "love." Freedom's meaning is misunderstood and has been stretched, changed, distorted, overused, cheapened, made merchandise, used to defend or promote conflicting purposes, and co-opted for support of principles and philosophies that are inherently in opposition to its real meaning.

Why is it that human beings value freedom so much? Before we can answer, we must realize that one's worldview will ultimately define his or her understanding of the concept of freedom. If a worldview is fundamentally flawed in that it is in conflict with truth, that worldview's concept of freedom will also be flawed and result in bondage of some type and degree. In Western civilization there are two worldviews contending for dominance—humanism and Christianity.

A Freedom that coerces

In the humanist worldview, man is encouraged to realize his own creative talents and desires and exercise maximum individual autonomy that is free from the mores, norms, tradition, and distant voices of the past. This freedom gives unbridled expression to self and senses. However, one must read the fine print in the humanists' promises of freedom which requires individual autonomy to be *consonant with social responsibility*. Therefore, humanists harness an individual's dignity, worth, and freedom to the principle of the greatest-happiness-for-the greatest-number which is hitched to the humanist belief that the highest moral obligation is to humanity as a whole. Freedom of the individual is subservient to his obligations to the larger society, and those obligations are determined and defined by the humanist intellectual elite. In other words, man replaces God as the defining authority for truth, and man's highest moral obligation is to humanity as a whole and not to God.[1]

The source of true and lasting freedom

To understand the Christian worldview as it relates to freedom, we must examine God's creation of man. Man was created with God's divine image stamped upon him. Man has an insatiable thirst for freedom because God made man with freewill. It was necessary for man to have freewill in order for love to exist. God did not create man out of need. Rather, it was a will to love, an expression of the very character of God, to share the inner life of the Trinity. By creating man with a free will meant the possibility of rejection of God and His love. Being God, He knew the course and cost of His creation would be the death of His Son on the cross. In other words freewill and the potential for rejection of God was the penalty for the possibility of love. So it is on the earthly plane, to risk love is to risk rejection.[2] Love is a choice because man has freewill, and true love reflects the divine in that it *focuses on relationships and not self.*

Now we begin to see the fundamental differences between humanism and Christianity that shape the disparities of how those worldviews define freedom. In the Christian worldview, freedom simply means a *lack of coercion but also implies self-restraint and deference* to relational patterns revealed in the mores, norms, tradition, and distant voices of the past. True freedom is found only when an individual chooses a right relationship with God through the acceptance of Christ as one's savior. In such relationship, man chooses to subordinate his own freewill to Christ, to accept Him, and to follow the road of freedom found in the revelation to the ancient Hebrews and first century Christians. From this foundation of a right relationship with God, man can find right relationships with his fellowman in family, community, and state.

In a contrary view of freedom that exalts self, humanists attempt to *release the individual from the relational patterns* flowing from those same mores, norms, tradition, and distant voices of the past. However, the subjugation of divinely ordered relational patterns to the god of self results in loneliness, pain, suffering, and loss in this life and eternity thereafter. In other words, true freedom is found in freely subduing one's will to that of God's will as opposed to the exaltation of self and the senses. Christ's words in Luke's gospel capture the essence of this seeming enigma.

...If any man would come after me, let him deny himself and take up his cross daily and follow me. For whoever would save his life will lose it; and whoever loses his life for my sake, he will save it. [Luke 9: 23-24. RSV]

Freedom lost

In twenty-first century America, the god of self rules the day. America's humanist masters have taken control of the nation and its institutions. Many Americans recognize there is something amiss with the country, but they take little time to look, listen, understand, and challenge the despoiling of America's central cultural vision upon which the nation was founded. Americans are much like Esau who sold his valuable birthright for a bowl of stew, that is, he traded what was important, godly, and honorable for temporary pleasures. America's hard-won two-hundred-plus year birthright of freedom is being willingly and rapidly surrendered to a growing legion of humanistic overlords in exchange for a bowl of entitlements, fleeting and licentious pleasures, self-centeredness, egotism, radical egalitarianism, imaginary rights, sloth, and an obsession for life-consuming leisure activities.

Fifty-six traitors to the crown signed their own death sentences and then fought to escape the hangman's noose. They were overwhelmingly Christian in worldview, and like God in His creation of man, the Founders knew the cost of freedom as revealed in the final words of the Declaration of Independence, "And for the support of this declaration, with a firm reliance on the Protection of Divine Providence, *we mutually pledge to each other our Lives, our Fortunes, and our sacred Honor.*"[3] [emphasis added]

> The 56 signers of the Declaration of Independence paid a tremendous price for our freedom: 5 were arrested by the British as traitors, 12 had their homes looted and burned by the enemy, 17 lost their fortunes, 2 lost sons in the Continental Army, and 9 fought and died during the Revolutionary War.[4]

Edmund Burke's famous observation of the eighteenth century still rings true today. "All that is necessary for the evil to triumph is for good men to do nothing."[5] To defend America's birthright of freedom, good and Godly men and women must once again depend on the providence of God and pledge their lives, their fortunes, and their sacred honor to subdue the humanistic apostles of self that are enslaving the nation.

The Fragility of Free Speech in America (3-21-14)

The First Amendment of the Constitution reads as follows: "Congress shall make no law respecting an establishment of religion, or prohibiting the free exercise thereof; or *abridging the freedom of speech*, or of the press; or the right of the people peaceably to assemble, and to petition the Government for redress of grievances." The free exercise of religion has been under assault by the liberalism for a number of years and the assault has accelerated significantly in the last two or three years. Attacks on free speech are increasing but of more recent occurrence.

Attacks on free speech increased significantly with efforts to classify certain opinions as hate speech. The problem with prohibiting hate speech is one of determining what is and what is not hate speech. Most often, the efforts at eliminating hate speech are aimed at the "content" of the speech rather than the intolerable mode of expressing the speech (e.g., violence). Here we are not talking about profanity or obscene language that offends the common decency of a civil society. Speech that is bad or hurtful may not be obscene or profane, and slander and libel laws are available where necessary. Also, enforced tolerance through limitations on the content of hate speech may have the opposite effect—that of promoting even more hateful speech or worse. Most importantly, any limit on free speech, however hateful or hurtful, is a slippery slope at whose base is an abyss in which free speech is not only lost but other liberties as well.

As America races toward a monolithic, all-powerful, all-knowing government, free speech is under attack in a variety of ways.

Government approved speech

A previous article ("The *New* Ministry of Truth 2014") described the federal government's tentative steps at limiting freedom of the press through proposed rules that would allow government monitoring of newsrooms to determine bias in the provision of critical information needs as determined by the Federal Communications Commission.

Government limits on speech through regulation

Government reach goes beyond the newsroom and into cyberspace. Health-wise, Steve Cooksey was a walking time bomb. He was obese, lethargic, asthmatic, chronically ill, and a pre-diabetic. Ignoring the advice of medical personnel and others, he chose to eat a high-carbohydrate, low-fat diet (beef, pork, chicken, leafy vegetables). He lost seventy-five pounds and no longer needed medications. He began sharing his dietary opinions on his Internet blog and interacting with his readers. When asked he would give his opinion, but the North Carolina Board of Dietetics/Nutrition got wind of his treachery and following a three-month investigation ordered him stop as he was "counseling" and needed a license to do so. The Institute for Justice defended Cooksey's First Amendment right of free speech citing the fact that Cooksey's speech "...involves no sensitive relationships (as in psychological counseling, no uniquely vulnerable listeners (as in potential legal clients forced to make snap decisions), and no plausible presumption that the listeners are unable to exercise independent judgment." Cooksey's advice was unpaid, freely sought, involved no professional-client relationships.[1]

Regulatory oversight is a necessary and proper function of government. However, under the expansive interpretation of the Constitution's general welfare clause beginning in 1936, much of regulatory oversight has become an autocratic function of a nanny-state bureaucracy intruding into the lives of a free people capable of making rational decisions without government interference.

Limiting when and where free speech may occur

Free speech is under attack on many of the nation's colleges and universities. Robert Van Tuinen, a student at Modesto Junior College, was stopped by campus police from distributing copies of the Constitution on the 226th anniversary of its signing. College officials told Van Tuinen that he could get permission to distribute the Constitution if he pre-registered for time in the "free speech zone" which reportedly was a small slab of concrete just big enough for two people. However, once registered, Van Tuinen would have to wait for an available opening. Effectively, administration officials used campus police to enforce an unconstitutional rule, declared the campus to be off limits for free speech except for a small "free speech" area, and limited when and how many could use so-called free speech area, all in violation of the First Amendment.[2]

Criminalizing free speech

Want to go to jail for your views—spoken or written? Lawrence Torcello, Assistant Professor of Philosophy at Rochester

Institute of Technology, suggests that some scientists and their financial backers may be both morally and criminally negligent if their views contradict a set of facts that the majority of scientists agree upon. As an example, Torcello believes that, "We have good reason to consider the funding of climate denial to be criminally and morally negligent. The charge of criminal and moral negligence ought to extend to all activities of the climate deniers who receive funding as part of a sustained campaign to undermine the public's understanding of scientific consensus."[3]

Torcello brushes aside free speech concerns by distinguishing between the protected voicing of one's unpopular beliefs and the funding of a strategically organized campaign to undermine the public's ability to develop and voice *informed* opinions. Torcello states that, "Protecting the latter as a form of free speech *stretches* the definition of free speech to a degree that *undermines* the very concept." But Torcello should read the First Amendment again. There is no limit on free speech because it is strategically organized and well-financed.[4] The Left questions the public's ability to develop and voice informed opinions without help from the liberal intellectual elites. The problem for the Left is that the public is getting wise to the liberal, radical environmentalist agenda and other pseudo-scientific pronouncements, and the Left's only recourse is silence their critics.

Writing seventy years ago in his seminal *Road to Serfdom*, F. A. Hayek identified the liberal necessity of group-think for the masses to achieve their ends.

> The most effective way of making everybody serve the single system of ends toward which the social plan is directed is to make everybody believe in those ends…Although the beliefs must be chosen for the people and imposed upon them, they must become *their* beliefs, a generally accepted creed which makes the individuals as far as possible act spontaneously in the way the planner wants.[5] [emphasis added]

For liberals, any public criticism or even expressions of doubt tend to weaken public support for the official doctrine, creed, values, or views of the regime. The acts of government must be sacrosanct and exempt from criticism. Even though the great majority may have surrendered independent thought, the minority's doubt, discontent, and criticisms must be suppressed or silenced.[6]

The suppression of free speech in America ranks high on the liberal agenda because the end of liberalism is socialism, and the end of socialism is totalitarianism. That is why those pesky three little words of "freedom of speech" in the First Amendment are so troubling to the liberal establishment.

Notes

BELIEFS HAVE CONSEQUENCES

Part I – The Christian and the culture

In Defense of Labels
[1] Max Lucado, "Simply 'Church'," *Max Lucado*, November 4, 2013. http://808bo.wordpress.com/2013/11/04/max-lucado-simply-church/ (accessed November 6, 2013).
[2] Matthew Henry, *Commentary on the Whole Bible*, Ed. Rev. Leslie F. Church, Ph.D., (Grand Rapids, Michigan: Zondervan Publishing House, 1961), p.1794.
[3] Richard Weaver, *Ideas Have Consequences*, (Chicago, Illinois: The University of Chicago Press, 1948), pp. 148-149, 152, 158, 163.

Tis the Season for Secular Silliness
[1] J. P. Duffy, "Post Office Manager Throws Christmas Carolers Out into the Cold," *Family Research Council*, December 12, 2011. http://www.frcblog.com/2011/12/post-office-manager-throws-christmas-carolers-out-into-the-cold/ (accessed December 10, 2013).
[2] Chris Deaton, "Victory: House members no longer prohibited from saying "Merry Christmas" in official mail," *Red Alert Politics*, December 4, 2013. http://redalertpolitics.com/2013/12/04/victory-house-members-no-longer-prohibited-from-saying-merry-christmas-in-official-mail/ (accessed December 10, 2013).
[3] Billy Hallowell, "N.J. School District That Banned Christmas Music With 'Religious Origins' Backs Down," *The Blaze*, November 6, 2013. http://www.theblaze.com/stories/2013/11/06/n-j-/school-district-that-banned-christmas-music-with-religious-origins-backs-down (accessed December 10, 2013).

How we choose to deal with our sin defines our destiny
[4] Edward J. Slattery, Bishop of Tulsa Diocese, "We are not defined by our sin," *Tulsa World*, October 18, 2014, A17; http://www.tulsaworld.com/opinion/readersforum/bishop-edward-j-slattery-defined-by-our/article_bb6fed60-fa34-581b-951c-5884295d6ffa.html (accessed October 20, 2014).
[5] Ibid.
[6] Gavin Newsom, et.al., Letter to Archbishop Salvatore Cordileone, June 10, 2014. https://docs.google.com/viewer?url=http://www.sfgate.com/file/829/829-ArchbishopLetter.pdf (accessed June 23, 2014).

[7] Slattery, "We are not defined by our sin," A17.
[8] Eric Metaxas, *Bonhoeffer*, (Nashville, Tennessee: Thomas Nelson, 2010), pp. 292-293.
[9] Erwin W. Lutzer, *When a Nation Forgets God*," (Chicago, Illinois: Moody Publishers, 2010), pp. 117-118.

Progressive Protestantism – Declining Faith

[1] Bill Sherman, "Christian church seeing 'major shift'," *Tulsa World*, January 24, 2015, A-9.
[2] Larry G. Johnson, "Strange Fire – The American church's quest for cultural relevance – Part I," *culturewarrior.net*, December 12, 2014. http://www.culturewarrior.net/2014/12/12/strange-fire-the-churchs-quest-for-cultural-relevance-part-i/
[3] Larry G. Johnson, "Strange Fire – The American church's quest for cultural relevance – Part II," *culturewarrior.net*, December 26, 2014. http://www.culturewarrior.net/2014/12/26/strange-fire-the-churchs-quest-for-cultural-relevance-part-ii/
[4] Sherman, "Christian church seeing 'major shift'," *Tulsa World*, A-9.
[5] Alexis De Tocqueville, *Democracy in America*, Gerald E. Bevan, Trans., (London, England: Penguin Books, 2003), pp. 346-347.
[6] Sherman, "Christian church seeing 'major shift'," *Tulsa World*, A-9.
[7] Ibid.
[8] Jim Cymbala with Jennifer Schuchmann, *Storm – Hearing Jesus for The Times We Live In*, (Grand Rapids, Michigan: Zondervan, 2014), pp. 14-15.
[9] Ibid., p. 15.

Criminalizing Christian beliefs and behavior

[1] Courtney Coren, "Washington Florist: State, ACLU 'Trying to bully me'," *Newsmax*, February 24, 2015. http://www.newsmax.com/Newsmax-Tv/Washington-state-florist-gay-marriage-ACLU/2015/02/24/id/626583/ (accessed April 6, 2015).
[2] Alan Gathright and Eric Lupher, "Denver's Azucar Bakery wins right to refuse to make anti-gay cakes," *7NewsDenver*, April 4, 2015. http://www.thedenverchannel.com/news/local- news/denvers-azucar-bakery-wins-right-to-refuse-to-make-anti-gay-cake (accessed April 7, 2015).
[3] "William J. Clinton - Remarks on Signing the Religious Freedom Restoration Act of 1993," *The American Presidency Project*. http://www.presidency.ucsb.edu/ws/?pid=46124 (Accessed April 3, 2015).
[4] "State Religious Freedom Acts," *Home School Legal Defense Association*, January 28, 2015. http://www.hslda.org/docs/nche/000000/00000083.asp (accessed April 3, 2015).
[5] TEXT: Indiana Religious Freedom Restoration Act: SENATE ENROLLED ACT No. 101Senate of the State of Indiana ^ | March 27, 2015 | Government of the State of Indiana. http://www.freerepublic.com/focus/f-news/3272850/posts (accessed April 6,

2015).
6 Tim Cook, "Opposing 'religious' bills requires courage," *Tulsa World*, April 3, 2015, A-17.
7 Eliana Dockterman, "Miley Cyrus: Indiana Religious Freedom Law Supporters 'Are dinosaurs, and they are dying off'," *Time*, March 31, 2015. http://time.com/3766436/miley-cyrus-on-indiana-law/ (accessed April 6, 2015).
8 William J. Federer, *America's God and Country*, (Coppell, Texas: Fame Publishing, Inc., 1996), pp. 10-11.
9 Ibid., p. 247.

Joseph – Man in the shadows

Creative Evolution – Screwtape's science for Christians – Parts I & II
1 Justin Phillips, *C. S. Lewis in a Time of War*, (New York: Harper San Francisco, 2002), pp. 38, 78.
2 Ibid., p. 78.
3 Lewis, *Mere Christianity* in *The Complete C. S. Lewis Signature Classics*, pp. 3-4, 6.
4 Daniel James Devine, "Interpretive dance," *World*, November 29, 2014, 35.
5 "Our History: 2006 to Today," *BioLogos*. https://biologos.org/about/history (accessed December 16, 2014).
6 "About the BioLogos Foundation," *BioLogos*. https://biologos.org/about (accessed December 16, 2014).
7 Ibid.
8 "Evolution & Christian Faith," *BioLogos*. https://biologos.org/ecf/overview (accessed December 17, 2014).
9 "Meet the Grantees," *BioLogos*. https://biologos.org/ecf/grantees (accessed December 17, 2014).
10 "Evolution & Christian Faith," *BioLogos*.
11 C. S. Lewis, *The Screwtape Letters*, *The Complete C. S. Lewis Signature Classics*, (New York: Harper One, 2007), pp. 185-187.
12 Lewis, *Mere Christianity* in *The Complete C. S. Lewis Signature Classics*, p. 31.
13 "Questions Categorized As "The First Humans," *BioLogos*. https://biologos.org/questions/category/the-first-humans (accessed December 17, 2014).
14 Devine, "Interpretive dance," *World*, 38.
15 "About the BioLogos Foundation," *BioLogos*.
16 "How does original sin fit with evolutionary history?" *BioLogos*. http://biologos.org/questions/original-sin (accessed December 17, 2014).
17 "Questions Categorized As "The First Humans," *BioLogos*.
18 Devine, "Interpretive dance," *World*, 39.
19 Weaver, *Ideas Have Consequences*, pp. 5-6.

I'm so ashamed! I was a member of a hate group and didn't know it.
1 Todd Starnes, "The Army's List of 'Domestic Hate Groups'," Fox News

Radio, April 10, 2013.
http://radio.foxnews.com/toddstarnes/top-stories/the-armys-list-of-domestic-hate-groups.html (accessed April 24, 2013).
[2] Ibid.
[3] "Are you an enemy of the state?" Family Research Council, April 11, 2013. http://www.frc.org/alert/are-you-an-enemy-of-the-state (accessed April 24, 2013).
[4] Ibid.

Part II – Worldview

Why I believe
[1] Lewis, *Mere Christianity* in *The Complete C. S. Lewis Signature Classics,* p. 116.
[2] Larry G. Johnson, *Ye shall be as gods – Humanism and Christianity – The Battle for Supremacy in the American Cultural Vision,* (Owasso, Oklahoma: Anvil House Publishers, 2011), p. 111.
[3] Lewis., *Mere Christianity* in *The Complete C. S. Lewis Signature Classics,* pp. 115-117.
[4] Weaver, *Ideas Have Consequences,*" p. 59.
[5] Johnson *Ye shall be as gods,* p. 176.

What is your purpose in life? Parts I & II
[1] Johnson, *Ye shall be as gods,* p. 401.
[2] Tocqueville, *Democracy in America,* pp. 346-347.
[3] Johnson, *Ye shall be as gods,* p. 70.
[4] Paul Kurtz, ed., *Humanist Manifestos I and II,* (Amherst, New York: Prometheus Books, 1973), pp. 14, 16.
[5] Johnson, *Ye shall be as gods,* pp. 306-307.
[6] Weaver, *Ideas Have Consequences,* pp. 41-42.

Thrill killers, the ACLU, Benjamin Spock, and C. S. Lewis
[1] Johnson, Ye shall be as gods, p. 367.
[2] "ACLU sues to remove Oklahoma 10 Commandments Monument" *Fox News.com,* August 22, 2013. http://www.foxnews.com/us/2013/08/22/aclu-sues-to-remove-oklahoma-10-commandments-monument/#ixzz2dHrcZwgM (accessed August 28, 2013).
[3] David Barton, *The Myth of Separation,* (Aledo, Texas: Wallbuilder Press, 1989), p. 32.
[4] Dr. Benjamin M. Spock, *A Better World for Our Children – Rebuilding American Family Values,* (Bethesda, Maryland: National Press Books, 1994), p. 15.
[5] C. S. Lewis, *The Abolition of Man* in *The Complete C. S. Lewis Signature Classics,* (New York: Harper One, 1944, 1947, 1971, 1974), p. 704.

Acts of God or Acts of Man?
[1] Ken Ham and Dr. Jonathan Sarfati, "Why is there death and suffering?" Creation Ministries International, http://creation.com/why-is-there-death-and-suffering#_ret4 (accessed August 8, 2014).
[2] "love," *Webster's Seventh New Collegiate Dictionary*, (Springfield, Massachusetts: G. & C. Merriam Company, Publishers, 1963), p. 501.
[3] Johnson, *Ye shall be as Gods*, p. 86
[4] Ibid., p. 158.
[5] Ronald Rhodes, "Tough Questions About Evil," *Who Made God?* Eds. Ravi Zacharias and NormanGeisler, (Grand Rapids, Michigan: Zondervan, 2003), p. 37.
[6] Corliss Lamont, *The Philosophy of Humanism*, Eighth Edition, Revised, (Amherst, New York: Humanist Press, 1997), pp. 13-14.
[7] William Lane Craig, *On Guard*, (Colorado Springs, Colorado: David C. Cook, 2010), p. 173.

Statistics: Facts often used to replace truth
[8] Leonard Pitts, "If GOP is so right, why are red states so far behind?" *Tulsa World*, September 4, 2014, A 13.
[9] Ibid.
[10] Ibid.
[11] Leonard Louis Levinson, *The Left Handed Dictionary*, (New York: Collier Books, 1963), p. 218.
[12] Robert J. Samuelson, "Do Dems run the economy better? Nope." *The Washington Post*, August 24, 2014. http://www.washingtonpost.com/opinions/robert-samuelson-do-democrats-run-the-economy-better-nope/2014/08/24/1e3d847c-2a0c-11e4-86ca-6f03cbd15c1a_story.html (accessed September 5, 2014).
[13] Ibid.
[14] Ibid.
[15] Weaver, *Ideas Have Consequences*, p. 58.

Part III – Conflict of Worldviews

Liberalism explained
[1] Christian Smith, "Introduction," *The Secular Revolution*, ed. Christian Smith, Berkeley, California: The University of California Press, 2003), pp. 53-54.
[2] J. M. Roberts, *The New History of the World*, (Oxford, England: Oxford University Press, 2003), p. 693.
[3] Paris Reidhead, "Ten Shekels and a Shirt," *Remnant Resource Network*. http://remnantradio.org/Archives/articles/Ten%20Shekels/tenshekels.htm (accessed December 18, 2010).
[4] Robert P. George, *The Clash of Orthodoxies*, (Wilmington, Delaware: ISI Books, 2001), p. 232
[5] Ibid.

[6] F. A. Hayek, *The Road to Serfdom – Text and Documents*, Ed. Bruce Caldwell, (Chicago, Illinois: The University of Chicago Press, 1944, 2007), p. 45.
[7] Smith, "Introduction," *The Secular Revolution*, pp. 52-55, 58, 66-67; Johnson, *Ye shall be as gods*, pp. 213-214.
[8] W. Cleon Skousen, *The 5000 Year Leap*, (www.nccs.net: National Center for Constitutional Studies, 1981), p. 175; Johnson, *Ye shall be as gods*, p. 249.
[9] Johnson, *Ye shall be as gods*, p. 249.
[10] Russell Kirk, *The Essential Russell Kirk – Selected Essays*, ed. George A. Panichas, (Wilmington, Delaware: ISI Books, 2007), p. 26; Johnson, *Ye shall be as gods*, pp. 215-216
[11] Ibid.
[12] Ibid.
[13] Ibid.

Conservatism explained
[1] Smith, "Introduction," *The Secular Revolution*, pp. 53-54.
[2] Johnson, *Ye shall be as gods*, pp. 216-217.
[3] Kirk, *The Essential Russell Kirk-Selected Essays,* pp. 7-9.
[4] Ibid., p. 7.
[5] Ibid.
[6] Ibid., p. 8.
[7] Ibid.
[8] Ibid., pp. 8-9.
[9] Ibid., p. 9.
[10] Weaver, *Ideas Have Consequences*, p. 52.
[11] Johnson, *Ye shall be as gods*, pp. 216-217.
[12] Russell Kirk, *The Roots of American Order*, (Washington, D. C.: Regnery Gateway, 1991), pp. 5-6.
[13] Lewis, *The Abolition of Man* in *The Complete C. S. Lewis Signature Classics*, p. 704.

Mainstream Environmentalism – The Dark Side – Parts I & II
[1] "Pentti Linkola*," penttilinkola.com*, http://www.penttilinkola.com (accessed July 5, 2014).
[2] Ibid.
[3] "Who was David Brower?" *David Brower Center.* http://www.browercenter.org/about/who-was-david-brower (accessed July 5, 2014).
[4] "David Brower," *Activist Facts*, https://www.activistfacts.com/person/3507-david-brower/ (accessed July 7, 2014).
[5] "deep ecology," *Merriam-Webster*. http://www.merriam-webster.com/dictionary/deep%20ecology (accessed July 7, 2014).
[6] Nicholas Riccardi, "Bird known for mating dance may decide Senate fate," *Associated Press*, July 5,
   2014. http://news.yahoo.com/bird-known-mating-dance-may-decide-senate-

election.html fate-124650685- (accessed July 7, 2014).
[7] Rhett Morgan, :Federal deal may hit rural fire departments hard," *Tulsa World*, July 5, 2014, A11.
[8] "deep ecology," *Merriam-Webster*. http://www.merriam-webster.com/dictionary/deep%20ecology
[9] Lamont, *The Philosophy of Humanism*, p. 35.
[10] Smith, "Introduction," *The Secular Revolution*, p. 54.
[11] Charles Colson with Nancy R. Pearcey, *A Dance with Deception*, (Dallas, Texas: Word Publishing, 1993), pp. 223-224.
[12] Ibid., p. 224.
[13] Christopher J. Bosso, *Environment, Inc.*, (Lawrence, Kansas: University Press of Kansas, 2005), pp. 23-24.
[14] Ibid., p. 24.
[15] "David Brower," *Activist Facts*. https://www.activistfacts.com/person/3507-david-brower/ (accessed July 7, 2014).
[16] Colson., p. 224.

Progressivism's Fatal Flaw
[1] Johnson, *Ye shall be as gods*, p. 213.
[2] Christian Smith, "Introduction," *The Secular Revolution*, p. 54. Quoted in *Ye shall be as gods*, p. 213.
[3] Johnson, Ye shall be as gods, p. 387.
[4] Ibid., pp. 219-220.
[5] Ibid., p. 219.

Liberal Hypocrisy – The Hollywood Ten and the Friends of Abe
[1] Reuters, "FBI doesn't plan charges over IRS scrutiny of Tea Party: WSJ," *Chicago Tribune*, January 13, 2014. http://articles.chicagotribune.com/2014-01-13/news/sns-rt-us-usa-tax-teaparty-20140113_1_fbi-director-james-comey-irs-cincinnati-irs-scrutiny (accessed January 28, 2014).
[2] Michael Cipley and Nicholas Confessore, "Leaning Right in Hollywood, Under a Lens," *New York Times*, January 22, 2014. http://www.nytimes.com/2014/01/23/us/politics/leaning-right-in-hollywood-under-a-lens.html?_r=0 (accessed January 28, 2014).
[3] Ibid.
[4] Ibid.
[5] John E. Haynes, *Red Scare or Red Menace? American Communism and Anticommunism in the Cold War Era*, (Chicago, Illinois: Ivan R. Dee, 1996), pp. 70-73.
[6] Ibid., pp. 72-73.
[7] Ibid., pp. 73-74.

End of the Citizen-Soldier?
[8] "New York Provincial Congress," George Washington's Mount Vernon. http://www.mountvernon.org/digital-encyclopedia/article/new-york-provincial-congress/

[9] Ken Klukowski, "Pentagon may court-marshal soldiers who share Christian faith," *Breitbart News*, May 1, 2013
http://www.breitbart.com/Big-Peace/2013/05/01/Breaking-Pentagon-Confirms-Will-Court-Martial-Soldiers-Who-Share-Christian-Faith (accessed May 7, 2013).
[10] Sally Quinn, "U.S. military should put religious freedom at the front," *The Washington Post*, April 26, 2013
http://www.washingtonpost.com/national/on-faith/us-military-should-put-religious-freedom-at-the-front/2013/04/26/c1befcea-ade2-11e2-8bf6-e70cb6ae066e_print.html (accessed May 3, 2013).
[11] Michael Weinstein, "Fundamentalist Christian Monsters: Papa's Got A Brand
New Bag," *HuffPost*, April 16, 2013
http://www.huffingtonpost.com/michael-l-weinstein/fundamentalist-christian-_b_3072651.html?view=print&comm_ref=false (accessed May 3, 2013).
[12] Federer, *America's God and Country*, p. 638.
[13] Ibid., p. 639.
[14] Ibid., p. 643.

Part IV - Language

Liberal language and the trashing of truth
[1] Weaver, *Ideas Have Consequences*, pp. 148, 158, 163.
[2] Paul Kurtz, *Toward a New Enlightenment – The Philosophy of Paul Kurtz*, (New Brunswick, New Jersey: Transaction Publishers, 1994), p. 70.
[3] Stefan F. Hayes, "The Benghazi Talking Points," *The Weekly Standard*, Vol. 18, No. 33, (May 13, 2013). On-line source:
http://www.weeklystandard.com/articles/benghazi-talking-points_720543.html?page=3 (accessed June 11, 2013).
[4] Ibid.
[5] Paul Greenberg, "Don't give up on the American language," *Tulsa World*, (June 9, 2013), G-3; On-line source:
Paul Greenberg, "The state of the language," *JewishWorldReview.com*, (June 5, 2013).
www.jewishworldreview.com/cols/greenberg060513.php3#.UbdQQpyi1qs (accessed June 9, 2013).
[6] V. I. Lenin, Quote, *The Great Quotations*, George Seldes, Comp., (New York: Pocket Books, 1968), p. 925.

Who owns the language?
[1] Jennifer Jacobs, "Palin compares federal debt to slavery at Iowa dinner," Video excerpts, *DesMoinesRegister.com*, November 10, 2013. Quote from video clip.
http://www.desmoinesregister.com/article/20131110/NEWS09/311100047/Pal-federal-debt-to-slavery-at-Iowa-dinner?Frontpage (accessed November

22, 2013).
[2] Tommy Christopher, "Martin Bashir Says Someone Should Sh*t in Sarah Palin's Mouth," *mediaite.com*, November 15, 2013. http://www.mediaite.com/tv/martin-bashir-says-someone- /should-sht-in-sarah-palins-mouth (accessed November 22, 2013).
[3] Ibid.
[4] Ibid.
[5] Ibid.
[6] Kathleen Parker, "Some things shouldn't be compared," *Tulsa World*, November 23, 2013, A-19.
[7] "servitude," *Webster's Seventh New Collegiate Dictionary*, (Springfield, Massachusetts: G. & C. Merriam Company, Publishers, 1963), p. 818.
[8] Ibid., p. 793.
[9] Weaver, *Ideas Have Consequences*, pp. 148, 151, 153.
[10] Ibid., pp. 151-153, 163.
[11] Richard M. Weaver, *The Southern Essays of Richard M. Weaver*, eds. George M. Curtis, III, and James J. Thompson, Jr., eds. (Indianapolis, Indiana: Liberty Fund, 1987), pp. 195-196.

The *New* Ministry of Truth 2014
[1] George Orwell, *1984*, (New York: Signet Classics, 1950).
[2] Ibid.
[3] Social Solutions International, Inc., "Research Design for the Study of Multi-Market Critical Information Needs," *Federal Communications Commission*, (Silver Springs, Maryland: Social Solutions International, Inc., April 2013). http://www.fcc.gov/encyclopedia/research-design-multi-market-study-critical-information-needs (accessed February 22, 2014)
[4] Ibid., pp. 2-3.
[5] Tony Perkins, "American Pai: FCC Chair Fights off Government Snoops," *Family Research Council*, February 21, 2014. http://www.frc.org/washingtonupdate/american-pai-fcc-chair-fights-off-govt-snoops (accessed February 22, 2014)
[6] Social Solutions International, Inc., "Research Design for the Study of Multi-Market Critical Information Needs," p. 61,
[7] See "Common Core Curriculum Standards: The devil is in the details."
[8] "Commissar," *Webster's Seventh New Collegiate Dictionary*, (Springfield, Massachusetts: G. & C. Merriam Company, Publishers, 1963), p. 166.
[9] Tocqueville, *Democracy in America*, pp. 807-808.

The most powerful weapon
[1] Weaver, *Ideas Have Consequences*, p. 148.
[2] Ibid.
[3] Ibid., pp. 148, 151.
[4] Weaver, *The Southern Essays of Richard M. Weaver*, p. 196-197.

Part V – Islam

Liberal defense of Islam
[1] Daniel Greenfield, "Howard Dean: Muslim Terrorists are as Muslim as Me," *Frontpage Mag*, January 7, 2015. http://www.frontpagemag.com/2015/dgreenfield/howard-dean-muslim-terrorists-are-as-muslim-as-me/ (accessed January 13, 2015).
[2] Erika Tucker, "Soldier killed in what Harper calls 'terrorist attack' in Ottawa," *Global News*, October 22, 2014. http://globalnews.ca/news/1628313/shots-fired-at-war-memorial-in- / ottawa-says-witness (accessed January 13, 2015).
[3] Michael Gerson, "The politics of homicide in France," *Tulsa World*, January 10, 2015, A-16.
[4] *The Meaning of The Illustrious Qur-an*, (Dar AHYA Us-Sunnah), p. 49.
[5] Kurtz, *Humanist Manifestos I and II*, pp.15-16.

Are Christianity and Islam morally equivalent? Parts I through IV
[1] "World Watch List Countries," *Open Doors*. http://www.worldwatchlist.us/ (accessed September 15, 2014).
[2] Sarah Eekhoff Zylstra, "Counting the Cost (Accurately)," *Christianity Today*, August 21, 2013. http://www.christianitytoday.com/ct/2013/september/counting-cost-accurately.html (accessed September 16, 2013).
[3] Jeremy Diamond, "Why President Obama won't call the fight on terror a war on radical Islam," *CNN*, February 1, 2015. http://www.cnn.com/2015/02/01/politics/obama-radical-islam-terrorism-war/index.html (accessed March 30, 2015).
[4] President Barak Obama, "Remarks of the President at the National Prayer Breakfast," *The White House – Office of the Press Secretary*, February 1, 2015. https://www.whitehouse.gov/the-press-office/2015/02/05/remarks-president-national-prayer-breakfast (accessed March 30, 2015).
[5] Roberts, *The New History of the World*, pp. 324-327.
[6] Raymond Ibrahim, *Crucified Again-Exposing Islam's New War on Christians*, (Washington, D.C.: Regnery Publishing, Inc., 2013), p. 9.
[7] Rodney Stark, *God's Battalions-The Case for the Crusades*, (New York: Harper One, 2009), pp. 12, 15-23.
[8] Ibrahim, *Crucified Again-Exposing Islam's New War on Christians*, p. 9.
[9] Ibid., p. 18.
[10] All quotations from the Quran are from the textless edition of the English translation of the Holy Qur-an: A. Yusuf Ali, *The Meaning of the Illustrious Qur-an*, Published by: Dar AHYA Us-Sunnah, Al Nabawiya.
[11] Ibrahim., *Crucified Again-Exposing Islam's New War on Christians*, p. 19.
[12] Ibid., p. 21
[13] Ibid.
[14] Ibid., pp. 22-23.
[15] Ibid., pp. 24-25.

[16] Jay Sekulow, "The Rise of ISIS & The New Caliphate," *The City*, Volume VII, Number 3, Winter 2015, 22-24.
[17] Sekulow, "The Rise of ISIS & The New Caliphate," *The City*, 22-24.; Roberts, *The New History of the World*, pp. 329, 333.
[18] "Compare Sunni and Shia Muslims," *Religions Facts*. http://www.religionfacts.com/islam/comparison_charts/islamic_sects.htm (accessed March 31, 2015).
[19] Stark, *God's Battalions-The Case for the Crusades*, p. 36-37.
[20] Ibrahim, *Crucified Again-Exposing Islam's New War on Christians*, p. 10.
[21] Ibid., p. 10-13.
[22] Stark, *God's Battalions-The Case for the Crusades*, p. 9.
[23] Ibid., pp. 2-4.
[24] Ibid.
[25] Ibid., p. 8.
[26] Ibid., p. 8.
[27] Ibid., pp. 117-118.
[28] President Barak Obama, "Remarks of the President at the National Prayer Breakfast," *The White House – Office of the Press Secretary*, February 1, 2015.
[29] Stark, *God's Battalions-The Case for the Crusades*, p. 8.
[30] Ibid., pp. 56-57.
[31] Ibid., p. 65.
[32] Ibid., pp. 65-66.
[33] Ibid., P. 66
[34] Alvin J. Schmidt, *How Christianity Changed the World*, (Grand Rapids, Michigan: Zondervan, 2004), pp. 8-9.

"Workplace violence" comes to Canada
[1] OSHA Fact Sheet, U.S. Department of Labor, Occupational Safety and Health Administration, 2002. https://www.osha.gov/OshDoc/data_General_Facts/factsheet-workplace-violence .pdf (accessed November 5, 2014).
[2] Billy Kenber, "Nidal Hasan sentenced to death for Fort Hood shooting rampage," *Washington Post*, August 28, 2013. http://www.washingtonpost.com/world/national-security/nidal-hasan-sentenced -to-death -for-fort-hood-shooting-rampage/2013/08/28/aad28de2-0ffa-11e3-bdf6-e4fc677d94a1_story.html (accessed November 5, 2014).
[3] Lindy Kyzer, "Gen. Casey on the strength of our diversity," *Army Live*, U.S. Army, November 8, 2009. http://armylive.dodlive.mil/index.php/2009/11/gen-casey-on-the-strength-of-our-diversity/ (accessed November 5, 2014).
[4] Erika Tucker, "Soldier killed in what Harper calls 'terrorist attack' in Ottawa," *Global News*, October 22, 2014. http://globalnews.ca/news/1628313/shots-fired-at-war-memorial-in-ottawa-says-witness/ (accessed November 5, 2014).
[5] *The Meaning of The Illustrious Qur-an*, (Dar AHYA Us-Sunnah), p. 49.

[6] Ibid., p. 98.
[7] Johnson, *Ye shall be as gods*, p 398.
[8] Ibid., pp. 189-190.

FINDING TRUTH IN THE MAZE OF FREEWILL

Part I – Marriage & Family

Marriage
[1] Johnson, *Ye shall be as gods*, Chapter 20, pp.305-321.
[2] Ibid., pp. 305-307.
[3] Weaver, *Ideas Have Consequences*, pp. 41-42.
[4] Johnson, Ye shall be as gods, p. 305.
[5] Ibid., p. 306.
[6] Ibid.
[7] Ibid.
[8] Ibid., pp. 306-307.
[9] Weaver, *Ideas Have Consequences*, pp. 35, 41-42.
[10] Johnson, *Ye shall be as gods*, p. 307.
[11] Albert M. Wolters, *Creation Regained*, (Grand Rapids, Michigan: William B. Eerdmans Publishing Company, 1985, 2005), p. 96.
[12] Johnson, *Ye shall be as gods*, p. 308.
[13] William J. Bennett, *The Broken Hearth*, (New York: Doubleday, 2001), pp. 44-50.
[14] Stephanie Coontz, *Marriage, a History*, (New York: Penguin Group, 2005), p. 7
[15] Johnson, *Ye shall be as gods*, p. 310.
[16] Bennett, *The Broken Hearth*, pp. 44-45, 174-178.
[17] Johnson, *Ye shall be as gods*, p. 311.
[18] Ibid., pp. 311-312.
[19] Bennett, *The Broken Hearth*, pp. 45-50, 53.
[20] Johnson, *Ye shall be as gods*, p. 312.
[21] Ibid.
[22] Bennet, *The Broken Hearth*, p. 188.
[23] Ibid., pp. 184-188.
[24] Ibid., pp. 186-187.
[25] Johnson, *Ye shall be as gods*, p. 313.
[26] Ibid.
[27] Gary Chapman, *Covenant Marriage*, (Nashville, Tennessee: Broadman & Holman Publishers, 2003), pp. 6-10.
[28] Johnson, *Ye shall be as gods*, pp. 313-314.
[29] Ibid., p. 314.
[30] Chapman, *Covenant Marriage*, pp. 11-16.
[31] Johnson, *Ye shall be as gods*, p. 314.
[32] Kurtz, *Humanist Manifestos I and II*, p. 18.

[33] Ryan T. Anderson, "Twelve Theses on Redefining Marriage – What comes Next," *The City*, Summer 2013, 16.
[34] Johnson, *Ye shall be as gods*, p. 315.
[35] Chapman, *Covenant Marriage*, pp. 17-21.
[36] Johnson, *Ye shall be as gods*, pp. 315-316.
[37] Ibid., p. 316.
[38] Ibid.
[39] Robert Rector, "The Collapse of Marriage and the Rise of Welfare Dependence," Panel Discussion, Lecture #959, The Heritage Foundation (May 22, 2006). www.heritage.org/research/welfare/hl959.cfm (accessed September 17, 2010).
[40] Robert Rector, "Marriage: America's Greatest Weapon Against Child Poverty," The Heritage Foundation, September 16, 2010, http://www.heritage.org/research/reports/2010/09/marriage-america-s-greatest-weapon-against-child-poverty (accessed September 21, 2010).
[41] Johnson, *Ye shall be as gods*, p. 17.
[42] Ibid., p. 319.
[43] Rector, "The Collapse of Marriage and the Rise of Welfare Dependence."
[44] Bennett, *The Broken Hearth*, pp. 2, 85.
[45] Lee Rainwater and William L. Yancey, *The Moynihan Report and the Politics of Controversy*, (Cambridge, Massachusetts: M.I.T. Press, 1967), p. 3.
[46] Bennett, *The Broken Hearth*, pp. 1-2.
[47] Johnson, *Ye shall be as gods*, p. 321.

Love and Commitment
[1] Ravi Zacharias, "Volume 4 - Establishing a Worldview," *Foundations of Apologetics*, DVD Video, (Norcross, Georgia: Ravi Zacharias International Ministries, 2007).
[2] Johnson, *Ye shall be as gods*, p. 158.
[3] Ibid.
[4] Bennett, *The Broken Hearth*, pp. 184-188; Johnson, *Ye shall be as gods*, p. 312.
[5] Bennett, *The Broken Hearth*, pp. 184-188; Johnson, *Ye shall be as gods*, pp. 312-313.
[6] Johnson, Ye shall be as gods, pp. 99-100.

Did father really know best?
[1] Stephanie Coontz, *Marriage, a History,* (New York: Penguin Group, 2005), pp. 4-5.
[2] Johnson, *Ye shall be as gods*, p. 323.
[3] Ibid., p. 323.
[4] Ibid., p. 325.
[5] Linda J. Waite and Maggie Gallagher, *The Case for Marriage*, (New York: Doubleday, 2000), p. 1.
[6] "The Founding of NOW," *National Organization of Women* website,

_http://now.org/about/history/founding-2/ (accessed July 16, 2014).
[7] "The National Organization for Women's 1966 Statement of Purpose," *National Organization of Women* http://now.org/about/history/statement-of-purpose/ (accessed July 16, 2014).
[8] Johnson, *Ye shall be as gods*, p. 391.
[9] Ibid.

Part II - Abortion

Postcard from Hell
[1] John Hayward, "Kermit Gosnell's House of Screams," *Human Events*, April 8, 2013.
http://www.humanevents.com/2013/04/08/kermit-gosnells-house-of-screams/ (accessed April 10, 2013).
[2] Tony Perkins, "Washington Update," *Family Research Council*, April 9, 2013.
http://www.frc.org/washingtonupdate/braking-news-media-halts-coverage-of-serial-killer (accessed April 10, 2013).
[3] "At Gosnell trial, Del. woman testifies scene 'freaked me out,'" *delawareonline.com*, April 9, 2013.
http://www.delawareonline.com/article/20130409/NEWS/304070067/ (accessed April 10, 2013).
[4] "Planned Parent Rep raises eyebrows in testimony on bill protecting babies born after botched abortion," *Fox News Politics*, March 29, 2013.
http://www.foxnews.com/politics/2013/03/29/planned-parenthood-rep-raises-eyebrows-in-testimony-on-bill-protecting-babies.html
[5] Johnson, *Ye shall be as gods*, p. 344.
[6] Ibid., p. 350.
[7] Ibid., p. 351.

Oh!? It's a matter of sanitation and not murder.
[1] Johnson, *Ye shall be as gods,* p. 35.
[2] Julie Pace and Mark Sherman, "Obama says no way to avoid gay marriage case," *Associated Press*, March 1, 2013. On-line source: http://news.yahoo-says-no-way-avoid-gay-marriage-case-172022149-politics.html (accessed March 5, 2013).
[3] Bennett, *The Broken Hearth*, pp. 105-107, 121, 138.
[4] Johnson, *Ye shall be as gods*, p. 365.

Part III - Homosexuality

Equality – The homosexual agenda's Trojan horse in its battle for cultural acceptance
[1] "Planned Parent Rep raises eyebrows in testimony on bill protecting babies born after botched abortion," *Fox News Politics*, March 29, 2013.
http://www.foxnews.com/politics/2013/03/29/planned-parenthood-rep-raises-

eyebrows-in-testimony-on-bill-protecting-babies.html
² Dr. Susan Berry, "Sen. Mike Lee resolves to address "Gosnell-type" abortion crime," Brietbart News, May 6, 2013
http://www.breitbart.com/Big-Government/2013/05/06/Sen-Mike-Lee-Resolves-To-Address-Gosnell-Type-Abortion-Crime (accessed May 10, 2013).
³ Blumenthal Delivers Floor Speech Objecting To Senator Lee's Abortion Resolution, Introduces Broader Resolution Condemning Criminal Acts And Malpractice In All Health Care Settings, *Richard Blumenthal, United States Senator – Connecticut*, May 8, 2013.
http://www.blumenthal.senate.gov/newsroom/press/release/blumenthal-delivers-floor-speech-objecting-to-senator-lees-abortion-resolution- all-introduces-broader-resolution-condemning-criminal-acts-and-malpractice-in-health-care-settings (accessed May 10, 2013).

Mr. Jones's Childish Things – Parts I & II
¹ Much of the discussion in Part I is based on the author's previous writing found in his book: Larry G. Johnson, *Ye shall be as gods – Humanism and Christianity – The Battle for Supremacy in the American Cultural Vision*, (Owasso, Oklahoma: Anvil House Publishers, 2011), pp. 229, 334-335, 354, 356.
² Mike Jones, "Childish things – It's time to end the divide over gay marriage," *Tulsa World*, (April 14, 2001), G1.
³ Richard M. Weaver, *Visions of Order*, (Wilmington, Delaware: Intercollegiate Studies Institute, 1964), pp. 22-23.
⁴ Jones, "Childish things – It's time to end the divide over gay marriage," *Tulsa World*, G1.

Is God Out of Touch with Mainstream Views?
¹ Mary Alice Parks, "This Week Panel: Are Evangelicals Out of Touch With Mainstream Views?" *ABC News*, April 20, 2014.
http://abcnews.go.com/blogs/politics/2014/04/this-week-panel-are-evangelicals-out-of-touch- with-mainstream-views/ (accessed April 20, 2014).
² Ibid.
³ Malcolm Muggeridge, *The End of Christendom*, (Grand Rapids, Michigan: William B. Eerdmans Publishing Company, 1980), p. 17.
⁴ Johnson, *Ye shall be as gods*, p. 374.

Does God lie?
¹Rev. Justin Alan Lindstrom and Rev. Robin R. Meyers, "Marriage equality is a matter of faith," *Tulsa World*, May 4, 2014, G-2.

Humanism's equality handcuffs freedom and violates the Constitution
[1] "Atlanta Fire Chief fired over controversial statements," *myfoxatlanta.com*, January 6, 2015. http://www.myfoxatlanta.com/story/27772986/mayor-holds-news-conference-on-fire-chiefs-future (accessed January 21, 2015).
[2] Todd Starnes, "Atlanta Fire Chief: I was fired because of my Christian faith," *Fox News*, January 7, 2015. http://www.foxnews.com/opinion/2015/01/07/atlanta-fire-chief-was-fired-because-my-christian-faith/ (accessed January 21, 2015).
[3] Ibid.
[4] Ibid.
[5] Ibid.
[6] The Editorial Board, "God, Gays, and the Atlanta Fire Department," *The New York Times*, January 13, 2015.
[7] Federer, *America's God and* Country, p. 642.
[8] Ibid., pp. 642-643.

Part IV – Education

Education in America – Parts I through III
[9] Common Core State Standards Initiative. http://www.corestandards.org/read-the-standards/
[10] "English Language Arts Standards," *Common Core State Standards Initiative.* http://www.corestandards.org/ELA-Literacy (accessed June 25, 2013).
[11] Josiah Quincy, LL.D., *History of Harvard University*, (Boston, MA: Crosby, Nichols, Lee, & Co., 1860), p. 515.
[12] Reprint of 1777 edition of *The New England Primer* by David Barton, (Aledo, Texas: Wallbuidler Press, May 2007).
[13] Jared Sparks, *The life of Gouverneur Morris*, Vol. III. (Boston, MA: Gray and Bowen, Vol. III), p. 483.
[14] Samuel Adams, "Letter of Samuel Adams to John Adams, October 4, 1790," *Writings of Samuel Adams*, Ed. Harry A. Cushing, (New York: Octagon Books, Inc., 1968), p. 4:343; Ira Stoll, *Samuel Adams – ALife*, (New York: Free Press, 2008), pp. 9-10, 240.
[15] Newt Gingrich, *Rediscovering God in America*, (Nashville, Tennessee, Discovery House, 2006, p. 46.
[16] Noah Webster, *American Dictionary of the English Language 1828*, Facsimile Edition, (San Francisco, California: Foundation for American Christian Education, 1967, 1995 by Rosalie J. Slater), p. 12.
[17] John H. Westerhoff III, *McGuffey and His Readers*, (Milford, Michigan: Mott Media, 1982), pp. 14-15.
[18] Kansas Historical Society, *Columbian History of Education in Kansas*, (Topeka, Kansas: Hamilton Printing Company, 1893), p. 82.
[19] Craig M. Gay, *The way of the (modern) world*, (Grand Rapids, Michigan: Wm. B. Eerdmans Publishing Co., 1998), pp. 204-205.

[20] Johnson, *Ye shall be as gods,* pp. 21-22, 24-25, 289, 291, 304.
[21] Charlotte Thomson Iserbyt, *the deliberate dumbing down of america*, (Ravenna, Ohio: Conscience Press, 1999), pp. 5-6, 345.
[22] Sidney Hook, *John Dewey – His Philosophy of Education and Its Critics*, (New York: Tamiment Institute, 1959), p. 3.
[23] Richard M. Weaver, *Visions of Order*, (Wilmington, Delaware: Intercollegiate Studies Institute, 1964), p. 117.
[24] Common Core State Standards Initiative.
[25] English Language Arts Standards," *Common Core State Standards Initiative.*
[26] "Implementing the Common Core State Standards," *Common Core State Standards Initiative.* http://www.corestandards.org/ (accessed June 25, 2013).
[27] Ibid.
[28] George M. Thomas, Lisa R. Peck, and Channin G. DeHaan, "Reforming Education, Transforming Religion, 1876-1931," in *The Secular Revolution*, ed. Christian Smith, (Berkeley, California: University of California Press, 2003, pp. 355-356, 362, 365, 377.
[29] Common Core State Standards Initiative.
[30] Ronald Reagan, *The Notes – Ronald Reagan's Private Collection of Stories and Wisdom*, Douglas Brinkley, ed., (New York: Harper, 2011), p.186.

Common Core Curriculum Standards – The devil is in the details
[31] U.S. Department of Education, "District-Level Race to the Top to Focus on the Classroom, Provide Tools to Enhance Learning and Serve the Needs of Every Student," *ED.gov,* May 22, 2012. ww.ed.gov/news/press-releases/district-level-race-top-focus-classroom-provide-tools-enhance-learning-and-serve (accessed October 30, 2013).
[32] "Race to the Top," *Truth in American Education,* http://truthinamericaneducation.com/race-to-the-top/ (accessed October 30, 2013).
[33] "District-Level Race to the Top–Race to the Top IV," *Truth in American Education.* http://truthinamericaneducation.com/race-to-the-top/district-level-race-to-the-toprace-to-the-top-iv/ (accessed October 30, 2013).
[34] Ibid.
[35] Ibid.
[36] Ibid.
[37] Ibid.
[38] Ibid.
[39] Dr. Allan Carlson, "Common Core: The Dangers of Federal Power in Education," Video Lecture, *Family Research Council,* September 25, 2013. http://www.frc.org/eventregistration/common-core-the-dangers-of-federal-power-in-education (accessed October 30, 2013).
[40] Ibid.
[41] U.S. Department of Education, "The Federal Role in Education," *ED.gov.*, http://www2.ed.gov/about/overview/fed/role.html (accessed October 30, 2013).

[42] Federer, *America's God and Country*, p. 698.
[43] George Will, "Clunker progressivism: Present, too, is prologue," *Tulsa World*, November 7, 2013, A-14.

Train up a child in the way he should go
[44] Johnson, *Ye shall be as gods*, pp 28, 311.
[45] Ibid., p. 11.
[46] Richard P. Adler, ed., *Understanding Television – Essays on Television as a Social and Cultural Force*, (New York: Praeger Publishers, 1981), pp. xi-xii.
[47] Michael Novak, "Television Shapes the Soul," *Understanding Television – Essays on Television as a Social and Cultural Force*, Richard P. Adler, ed., (New York: Praeger Publishers, 1981), pp. 20, 26-27.
[48] Richard Croker, *The Boomer Century 1946-2046*, (New York: Springboard Press, 2007), p. 20.
[49] David Elkind, Ph.D., *The hurried child – growing up too fast too soon,*" (Cambridge, Massachusetts: Da Capo Press, 2007), pp. ix-x.
[50] Weaver, *Visions of Order – The Cultural Crisis of Our Time*, p. 41.
[51] Johnson, *Ye shall be as gods*, pp. 336-337.
[52] Federer, *America's God and Country*, p. 21.
[53] Ibid., pp. 23-24.
[54] Robert J. Roth, *John Dewey and Self-Realization*, (Westport, Connecticut: Greenwood Press, Publisher, 1962), pp. 100-101.
[55] Ibid., p. 101.
[56] Elkind, *The hurried child – growing up too fast too soon*, p. xiii.
[57] U.S. Department of Education, "16 States and D.C. Submit Applications for the Race to the Top-Early Learning Challenge," *ED.gov*, October 18, 2013. http://www.ed.gov/news/press-releases/16-states-and-dc-submit-applications-race-top-early-learning-challenge (accessed November 14, 2013).
[58] Ibid., p. 3.
[59] Ibid., pp. 49-50.
[60] Ibid., pp. 50-51.
[61] Ibid., p. 221.

Shake and Bake History - Engineering the future while forgetting the past
[1] David Turnoy, "When can we introduce children to honest history?" *Tulsa World*, June 8, 2014, A14.
[2] Ibid.
[3] Daniel Burnett, "Historical amnesia: Let us never forget D-Day," *Tulsa World*, June 6, 2014, A14.
[4] Robert B. Talisse, *On Dewey*, (Belmont, California: Wadsworth/Thompson Learning, 2000), pp. ix, 1, 4.
[5] Johnson, *Ye shall be as gods*, pp. 23-25.
[6] Smith, "Introduction," *The Secular Revolution*, p. 54.
[7] Johnson, *Ye shall be as gods*, p. 300.
[8] Kirk, *The Essential Russell Kirk*, p. 400.
[9] Weaver, *Visions of Order*, p. 117.

Progressive view of American history: The good old days were all bad.
[1] Murray N. Rothbard, "The Progressive Theory of History," Ludwig von Mises Institute, September 14, 2010. http://mises.org/daily/4708 (accessed October 28, 2014).
[2] College Board, https://www.collegeboard.org/about (accessed October 14, 2014).
[3] Colleen Slevin, "Colorado board backs review of curriculum," *Tulsa World*, October 3, 2014, A9.
[4] Colleen Slevin, "Critics slam school board over history course review," *Tulsa World*, October 4, 2014, A4.
[5] Johnson, *Ye shall be as gods*, pp. 23-24, 289-290.
[6] Slevin, "Critics slam school board over history course review," A4.

FREEDOM ABUSED IS FREEDOM LOST

Part I - Government

Our Play-Doh® Constitution
[1] James E. Person, Jr., *Russell Kirk, A Critical Biography of a Conservative Mind*, (Latham, Maryland: Madison Books, 1999), p. 105
[2] Cheryl K. Chumley, "N.Y. Mayor Michael Bloomberg: Constitution 'must change' to give government more power," *The Washington Times*, April 23, 2013. http://www.washingtontimes.com/news/2013/apr/23/ny-mayor-michael-bloomberg-constitution-must-chang/ (accessed April 27, 2013).
[3] Sherwood Eddy, *The Kingdom of God and the American Dream*, (New York: Harper & Brothers Publishers, 1941), p. 124.
[4] Kirk, *The Roots of American Order*, p. 29.
[5] Federer, *America's God and Country*, p. 247.
[6] Cheryl K. Chumley, "NYC Mayor Bloomberg: Government Has Right To 'Infringe On Your Freedom'," *The Washington Times*, March 25, 2013, http://www.washingtontimes.com/news/2013/mar/25/nyc-mayor-bloomberg-government-has-right-infringe-/ (accessed April 27, 2013).

Death of the American Constitution
[1] Much of the discussion in this article is based on the author's previous writing found in his book: Johnson, *Ye shall be as gods*, pp. 401-404.
[2] Benjamin Rush, *Essays, Literary, Moral & Philosophical*, (Philadelphia: Thomas and Samuel F. Bradford, 1798), 93. Online source: http://fromthisconservativesviewpoint.blogspot.com/2013/01/the-only-foundation-for-republic.html (accessed May 9, 2013)
[3] "Letter of Charles Carroll to James McHenry," dated November 4, 1800. Bernard C. Steiner, *The Life and Correspondence of James McHenry*, (Cleveland: The Burrows Brothers, 1907, 475.

Online source: Quoted by Dave Miller, Ph.D., *Apologetics Press*
http://www.apologeticspress.org/apcontent.aspx?category=7&article=1508
(accessed May 9, 2013)

[4] John Adams, "Letter to Zabdiel Adams, Philadelphia, 21 June 1776," in *The Works of John Adams – Second President of the United States*, ed. Charles Francis Adams, Vol. IX, p. 229, October 11, 1798, (Boston: Little, Brown & Co., 1854). Online Source: http://historicwords.com/american-history/john-adams/ (accessed May 9, 2013).

Government is not the problem, however…

[5] Washington Wire, "Transcript: Obama speech at Ohio State University," *The Wall Street Journal*, May 16, 2013.
http://blogs.wsj.com/washwire/2013/05/06/transcript-obamas- /commencement-speech-at-ohio-state (accessed May 16, 2013).

[6] Noah Webster, "Politics," *American Dictionary of the English Language*, 1828, Facsimile Edition, (San Francisco, California: Foundation for American Christian Education, 1995).

[7] *The Works of James Wilson*, Bird Wilson, editor (Philadelphia: Bronson and Chauncey, 1804), Vol. I, pp. 104-106 as quoted from online source: http://www.partyof1776.net/p1776/fathers/WilsonJames/quotes.html (accessed May 16, 2013).

[8] Illinois State Senator Barak Obama, "Our Future and Vision for America", *About.com US Liberal Politics*, June 28, 2006.
http://usliberals.about.com/od/faithinpubliclife/a/ObamaReligion_4.htm (accessed May 16, 2013).

The Christian's Role in Politics and Government

[9] Noah Webster, "Politics," *American Dictionary of the English Language*, 1828, Facsimile Edition, (San Francisco, California: Foundation for American Christian Education, 1995).

[10] Joseph Story, *Commentaries on the Constitution of the United States*, (Boston: Hilliard, Gray, & Co., 1833). Vol. III, p. 728, paragraph 1871.

[11] Wayne Gruden, "Why Christians should seek to influence the government for good." Booklet adapted from Wayne Gruden, *Politics – According to the Bible – A Comprehensive Resource for Understanding Modern Political Issues in Light of Scripture*, (Grand Rapids, Michigan: Zondervan, 2010).

[12] Johnson, *Ye shall be as gods*, p. 224.

[13] Tocqueville, *Democracy in America*, pp. 343, 345.

[14] Ibid.

Would Jefferson label the modern Judiciary as the "Despotic Branch"?

[15] George Will, Huckabee's 'appalling' crusade for nullification," *Tulsa World*,
May 15, 2015, A-15.

[16] Richard B. Morris, ed., *Encyclopedia of American History*, (New York: Harper & Brothers, Publishers, 1953), pp.167-168.

[17] Ibid., p. 173.

[18] Ibid.
[19] David Barton, *Original Intent*, (Aledo, Texas: Wallbuilder Press, 2008), pp. 275-176.
[20] Barton, *Original Intent*, p. 271. Quoting: Thomas Jefferson, *Writings of Thomas Jefferson*, Albert Ellery Bergh, ed., (Washington, DC: Thomas Jefferson Memorial Association, 1904), Vol. XV, p. 213, to Spencer Roane, September 6, 1819.
[21] Ibid.
[22] Morris, *Encyclopedia of American History*, pp. 221-222.
[23] Barton, *Original Intent*, p. 272.
[24] Ibid.
[25] Barton, *Original Intent*, pp. 271-272. Quoting: Thomas Jefferson, *Memoir, Correspondence, and Miscellanies*, Thomas Jefferson Randolph, ed., (Boston: Gray and Bowen, 1830), Vol. IV, p. 27, to Abigail Adams, September 11, 1804.

Helicopter government – Parts I through V
[26] "helicopter parenting," *Dictionary.com* http://dictionary.reference.com/browse/helicopter+parenting (accessed March 24, 2014).
[27] Jason Ashley Wright, "Nurturing in Excess," *Tulsa World*, March 24, 2014, D1.
[28] Hara Estroff Marano, "A Nation of Wimps," *Psychology Today*, November 1, 2004. http://www.psychologytoday.com/articles/200411/nation-wimps (accessed March 31, 2014).
[29] Paul Kurtz, *In Defense of Secular Humanism*, (Amherst, New York: Prometheus Books, 1983), p. 68.
[30] Kurtz, ed., *Humanist Manifestos I and II*, p. 20.
[31] Lamont, *The Philosophy of Humanism*, p. 272.
[32] Arthur Brooks, "The right must reclaim social justice," *Tulsa World*, April 1, 2014, A-14.
[33] Johnson, *Ye shall be as gods*, pp. 252-253.
[34] Robert J. Samuelson, *The Good Life and Its Discontents*, (New York: Vintage Books, 1995, 1997), p. 141-142.
[35] Alan Petigny, *The Permissive Society – America, 1941-1965*, (Cambridge, England: Cambridge University Press, 2009), pp. 226, 238-239.
[36] Jason Ashley Wright, "Nurturing in Excess," *Tulsa World*, March 24, 2014, D1.
[37] Robert Bork, *Slouching Towards Gomorrah*, (New York: Regan Books, 1996), p. 243.
[38] Marano, "A Nation of Wimps," *Psychology Today*, November 1, 2004; Hara Estroff Marano, *A Nation of Wimps*, (New York: Broadway Books, 2009), pp. 243-244.
[39] Marano, "A Nation of Wimps," *Psychology Today*.
[40] Weaver, *Visions of Order – The Cultural Crisis of Our Time*, pp. 136-145.

[41] Johnson, *Ye shall be as gods*, pp. 222-223.
[42] Ibid., pp. 220, 221-222.
[43] Ibid., p. 158.
[44] Weaver, *Ideas Have Consequences*, p. 113.
[45] Johnson, *Ye shall be as gods*, p. 3. Quoted material from: Robert J. Samuelson, *The Good Life and Its Discontents*, (New York: Vintage Books, 1995, 1997), pp. 46-47.
[46] Larry Schweikart and Michael Allen, *A Patriot's History of the United States*," (New York: Sentinel, 2004), pp. 687-688.
[47] Kurtz, *Humanist Manifestos I and* II, p. 20.
[48] Johnson, *Ye shall be as gods*, p. 406.
[49] Samuelson, *The Good Life and Its Discontents*, p. 218.
[50] Leonard Steinhorn, *The Greater Generation – In Defense of the Baby Boom Legacy*, (New York: Thomas Dunne Books, 2006), p. 69.
[51] Johnson, *Ye shall be as gods*, p. 41.
[52] Ibid., p. 3.
[53] David Elkind, Ph.D., *The hurried child – growing up too fast too soon*, (Cambridge, Massachusetts: Da Capo Press, 2007), p. 221.
[54] Marano, *A Nation of Wimps*, pp. 86-87.
[55] Elkind, *A Nation of Wimps*, p. 214.
[56] Johnson, *Ye shall be as gods*, p. 243.
[57] "What is the Real Size of the U.S. Federal Tax Code," *Isaac Brock Society*, February 12, 2012. http://isaacbrocksociety.ca/2012/02/12/what-is-the-real-size-of-the-u-s-federal-tax-code/ (accessed April 9, 2014).
[58] James Thurber, "The Secret Life of Walter Mitty," *Introduction to Literature*, 4th Edition, (eds., Louis G. Locke, William M. Gibson, and George Arms, (New York: Holt, Rinehart and Winston, 1962), p. 418-421.

This was done by ordinary people – Parts I through IV
[59] Metaxas, *Bonhoeffer*, pp. 145, 148-149.
[60] Ibid., pp. 149-150.
[61] Ibid., pp. 150-151, 156-157, 160.
[62] Roberts, *The New History of the World*, pp. 954, 1150.
[63] Ibid., p. 964.
[64] Ravi Zacharias, "God, Evil, and Suffering," *Foundations of Apologetics*, Vol. 10, DVD Video, (Norcross, Georgia: Ravi Zacharias Ministries International, 2007).
[65] Metaxas, *Bonhoeffer*, pp. 33-34.
[66] Ibid., p. 141.
[67] Johnson, *Ye shall be as gods*, p. 139.
[68] Ibid., pp. 92-93, 287.
[69] Metaxas, *Bonhoeffer*, p. 85.
[70] Ibid., p. 156.
[71] Michael Scherer, "Chic-Fil-A meets a First Amendment buzz saw in Chicago," *Time*, July 26, 2012. http://swampland.time.com/2012/07/26/chick-fil-a-meets-a-first-amendment-/buzzsaw-in-chicago (accessed May 21, 2014).

72 Metaxas, *Bonhoeffer*, p. 160.
73 Jeremy Tedesco, "The Julea Ward Settlement: A Win for Religious Liberty," *Townhall.com*, January 4, 2013. http://townhall.com/columnists/jeremytedesco/2013/01/04/the-julea-ward-settlement--a-win-for-religious-liberty-n1478423 (accessed May 22, 2014).
74 Metaxas, *Bonhoeffer*, p. 160.
75 "Court orders UNC–Wilmington to pay, promote professor after retaliating against him" Alliance Defending Freedom, April 9, 2014. http://www.alliancedefendingfreedom.org/News/PRDetail/3901 (accessed May 22, 2014).
76 Metaxas, *Bonhoeffer*, p. 160.
77 Mark A. Kellner, "Pasadena's medical director on leave after his Protestant sermons surface." *NewsOK*, May 9, 2014. http://newsok.com/pasadenas-medical-director-on-leave-after-his-protestant-sermons- surface/article/4747892 (accessed May 24, 2014).
78 Metaxas, *Bonhoeffer*, p. 160.
79 Ann Oldenburg, "Bentham brothers: If faith cost us TV show, so be it," *USA Today*, May 8, 2014. http://www.usatoday.com/story/life/tv/2014/05/07/hgtv-nixes-benham-brothers-series-anti-gay-extremist-abortion/8810393/ (accessed May 22, 2014).
80 Metaxas, *Bonhoeffer*, p. 160.
81 Barry Horn, "Craig James' anti-gay stance during political campaign reason for quick exit from FOX Sports SW," *SportsDayDFW*, September 6, 2013. collegesportsblog.dallasnews.com/2013/09/craig-james-anti-gay-stance-during-political-campaign-reason-for-his-quick-exit-from-fssw-college-football-duties.html/ (accessed May 22, 2014).
82 Metaxas, *Bonhoeffer*, p. 161.
83 "Barak Obama Quotes," *Notable Quotes*. http://www.notable-quotes.com/o/obama_barack.html (accessed May 28, 2014).
84 Metaxas, *Bonhoeffer*, pp. 165-166.
85 Lutzer, *When a Nation Forgets God*," p. 44.
86 Metaxas, *Bonhoeffer*, pp. 151-152, 176.
87 Lutzer, *When a Nation Forgets God*, pp. 19-20.
88 Ibid., p. 21.
89 Metaxas, *Bonhoeffer*, pp. 293, 295.
90 Ibid., p. 85.
91 Lutzer, *When a Nation Forgets God*, pp. 117-118.
92 Ibid., p. 33.
93 Ibid., pp. 120-121.
94 Metaxas, *Bonhoeffer*, p. 153.
95 Ibid., pp. 152-153.
96 Ibid., pp. 153-154.

Part II – Socialism

The New Despotism – Parts I & II
[97] Russell Kirk, *The Conservative Mind*, (www.bnpublishing.net, 2008), pp. 82-
   83.
[98] Kurtz, ed., *Humanist Manifestos I and II*, p. 20.
[99] Ibid.
[100] Tocqueville, *Democracy in America*, pp. 805-806.
[101] Kurtz, *Humanist Manifestos I and II*, p. 10.
[102] Tocqueville, *Democracy in America*, p. 808.

March Madness: Nanny State 1 – Freedom 0
[103] Dylan Goforth, "Tooth Fairy to be extracted," *Tulsa World*, March 22, 2014,
   A-1.
[104] Ibid.
[105] Ibid.
[106] "Oklahoma State Agencies, Boards, and Commissions," *Oklahoma Department of Libraries*, September 2, 2013.
   http://www.odl.state.ok.us/sginfo/abc/index.htm (accessed March 24, 2014).
[107] Tocqueville, *Democracy in America*, pp. 805-806.

Work
[108] Schmidt, *How Christianity Changed the World*, pp. 194-196.
[109] Ibid.
[110] Johnson, *Ye shall be as gods*, p. 88.
[111] Schmidt, *How Christianity Changed the World*, pp. 198-199.
[112] Johnson, *Ye shall be as gods*, p. 247.
[113] Patrick Buchanan, "Is this end of the line for the welfare state?" *Tulsa World*,
   February 12, 2014, A-14.
[114] Wanda Carruthers, "Joe Scarborough: CBO Report Shows Obamacare 'Still Red Hot Mess'," *Newsmax.com*, February 6, 2014.
   http://www.newsmax.com/Newsfront/cbo-work-obamacare-disincentive (/2014/02/06/id/551246#ixzz2tEpiNt4b accessed February 13, 2014).
[115] Johnson, *Ye shall be as gods*, p. 247.

Newspeak **2014: The Language of Socialism**
[116] Johnson, *Ye shall be as gods*, p. 392.
[117] Ibid., pp. 392-393.
[118] Merriam-Webster, "newspeak," *w-m.com*. http://www.merriam-webster.com/
   dictionary/ newspeak (accessed March 3, 2014).
[119] Orwell, *1984*, pp. 299-300.
[120] Hayek, *The Road to Serfdom – Text and Documents*, pp. 54-55.
[121] Ibid., pp. 171-172.
[122] Ibid., p. 174.
[123] Ibid., p. 174-175.

[124] Weaver, *Ideas Have Consequences*, pp. 150-151.
[125] Weaver, *The Southern Essay of Richard M. Weaver*, pp. 195-196.

Part III - America

Disunited States of America
[126] Henry Steele Commager, ed., *Documents of American History – Vol. 1 to 1865*, (New York: F. S. Crofts & Co., 1935), pp. 170, 173.
[127] Ibid.
[128] Ibid.
[129] Ibid., p. 173.

American Exceptionalism – Parts I through III
[130] Tocqueville, *Democracy in America*.
[131] Terrence McCoy, "How Joseph Stalin Invented "American Exceptionalism,"
The Atlantic, May 15, 2012,
http://www.theatlantic.com/politics/archive/2012/03/how-joseph-stalin-invented-american-exceptionalism/254534/ (accessed April 7, 2013).
[132] Tyler Gobin, "American Exceptionalism," *Technician Online*, April 2, 2013,
http://www.technicianonline.com/opinion/columnists/article_c3994862-9b4b-11e2-9c65-0019bb30f31a.html (accessed April 7, 2013).
[133] Ibid.
[134] Skousen, *The 5000 Year Leap*, p. iii.
[135] Peter H. Schuck and James Q. Wilson, eds., *Understanding America: The Anatomy of an Exceptional Nation*, (New York: Public Affairs, 2008), pp. 627-643.
[136] Karlyn Bowman, "Understanding American Exceptionalism," *The American
– The Online Magazine of the American Enterprise Institute,* April 28, 2008.
http://www.aei.org/publication/understanding-american-exceptionalism-2/
[137] Federer, *America's God and Country*, p. 18.
[138] "In God We Trust", *Tulsa World*, July 4, 2012, A 17.
[139] Tocqueville, *Democracy in America*, pp. 340, 343, 345.
[140] Federer, *America's God and Country*, pp. 10-11.
[141] Ibid., p. 247.

Freedom
[1] Johnson, *Ye shall be as gods*, p. 389.
[2] Ibid, p. 158.
[3] Commager, *Documents of American History*, Volume 1 to 1865, p. 102.
[4] Federer, *America's God and Country*, p. 144.
[5] Ibid., p. 82.

The Fragility of Free Speech in America

[1] George Will, "An attack on free speech in North Carolina," *Tulsa World*, September 27, 2012, A-16.
[2] Charles C. Haynes, "On college campuses, zoning out free speech," *First Amendment Center*, October 14, 2013. http://www.firstamendmentcenter.org/on-college-campuses-zoning-out-free-speech (accessed 3-19-14).
[3] Ibid.
[4] Ibid.
[5] Hayek, *The Road to Serfdom – Text and Documents*, p. 171.
[6] Ibid., pp. 175-176.

Selected Bibliography

This bibliography is a substantial but not a complete record of all the works and sources consulted in writing this book. It represents the substance and range of reading which have formed the ideas presented. It is intended that these sources serve as a convenience for those who wish to pursue further research and study on the concepts and ideas presented.

Barton, David. *The Myth of Separation*. Aledo, Texas: Wallbuilder Press, 1989.

_____. *Original Intent*. Aledo, Texas: Wallbuilder Press, 2008.

Bennett, William J. *The Broken Hearth*. New York: Doubleday, 2001.

Bible. Scripture quotations marked KJV are taken from the Holy Bible, King James Version.

Bible. Scripture quotations marked ML (*Modern Language Bible*), LB (*Living Bible*), and RSV (Revised Standard Version) are taken from *The Layman's Parallel Bible*. Grand Rapids, Michigan: Zondervan Bible Publishers, 1973.

Bible. Scripture quotations marked NIV (New International Version) and TM (The Message) are taken from the *NIV/The Message Parallel Bible*. Grand Rapids, Michigan: Zondervan, 2004, 2006.

Blackstone, William. *Commentaries on the Laws of England*, Vol. 1-Book I & II. Philadelphia: J. B. Lippincott Company, 1910.

Bork, Robert H. *Slouching Towards Gomorrah – Modern Liberalism and American Decline*. New York: Regan Books, 1996.

Chapman, Gary. *Covenant Marriage*. Nashville, Tennessee: Broadman & Holman Publishers, 2003.

Colson, Charles and Nancy Pearcey. *How Now Shall We Live?* Wheaton, Illinois: Tyndale House Publishers, Inc., 1999.

Colson, Charles with Nancy Pearcey. *A Dance with Deception*. Dallas, Texas: Word Publishing, 1993.

Commager, Henry Steele, ed., "Mayflower Compact." *Documents of American History*, Vol. 1 & II. New York, F. S. Crofts & Co., 1934.

Coontz, Stephanie. *Marriage, a History*. New York: Penguin Group, 2005.

Craig, William Lane. *On Guard*. Colorado Springs, Colorado: David C. Cook, 2010.

Croker, Richard. *The Boomer Century 1946-2046*. New York: Springboard Press, 2007.

Cymbala, Jim. *Fresh Power*. Grand Rapids, Michigan: Zondervan, 2001.

Cymbala, Jim, with Jennifer Schuchmann. *Storm – Hearing Jesus for The Times We Live In*. Grand Rapids, Michigan: Zondervan, 2014.

Douthat, Ross. *Bad Religion – How We Became a Nation of Heretics*. New York: Free Press, 2012.

Elkind, David, Ph.D. *The hurried child – growing up too fast too soon*. Cambridge, Massachusetts: Da Capo Press, 2007.

Eddy, Sherwood. *The Kingdom of God and the American Dream*. New York: Harper & Brothers Publishers, 1941.

Federer, William J. *America's God and Country*. Coppell, Texas: Fame Publishing, Inc., 1996.

Flory, Richard W. "Promoting a Secular Standard." *The Secular Revolution*. Edited by Christian Smith. Berkeley, California: University of California Press, 2003.

Gay, Craig M. *The way of the (modern) world*. Grand Rapids, Michigan: William B. Eerdmans Publishing Company, 1998.

Gruden, Wayne. *Politics – According to the Bible – A Comprehensive Resource for Understanding Modern Political Issues in Light of Scripture*. Grand Rapids, Michigan: Zondervan, 2010.

Hayek, F. A. *The Road to Serfdom – Text and Documents*. Edited by Bruce Caldwell. Chicago, Illinois: The University of Chicago Press, 1944.

Henry, Matthew. *Commentary on the Whole Bible*. Edited by Rev. Leslie F. Church, Ph.D. Grand Rapids, Michigan, Zondervan Publishing House, 1961.

Hook, Sidney. *John Dewey – His Philosophy of Education and Its Critics*.

New York: Tamiment Institute, 1959.

Ibrahim, Raymond. *Crucified Again – Exposing Islam's New War on Christians*. Washington, D.C.: Regnery Publishing, Inc., 2013.

Iserbyt, Charlotte Thomson. *the deliberate dumbing down of america*. Ravenna, Ohio: Conscience Press, 1999.

Johnson, Larry G. *CultureWarrior.net*.

_____. *Ye shall be as gods – Humanism and Christianity – The Battle for Supremacy in the American Cultural Vision*. Owasso, Oklahoma: Anvil House Publishers, 2011.

Johnson, Paul. *A History of Christianity*. New York: Simon & Schuster, 1976.

_____. *A History of the American People*. New York: HarperCollins Publishers, 1997.

Kirk, Russell. *The Essential Russell Kirk – Selected Essays*. Edited by George A. Panichas. Wilmington, Delaware: ISI Books, 2007.

_____. *The Roots of American Order*. Washington, D.C.: Regnery Gateway, 1991.

Kemeny, P. C. "The Destruction of Moral Reform Politics." *The Secular Revolution*. Edited by Christian Smith. Berkeley, California: University of California Press, 2003.

Kuiper, B. K. *The Church in History*. Grand Rapids, Michigan: Wm. B. Eerdmans Publishing Co., 1951, 1964.

Kurtz, Paul, ed. *Humanist Manifestos I & II*. Amherst, New York: Prometheus Books, 1973)

_____. *Toward a New Enlightenment – The Philosophy of Paul Kurtz*. New Brunswick, New Jersey: Transaction Publishers, 1994.

Lamont, Corliss. *The Philosophy of Humanism*, 8th Edition. Amherst, New York: Humanist Press, 1997.

Lewis, C. S. *Mere Christianity* from *The Complete C. S. Lewis Signature Classics*. New York: Harper One, 2002.

_____. *The Abolition of Man* from *The Complete C. S. Lewis Signature Classics*. New York: Harper One, 2002.

———. *The Problem of Pain* from *The Complete C. S. Lewis Signature Classics*. New York: Harper One, 2002.

———. *The Screwtape Letters* from *The Complete C. S. Lewis Signature Classics*. New York: Harper One, 2002.

Lutzer, Erwin W. *When a Nation Forgets God.* Chicago, Illinois: Moody Publishers, 2010.

Meador, Keith G. "My Own Salvation." *The Secular Revolution.* Edited by Christian Smith. Berkeley, California: University of California Press, 2003.

Metaxas, Eric. *Bonhoeffer.* Nashville, Tennessee: Thomas Nelson, 2010.

Marano, Hara Estroff. *A Nation of Wimps.* New York: Broadway Books, 2009.

Muggeridge, Malcolm. *The End of Christendom*. Grand Rapids, Michigan: William B. Eerdmans Publishing Company, 1980.

Nicole, Roger. "James I. Packer's Contribution to the Doctrine of the Inerrancy of Scripture." *Doing Theology for the People of God.* Edited by Donald Lewis & Alister McGrath. Downers Grove, Illinois: InterVarsity Press, 1996.

Orwell, George. *1984.* New York: Signet Classics, 1950.

Qur-an. Ali, A. Yusuf. *The Meaning of the Illustrious Qur-an*, Published by: Dar AHYA Us-Sunnah, Al Nabawiya.

Packer, J. I. *Knowing God.* Downers Grove, Illinois: IVP Books, 1973.

Pearcey, Nancy. *Total Truth.* Wheaton, Illinois: Crossway, 2004, 2005.

Petigny, Alan. *The Permissive Society – America, 1941-1965*. Cambridge, England: Cambridge University Press, 2009.

Rainwater, Lee, and William L. Yancey. *The Moynihan Report and the Politics of Controversy*. Cambridge, Massachusetts: M.I.T. Press, 1967.

Randall, Jr. John Herman. *The Making of the Modern Mind.* New York: Columbia University Press, 1926, 1940.

Rhodes, Ronald. "Tough Questions About Evil." *Who Made God?* Edited by Ravi Zacharias and Norman Geisler. Grand Rapids, Michigan: Zondervan, 2003.

Roberts, J. M. *The New History of the World.* New York: Oxford University

Press, 2003.

Roth, Robert J. *John Dewey and Self-Realization*. Westport, Connecticut: Greenwood Press, 1962.

Rush, Benjamin. *Essays, Literary, Moral & Philosophical*. Philadelphia, Pennsylvania: Thomas and Samuel F. Bradford, 1798.

Schaeffer, Francis A. *The Great Evangelical Disaster.* Westchester, Illinois: Crossway Books, 1984.

_____. *How Should We Then Live?* Wheaton, Illinois: Crossway Books, 1976.

_____. "Interview with Francis & Edith Schaeffer – God's Leading in L'Abri & Our Lives." *How Then Should We Live?* DVD - Gospel Communications International, Inc. Worchester, Pennsylvania: Vision Video, 1977.

Schmidt, Alvin J. *How Christianity Changed the World.* Grand Rapids, Michigan: Zondervan, 2004.

Schweikart, Larry and Michael Allen. *A Patriot's History of the United States.* New York: Sentinel, 2004.

Skousen, W. Cleon. *The 5000 Year Leap*. www.nccs.net: National Center for Constitutional Studies, 1981

Smith, Christian. "Introduction: Rethinking the Secularization of American Public Life." *The Secular Revolution.* Edited by Christian Smith. Berkeley, California: University of California Press, 2003.

_____. "Secularizing American Higher Education." *The Secular Revolution.* Edited by Christian Smith. Berkeley, California: University of California Press, 2003.

Spock, Benjamin. *A Better World for Our Children – Rebuilding American Family Values*. Bethesda, Maryland: National Press Books, 1994.

Stark, Rodney. *God's Battalions – The Case for the Crusades*. New York: Harper One, 2009.

Steinhorn, Leonard. *The Greater Generation – In Defense of the Baby Boom Legacy*. New York: Thomas Dunne Books, 2006.

Tocqueville, Alexis De. *Democracy in America.* Translated by Gerald E. Bevan. London, England: Penguin Books, 2003.

Tozer. *Man—The Dwelling Place of God.* Camp Hill, Pennsylvania: WingSpread Publishers, 1986, 2008.

_____. *The Radical Cross*. Camp Hill, Pennsylvania: WingSpread Publishers, 2005, 2009.

_____. *The Root of the Righteous.* Camp Hill, Pennsylvania: WingSpread Publishers, 1955, 1966.

Weaver, Richard M. *Ideas Have Consequences.* Chicago, Illinois: The University of Chicago Press, 1948.

_____. *The Southern Essays of Richard M. Weaver*. Edited by George M Curtis, III, and James J. Thompson. Indianapolis, Indiana: Liberty Fund, 1987.

_____. *Visions of Order*. Wilmington, Delaware: ISI, 1964.

Wolters, Albert M. *Creation Regained*. Grand Rapids, Michigan: William B. Eerdmans Publishing Company, 1985, 2005.

www.ingramcontent.com/pod-product-compliance
Lightning Source LLC
Chambersburg PA
CBHW030218170426
43201CB00006B/130